Practical Strategies For Managing A Diverse Classroom, K–6

Practical Strategies for Managing a Diverse Classroom, K–6

The Teacher's Toolkit

Wendy W. Murawski

Kennet Fröjd

Jennifer L. Austin

Forewords by John Hattie and David Mitchell

For information:

Corwin
A Sage Company
2455 Teller Road
Thousand Oaks, California 91320
(800) 233-9936
www.corwin.com

Sage Publications Ltd.
1 Oliver's Yard
55 City Road
London EC1Y 1SP
United Kingdom

Sage Publications India Pvt. Ltd.
Unit No 323-333, Third Floor, F-Block
International Trade Tower, Nehru Place
New Delhi 110 019
India

Sage Publications Asia-Pacific Pte. Ltd.
18 Cross Street #10-10/11/12
China Square Central
Singapore 048423

Printed in the United States of America

Paperback ISBN 978-1-0719-3720-4

This book is printed on acid-free paper.

Vice President and Editorial Director: Monica Eckman
Senior Publisher: Jessica Allan
Senior Content Development Editor: Mia Rodriguez
Senior Editorial Assistant: Natalie Delpino
Production Editor: Vijayakumar
Copy Editor: Pam Schroeder
Typesetter: TNQ Tech Pvt. Ltd.
Proofreader: Girish Sharma
Indexer: TNQ Tech Pvt. Ltd.
Cover Designer: Scott Van Atta
Marketing Manager: Olivia Bartlett

24 25 26 27 28 10 9 8 7 6 5 4 3 2 1

CONTENTS

Note From the Publisher: The authors have provided web content throughout the book that is available to you through QR (quick response) codes. To read a QR code, you must have a smartphone or tablet with a camera. We recommend that you download a QR code reader app that is made specifically for your phone or tablet brand.

FOREWORD

I recall teaching an undergraduate class of about 300 students, and in the middle of the session, a phone starting ringing. I expected the usual shuffling to quiet it, but no, the student actually stood up and demanded quiet from me and the class while she had a loud conversation with a colleague about her upcoming hair appointment. How to react? This was a minor form of disruption, but I felt my credibility and skills as a teacher were on the line, especially because the class was, ironically, about classroom management. This student interrupted my flow, which affected fellow students (who thought it was funny but in a stunned silence kind of way), and all were looking for my reaction. The problem on that day was me. As much as I want to personify the problem as the student, it was up to me and my skills to deal with disruption—if only I'd had this book then!

We have all experienced disruptive students. Sometimes they are seeking attention for themselves, sometimes stopping your flow because they can, and sometimes expressing boredom and anger in extreme fashion. Every beginning teacher worries about "controlling" their class, and about 25% of classroom time is engaged in "managing" the class in positive and negative ways. Disruptive students are not engaged in class learning, and particularly, as teenagers, they gain much enhancement of their reputations as "naughty students" from engaging in these activities. There are many Oscars in our classes. (You will meet Oscar in Chapter 1 and then meet 20 of his disruptive peers.)

We seek a balance. We do not want overcompliance; by age 8, most students learn that teachers welcome those who come prepared, sit up straight, answer questions correctly, and watch the teacher work. We also want curiosity, that is, students asking "why" (more than "what") questions. That is why so many graduation speeches implore students to question all they have been taught and to invent new ways of thinking and doing. Employers now are asking for graduates who can question, probe, work in teams, explain to others, deal with others (sometimes difficult people), and stand critically in the shoes of others and entertain views different from their (sometimes cherished) ideas. We need to welcome disruptive thinking and disruptive ideas but be less welcoming of people who disrupt to stop their or others' learning. A theme throughout this book is that there are no disruptive students, but there are disruptive problems—and thinking this way we can deal with these problems.

Wendy Murawski, Kennet Fröjd, and Jennifer Austin outline 30 tools for the top 10 challenges, using lifelike scenarios to introduce the challenges, provide three immediate strategies, and then in the second part of the book, dive deeper. That part is resplendent with resources, applications, and activities. This structure sets this work apart from the many books and resources that identify problems with disruptive students and other dilemmas experienced in classes. This is an unusually powerful book because it does not only identify the problem (the first step to improvement) but is laser specific in recommending solutions. Further, the dilemmas identified are commonplace, and to have a book so firmly evidence based, practical, and scalable is a rarity.

We all want our students to enjoy the struggle of learning, smell the roses of meeting success criteria, and enjoy the love of learning. In many ways, our role is to disrupt their current thinking, and this means we need to find strategies to engage them in learning new and better ways about that which we cherish. Engagement is a well-rehearsed concept in our literature, but too often it is seen in terms of "doing"—for example, the students are doing the work; they have completed it; the work is long, neat, and handed in. Sadly, in a lot of doing, there can be little learning, especially as Nuthall (2004) noted that about 40% of all we teach in a class the students know already (hence, the work is often too easy). And why would a student bother to engage in doing if they think their chances of being successful are low? In either of these scenarios (too easy or too hard), I would personally be distracted, turn off, seek other sources of stimulation, and probably disrupt those around me. Berry (2020) devised a model of engagement to help move students along the continuum from disruptive to driving. Her recommendation is to aim for small steps: from disruptive to avoiding, to withdrawing, to participating, to striving, to driving the learning. Many of the messages throughout this book apply as much to those students who avoid or withdraw as to the disruptive student; in each instance the strategies are designed to help move students to at least participate.

Understanding the students' level of confidence, their disposition for dealing with challenges and the unknown, and their motivations for learning are critical. Students walk into classrooms with high levels of motivation resources. The problem is that some do not want to engage in what teachers want them to learn. They still can be motivated to learn—watch them learn and engage in video games, sports, and social skills! Hence, care is needed before we as teachers classify students as "not motivated" or "lazy," or say they are "not putting in an effort." Our task as educators is to figure out how to make the tasks more attractive to the students, reduce the risk of public failure, scale and scaffold the degree of challenge, target mastery, and focus more on intrinsic than performance or external attributes. The sections in this book on developing these skills are powerful.

The tension between positive and negative disruption is increasing. The COVID-19 pandemic highlighted the issues raised throughout these chapters. Even online, and at times, even more so online, teachers experienced students who withdrew, avoided, or disrupted class. Our classes also are becoming more worldly with more cultural diversity, countries, and languages present. These can create differences because one society's norms may not be another society's norms; some are less tolerant of diversity, although the desired mind frame is to see differences as opportunities to learn. Henrich (2020) has used the notion of WEIRD—Western, educated, industrialized, rich, and democratic—to contrast with the Global South (the new term for developing countries). He argued that the ways of thinking are different across these cultures, in that WEIRD people are more analytical thinkers and less wholistic or relational, more likely to attribute actions to internal or personal than external factors, and value independence, nonconformity, overconfidence, and self-promotion. Thus, in any one class, you could have a clash of cultures, or more specifically a difference in how we think, how we relate to others, what we consider to be disruption, and what we value. Classes now have greater diversity, and more "categories" of students to add to the mix. We need to follow many of the suggestions in this book to see these as positive influences. Solutions like "make it a game," "mix it up to build motivation," "play cards," "create a village," and "call all kids" are a few of the suggestions offered here by Murawski, Fröjd, and Austin. Read on to increase your own teaching tool kit from these auspicious authors!

—John Hattie

FOREWORD

The COVID-19 pandemic—these words have caused and continue to cause apprehension, even fear, in many of us. Most of us know of someone who became stricken with COVID-19; some of us, including myself, sadly know of someone who died because of it. The threat posed by this disease, particularly to those of us with heightened vulnerability, directed my attention to the meaning of our lives. What is it all about—this living? What is the purpose, if any, of our existence? What drives us to engage in our lives? Surely, the rationale for our existence goes beyond perpetuating our species, a purpose shared by all other living creatures? Nor do I believe that some supernatural being has designed our lives for us.

These questions arose against the backdrop of my professional career as an educational psychologist, which took me into research on how children learn and what motivates them. This has culminated in my academic writing on human diversity, inclusive education, and evidence-based pedagogy. I am now asking myself, what assumptions was I making about human nature, particularly about the young of our species, in this writing?

My tentative answer to the preceding questions is based on two premises: first, that *Homo sapiens* have evolved to achieve a high level of understanding of the world and are continuing to advance that understanding with increasing rapidity. Second, these accomplishments reflect the working of our species' unique brains that are "pre-wired" to perform an enormous range of cognitive and social functions *once we are motivated by our inner drives and external stimulation to do so.*

My personal view of the meaning of life is summed up in the concept of *potentiality*, which I define as *the potential to pursue social virtues and cognitive excellence to the best levels within us.* I believe that it is this quality that explains how our species has evolved to cope with and master the myriad challenges it has faced and will continue to face in the future.

Potentiality exists within all of us. It is expressed to different degrees at different times. It varies from individual to individual. It is an ongoing process rather than an end state. It is facilitated or inhibited by a person's physical and social environments and their will, or drive.

Social virtues are both biologically and culturally determined. They center on our inborn drive to be cooperative beings, a quality that has contributed to our survival as a species. However, we vary in our social sensitivity. We are exposed to different levels of social press. All of us, except the most sociopathic among us, have the potential to express social virtues. Their nature varies according to our sphere of identity at any one time. In children, this varies from their immediate families to their extended families, neighborhoods, communities, and importantly, peer groups. As they grow older, these spheres will widen to include their country and, perhaps, the world. Increasingly, these identity spheres have been augmented, even supplemented, by virtual communities operating through social media.

Cognitive excellence is a universal attribute largely based on reason, or rationality, according to Stephen Pinker (2013). After all, *Homo sapiens* does mean "wise man." We vary in our ability to express our cognitive skills. Some of us will excel in comparison to others—past and present—and advance or disperse new knowledge. The ast bulk of us will simply manage our day-to-day existence, dealing with comparatively simple problems. Still others of us will irrationally refuse to follow evidence, relying instead on conspiracy theories, falsehoods, and disinformation.

The best levels within us vary according to our drives, which are in turn, influenced by environmental circumstances (physical and cultural) and our personal motivation.

My hypothesis is that when we achieve a certain level of cognitive performance or engage in a certain kind of social relationship, we feel satisfied to some degree. Those actions that meet or exceed our expectations probably result in the release of endorphins, dopamine, and oxytocin, yielding feelings of well-being and motivating us to repeat that or a similar behavior in the future. When we feel we have failed in our endeavors, this can lead to stress, resulting in the release of cortisol, which puts the brain into survival mode so that it can deal with the source of stress, which distracts us from the task in hand.

This potentiality philosophy was uppermost in my mind as I approached the text of this admirable book. As I read about the individual children, I asked myself these questions:

Social virtues:

- What do they think and feel about their social environments—home, school, neighborhood, peer group, and virtual?

- How do they see themselves in those social environments?

- How would they like to relate to those social environments?

- What is preventing them from fulfilling their potential to relate to those social environments?

- What could I, as a teacher, do to help them to fulfill their social potential?

Cognitive excellence:

- What do they think and feel about their cognition?

- How would they like to improve their cognition?

- What is preventing them from fulfilling their cognitive potential?

- What can I, as a teacher, do to help them fulfill their cognitive potential—generally and with reference to specific areas of the curriculum?

Thus, when I look at Oscar (and others with "disruptive" behaviors as described in this book), it seems that it is his social behavior rather than his cognition that is of concern, but of course, the two are closely related. I would therefore be seeking answers to these questions by (a) observing him in different settings, (b) talking with him about these matters, and (c) interviewing (and observing) his parents and caregivers:

- What does he think and feel about his social environments—home, school, neighborhood, peer group, and virtual? I would broaden the focus beyond the immediate setting of the classroom as portrayed in the description. I would also be interested in how the parents and caregivers think and feel about their social environments.

- How does he see himself in those social environments? Does he see himself as a disrupter or as someone who makes a positive contribution to the culture of the classroom?

- How would he like to relate to those social environments? Is the role he appears to be playing satisfying to him? What else would give him satisfaction?

- What is preventing him from fulfilling his potential to relate more acceptably to those social environments? Is he motivated to change his image? How does he feel about the role that I, his teacher, would like him to play?

- What could I, as a teacher, do to help him fulfill his social potential? How does Oscar see me in the context of the class dynamics? How does he see his relationship with me? Is it different with other adults in his life—parents, caregivers, or other teachers?

I present these suggestions as supplements to the approaches taken by the authors of this innovative book. I am suggesting that, like anthropologists or David Attenborough, you should occasionally stand back from the immediacy of your classroom with all its challenges, successes, failures, sadness, worries, and joy, and ask yourself, what is really going on here? What does it tell us about human nature and our evolution as a species? What do my reactions tell me about me?'

As teachers you are faced with the challenge of intervening in children's lives, often with the intention of changing them. Society has granted you that privilege and with it all the responsibilities that it entails. I am confident that this thoughtful, evidence-based book will assist you to help your learners pursue social virtues and cognitive excellence to the best levels they are capable of achieving—their potential. And, in doing so, your potential will also be realized.

This book provides you with a handy tool kit that is a blend of strategies based on sound evidence and the practical experience of the authors. It combines scenarios of learners' behavior that are familiar to every teacher with easy-to-follow intervention strategies that all educators should have in their repertoire. Enjoy.

—David Mitchell

PREFACE

The Students

We start our book where every good book on education should start—with a focus on the students themselves. As mentioned in the introduction, we wanted this book to "flip the script"—offering challenges and solutions before we offer the literature base, research, or rationale for those solutions. We also wanted this book to be extremely practical and grounded in real-world issues. What is more real world than a class of diverse students? On the next pages, we offer a brief introduction to our students. We do not put them in any particular grade level because we want our solutions and strategies to span many grade levels and abilities. However, we do note when some students are working above or below the typical grade level.

Students are so much more than their academic scores. Thus, you will also note that we have provided a small amount of information about their personalities and interests. We cannot emphasize enough how much knowing your students, getting to know them as people and not only as learners, can help with instruction, class management, and addressing social-emotional needs. In his foreword, David Mitchell implores educators to get to know their students beyond the classroom; when possible, learn about their families, neighborhoods, and outside activities. We completely agree—although the focus of this book is primarily within the walls of the school. This class of students will come up throughout the "Challenges" in Part I. We provide you with scenarios we are certain you will connect with and then follow up those scenarios with potential solutions based not only on evidence-based best practice but also on what we know about our kids.

Get to know this class, and feel free to bookmark these pages. Come back to them frequently, much as we hope you make notes about your own students and come back to those notes time and again as you seek to determine how to improve your connections. We hope you enjoy this class and that these students become familiar to you as you continue throughout the book.

	NAME	ETHNICITY	LABEL	MATH	READING	DESCRIPTION
1.	Oscar	American	Typical	+0	+0	The class clown; well-liked by peers and teachers; likes to be helpful
2.	José	Latinx	ADHD	+0	−1	Energetic; enthusiastic; always on the move
3.	Kenneth	American	Gifted	+2	+2	Bored easily; kind; loves sports; extroverted; does homework
4.	Hannah	American	Typical	+0	+0	Into her phone, movies, and TV; lots of friends; funny
5.	Lisa	American	Autism	+0	− 1	Likes structure; hard worker; loves animals; strong auditory comprehension skills
6.	Camila	Latinx	English Learner (EL)	+0	−2	Diligent worker; speaks multiple languages; likes horses and cooking
7.	Susana	German	EL	−1	− 1	Interested in anime; likes to talk to adults; prefers to work alone

	NAME	ETHNICITY	LABEL	MATH	READING	DESCRIPTION
8.	Anna	American	Gifted/ADHD	+1	+3	Loves reading and writing; writes poetry; interested in many topics; likes groupwork
9.	Matteo	Latinx	EL	−1	−2	Loves soccer; prefers to work alone typically; likes structure
10.	John	American	Typical	−1	−1	Athletic; good with his hands; prefers activities to academics
11.	Flora	American	Intellectual Disability	−4	−5	Happy; speaks loudly; loves TV and TV characters; quotes often
12.	Eva	American	Typical	+0	+0	Interested in fashion; quiet but makes friends easily; funny
13.	Linda	Swedish	Gifted	− 1	+2	Loves dogs and reading; extrovert; loves working with others; takes charge
14.	Monica	American	Typical	+0	+0	Funny; positive; hard worker; works well with others
15.	Fatima	Syrian	EL	−3	−4	Quiet; likes to color; prefers repetition and structure
16.	Tom	American	Autism	+2	+0	Strong at patterns and

(Continued)

(Continued)

	NAME	ETHNICITY	LABEL	MATH	READING	DESCRIPTION
						spatial activities; loves music; quiet; needs structure
17.	Ivan	Ukrainian	EL	+0	−1	Interested in photography and music; plays instruments; has twin older sisters
18.	Kiernan	Irish	Gifted/ADHD/EL	+2	+1	Loves soccer; athletic; does minimal work required; inquisitive; strong vocabulary; strong English skills
19.	Luis	Hispanic	EL	+0	+0	Artistic; loves fishing; great sense of humor
20.	Amy	American	ID	−4	−4	Sweet; people-pleasing; loves music and horses
21.	Mohammad	Iranian	EL	−1	−3	Introvert; quiet; gets along well with Matteo; enjoys cooking
22.	Isak	Iranian	Gifted	+1	+2	Articulate; extrovert; works well with others; likes basketball
23.	Hassan	Somalian	Typical	+1	+0	Good at mathematics; likes writing and illustrating books; enjoys participating in class

ABOUT THE AUTHORS

Wendy W. Murawski, PhD, EdS, MBA, MEd, is the executive director and Eisner Endowed Chair for the Center for Teaching and Learning at California State University, Northridge (CSUN), where she is also a full professor in the Department of Special Education and the director of SIMPACT Immersive Learning. Dr. Murawski is the national past president of the Teacher Education Division (TED) of the Council for Exceptional Children (CEC) and an internationally known speaker and author, presenting in Europe, Asia, Africa, and North America. Her research focuses on co-teaching and inclusive practices nationally and internationally. She has published extensively about inclusive education, co-teaching, collaboration, and Universal Design for Learning, including 18 books and numerous chapters, blogs, and peer-reviewed articles. She is the CEO of 2Teach® Global (www.2TeachGlobal.com), an educational consulting company dedicated to promoting inclusive education around the world. In her personal life, Dr. Murawski enjoys traveling with her husband, learning languages, reading, drinking merlot, seeing movies, going to book club, visiting her college-bound son Kiernan, and pretending she is going to work out.

Kennet Fröjd has worked toward inclusion based on evidence-informed learning and teaching strategies for more than 30 years. He has his main specialties in adapted physical activity and in teaching with a particular focus on sensory motor development. Another specialty is stress management.

For many years, Mr. Fröjd taught his specialties, among other things, directly in schools via professional development for staff. He has also presented and lectured in several European countries as well as in Africa, North America, South America. and Oceania. During the same period of time and parallel to his work on inclusion and learning, Mr. Fröjd worked as a director and with leadership for different groups and organizations both nationally and internationally.

Since 2018, he has worked as a principal at the Celsius School (Celsiusskolan) in Edsbyn, Sweden—always keeping one foot in the practice of sensory motor development.

Jennifer L. Austin, PhD, BCBA-D, has been applying the science of behavior analysis to improve outcomes for children and their teachers for more than 20 years. Both her research and clinical work focus on how behavior analytic assessment and intervention strategies can be applied in inclusive classrooms with a specific focus on ensuring the behavior change process is collaborative and acceptable to both teachers and students. She has worked with numerous schools in the United States and the United Kingdom, focusing primarily on those in disadvantaged communities. Dr. Austin served as professor of psychology and head of behavior analysis at the University of South Wales in the UK before joining the faculty at Georgia State University in the United States. She has published more than 30 peer-reviewed articles and is a former associate editor of the *Journal of Applied Behavior Analysis* and *Behavior Analysis in Practice.*

ABOUT THE CONTRIBUTOR

Adrienne Gear has been an elementary teacher with the Vancouver School District for more than 25 years. She is passionate about literacy, learning, and inspiring teachers to reflect and refine their practice to best support their students. Her practical and engaging workshops and webinars are in high demand both in and outside of Canada. She has presented internationally in the United States, UK, Australia, and Sweden. Adrienne is the author of eight professional books for elementary teachers that focus on best practices in literacy instruction. Her latest book, *Powerful Thinking* (Pembroke, 2024) will be released in early spring.

INTRODUCTION

It does not matter where you teach, what age students you teach, or what subject you teach—every teacher wants to increase their "tool kit." Every teacher wants strategies to help them do better: to teach better, to have better classroom management, to engage their students better, and to do a better job managing their stress. The need to "do better" is ubiquitous and transcends countries, topics, and school boundaries. The desire for a strategy—any strategy—that may help increase students' success is shared by educators in all fields. Administrators, counselors, school psychologists, and other educational specialists share in the desire to identify educational techniques that support their work with students. Knowing this, the field is overwhelmed by books offering to do just that—provide strategies to help educators do better.

How is this book different then? When first conceptualizing this book, we knew we wanted to combine our years of experience in education with our diverse backgrounds and areas of specialization. Kennet is a principal in Sweden, Wendy is a professor of special education in the United States, and Jenn was a professor of behavior analysis in South Wales during this writing (she has since taken a position as a professor in Georgia in the United States). We had a plethora of strategies at our fingertips, but we also wanted to be certain our text was steeped in research and evidence-based practices. It was equally important to us that we were creating a text that would support an inclusive classroom. Although Wendy and Jenn work with teachers on a regular basis, Kennet is in a school every single day and knows that teachers are desperate for ideas they can implement immediately. He appreciates the need to provide the research support but suggested that we flip the script and provide the strategies first.

We began to call this book our "unique book project." Instead of requiring busy educators to read copious amounts of research and theory to support the few strategies that are ultimately offered, we took Kennet's idea and flipped the script. We decided to provide something rather unique: a book that essentially gives the answers *first* and *then* describes the problems.

This text opens with a typical class. We give names of students and their learning profiles so that we can describe real situations and needs and abilities. The class we offer is diverse and inclusive. Students who are gifted, twice exceptional, second language learners; those who have disabilities; and typical learners are all present, much as they are in classrooms across the world.

After introducing the students, the text sets up common scenarios that require immediate attention. Teachers will see familiar situations play out that they often have to deal with daily. From students who are misbehaving to individuals who are struggling to read, teachers will recognize common issues. For each situation, we offer three concrete strategies to address the scenario. The strategies are provided in a "use now" format. Educators can take the ideas and run with them without any additional reading required. With each strategy, however, we link the concept to a chapter that follows, which focuses on providing the research rationale and evidence base for that strategy. In this way, teachers can learn more about *why* the strategy works and how to later build on that information as they create their own strategies. Our goal is to hook readers with the practical strategies and then provide the real teaching as they read on to learn more.

One of the beautiful aspects of teaching and learning is how many concepts interconnect. Throughout the text, we make explicit links to other chapters or topics or strategies. For example, co-teaching and cooperative learning cannot occur without collaboration and communication. A well-managed class requires a solid understanding of applied behavior analysis. Academic success goes hand in hand with students' social and emotional well-being. Although chapters focus on particular topics, we interweave connections so that it is clear that these are not a bunch of individual areas but rather interdependent aspects of any educator's tool kit.

Educators are as diverse as the student bodies with whom they work. Some readers will want to read the text from beginning to end in a linear fashion. Others will want to pick and choose chapters and topics based on specific needs as they arise. Still others may want to implement one strategy at a time, reading the corresponding chapter and delving deep into its theoretical and evidence-based underpinnings. No matter how you choose to interact with this text, we hope that you will find the cutting-edge topics, current research, and practical strategies useful in your profession.

PART I

CHALLENGES AND SOLUTIONS

TOP 10 CHALLENGES AND 30 PRACTICAL TOOLS

DEALING WITH DISRUPTIVE BEHAVIOR

Defining the Problem and Finding Solutions

All teachers expect to encounter some student disruptions in their classrooms, such as calling out without permission, making noises, or chatting with peers. However, newer teachers are often surprised by the sheer volume of disruptions they must deal with on a daily basis and how a relatively minor issue suddenly can become a major problem. A recent survey of teachers across 30 countries indicated that only an average of 78% of allocated teaching time is devoted to teaching; much of the remaining time is spent trying to maintain order in the classroom (Organization for Economic Cooperation and Development, 2019). In the United Kingdom, a government report estimated that some students were losing up to an hour of instruction per day—a loss of 38 days of instruction per school year—due to disruptive behavior (Office for Standards of Education, 2014).

Without effective strategies to address persistent disruptions, students and their teachers are at risk. Disruptive students spend less time engaged with academic tasks and often have fewer positive relationships with peers and teachers (Evertson & Weinstein, 2006). Further, these students may negatively affect learning environments by distracting peers and requiring teachers to allocate precious teaching time to dealing with problem behavior (Guerra & Smith, 2006; Office for Standards of Education, 2014). Disruptive classroom behavior also is associated with greater teacher stress and burnout (Abel & Sewell, 1999), and the inability to effectively manage these behaviors, or managing them in a way that doesn't meet their needs, can lead to over-referring children for special education assessment and disparate outcomes for discipline policies and practices (White et al., 2024).

Whether teachers have a few or many disruptive behaviors in their classrooms, strategies for effectively dealing with these problems is essential. Given that disruptions might occur for a range of reasons (e.g., the student likes the attention, the student is bored, the student has difficulty sustaining attention for long periods of time), having a range of strategies can help teachers feel better equipped to manage these behaviors in ways that suit both them and their students. Let's jump into a few scenarios that may feel familiar. Don't worry—we'll follow them up immediately with some potential solutions!

Disruptive Behavior: Scenario 1

It's math class, and you ask the class a question related to fractions. Oscar, your likable, helpful, extremely tiring, and verbal student, yells out "an elephant's butt" as his answer. As per usual, his peers laugh, and Oscar grins. Oscar loves to make people laugh and spends much of his time making comments or noises that he hopes others will find funny. You and the other teachers even agree that Oscar is quite witty and often says things that are genuinely humorous, but his nearly constant antics make teaching difficult. You don't know what to do because when you remind Oscar of the classroom rules or tell him that he is disturbing others, it only seems to make the problem worse. Telling other students not to laugh or to ignore Oscar also does not work because many of the students find his behavior entertaining. What's additionally frustrating is that Oscar typically gets his work done in class to a good standard, completing unfinished work during breaks or as homework when his joking around takes up class time. Unfortunately, not all of his peers are able to finish their work and are distracted by Oscar's antics. Although Oscar is well liked by teachers and peers, both are beginning to get annoyed with his disruptive behavior. What can you do?

Scenario 1 Solution: Give Him Attention!

It is clear that Oscar likes attention from both adults and peers. It also seems reasonable to assume that Oscar has learned that being funny is a good way to get that attention. Given that Oscar does not seem to have difficulty completing his work, it is unlikely that his behaviors are aimed at avoiding tasks that might be too easy or too difficult. When he does not finish his work, it is typically because he has spent his time doing other things.

It makes sense that giving Oscar attention when he is disruptive (e.g., reminding him of rules, other children laughing) makes the problem worse. We know that Oscar likes attention, so if disruptions lead to attention, then he is more likely to keep doing those behaviors. Controlling the reactions of peers (e.g., telling them not to laugh) is a losing battle for any teacher. Teachers who try these strategies often find they begin punishing students who were not initially responsible for the problem, for instance, by scolding children who laugh when another child does something that they find funny.

Although Oscar has learned how to get attention by being disruptive, he also has other skills that could potentially result in the same outcome. Teachers naturally focus their attention on problem behavior more than appropriate behavior because problem behaviors often *require* a response, whereas appropriate behaviors do not. However, if they can shift their focus, they might find they have fewer problem behaviors that require their attention.

For students like Oscar, the key is to find another behavior that will lead to the same outcome as his disruptions. Given that Oscar is competent with academics, allowing him to support a less academically competent peer might give him the peer attention he craves. When he is working well alongside his peer, you could offer praise, thus giving Oscar the adult attention he is seeking. Even when Oscar is not supporting a peer, you should be proactive about looking for opportunities to praise appropriate behavior. Setting a timer or using a Motivaider® can be helpful in reminding busy teachers to look for good behavior. It is important that these devices be set to short intervals (e.g., 4–5 minutes) initially because waiting too long to praise good behavior will inevitably lead to the student engaging in problem behavior.

You might also try allowing Oscar to make people laugh in a more appropriate context. For instance, you might set a rule whereby Oscar can tell a joke to the class if he finishes his work and does not disrupt the lesson. Again, timing is everything. Oscar should be allowed to tell his joke as soon as the lesson has ended, provided he followed the rule; if he has to wait too long, he may try disruptive behavior instead.

These strategies are referred to as *differential reinforcement* (Flood et al., 2002). They come from an area of psychology called applied behavior analysis (ABA). You can read more about these strategies in Chapter 3.

José seems as though he is being run by a motor, and it is driving you crazy. He is constantly on the move, whether it be getting up dozens of times during a lesson to locate materials, checking in with peers to see what they are doing, or incessantly tapping his pencil on the desk. José likes to learn but cannot seem to be still even during lessons that he enjoys. If a thought pops into José's head, it seems to immediately come out of his mouth. He has difficulty waiting his turn to speak and gets frustrated if he is not immediately called on during group discussions. His academic skills are good, although he is a bit below average for his age in reading.

The great thing about José is that he is constantly enthusiastic and eager to learn. He has a few good friends, but many of his peers are weary of his disruptive behavior and are beginning to comment negatively about him disturbing them when they are trying to work. You've tried using a sticker chart to reward staying in his space and completing his work, but José lost interest in the chart after a day. You've also tried letting him work in the hallway (ostensibly to reduce the number of distractions in class) but found that he often wandered away instead of doing his work. What can you do?

Scenario 2 Solution: Let Him Move!

Behavior always occurs for a reason. You can consider it a method of communication. Students might do particular things to get what they want or to escape from something they don't want, or it can be a combination of the two. However, behavior can also be related to our biological needs, including sensory ones. For José, it is possible that he feels a need to move around because doing so helps him regulate himself. Trying to make him stay in one space likely makes him feel a bit unbalanced, and even if you could make him stay, sitting is not the same as learning. José will need opportunities to move in ways that help him focus more on his academic tasks but not cause a distraction for his peers.

One potential solution is a bicycle chair, which does not make much noise but allows José to be physically active while he works. Activities that activate the vestibular system also can be helpful. Our vestibular systems give our bodies information about where we are in space, where our heads are, and whether we are moving. It helps us balance and lets us know when we aren't. Moving your head or accelerating your body activates the vestibular system. From that perspective, running around the classroom could work quite well for José, but it is difficult to do work when you're running, not to mention the disruptions to José's peers!

A more reasonable option that could achieve the same outcome is having a mini-trampoline in the classroom. You could give José small trampoline breaks every lesson, which would activate his vestibular system and make him feel more balanced and regulated. In the beginning, you would probably need to organize the breaks, paying particular attention to how frequently José seems to become restless. After a while, you should be able to allow José to choose when he needs a break, within reason. For instance, you might allow him to have 5 minutes of trampoline time during each lesson. It is likely that other students in the class also will want a turn on the trampoline regardless of their sensory needs. You can simply work out a schedule whereby everyone gets some trampoline time each week, allocating more time for the students who need it the most, like José. You can read more about strategies for students like José in Chapter 1.

Disruptive Behavior: Scenario 3

You know that research supports students working in small groups, and it is clear that many of your own students are eager to do so. In fact, when you do whole-group instruction, many appear bored—no matter how engaging you try to make the instruction! But when you allow them to work in small groups, it feels like you've lost control of the lesson. Isak, Kiernan, Linda, and Kenneth immediately jump to work together; as your extroverts, this group can be boisterous and disruptive, even when they are getting their work done. Sometimes you'll even catch a few of your students moving their chairs to work together when you haven't given direct instruction to work in pairs or groups, and their cute response is, "What's wrong? We're just collaborating!" All of this "collaborating" sounds good in theory, but it is resulting in students moving desks, talking, and generally disrupting your nice, quiet classroom.

Scenario 3 Solution:
Use Station Teaching!

Station Teaching is an approach to co-teaching that will be described in full in Chapter 5. Station Teaching involves having small groups of students rotate through multiple activities. Students can choose their own groups, you can choose the groups, or you can use a combination of both strategies. Chapter 5, p. 134, provides a strategy for creating groups that incorporate student preferences but also allows the teacher to select groups. Each station should offer activities that engage learners and instruct them on the objective of the day. For example, in a reading class, one station might be a reading passage that asks comprehension questions, another might be a video teaching about metaphors and similes, a third might ask students to highlight nouns and verbs on a page in different colors, and a fourth might be a direct instruction lesson on figurative language by you or another teacher.

As noted in the Scenario 3, research supports the use of small-group instruction and shows that it facilitates smaller student–teacher ratios, encourages the use of differentiation techniques, and increases cognitive engagement of learners (Karten & Murawski, 2020; Lochner et al., 2019). However, simply creating small groups is insufficient and can lead to chaos, like in Scenario 3! When Station Teaching, you and your co-teachers can work collaboratively to create small-group instruction that maximizes student engagement but also is mindful of managing behavior. Be sure to review the classroom rules for noise and transitions while also reminding students which types of collaboration and interaction are appropriate and which are not. You can also provide collaborative roles (described in more detail in Chapter 7 on cooperative learning) to minimize one or two students taking charge and doing the work for their peers.

In addition to teaching students how stations work and the rules for engaging collaboratively, you and your co-teacher also need to proactively identify the work for each station. Although some stations can be led by a teacher or paraprofessional, and thereby manage behavior directly, others will need to facilitate students working independently. These might involve students watching an instructional video, working on independent materials, or even playing a collaborative instructional game together. In all cases, you will need to build in accountability for each station so that students are motivated to stay on task and complete quality work. Accountability measures, such as completing a Google Doc or other form to turn in after each station, can be helpful to manage behavior and are also excellent examples of formative assessments (read more about that in Chapter 2). Once you and your co-teacher have identified stations and groups, selected the materials needed, and instructed students on roles and accountability requirements, they are ready to go! Now students can work collaboratively, while the adults in the room help manage behavior, teach small groups, and avoid any more headaches.

DEALING WITH NONCOMPLIANCE AND DISRESPECTFUL BEHAVIOR

Defining the Problem and Finding Solutions

Every teacher's life would be easier if students did what we asked them to do when we asked them to do it. Unfortunately, most teachers deal with noncompliance on a regular basis. Whether it is a student refusing to stay in their space, begin their work, or line up after lunch, having to provide repeated instructions to students who do not comply can be both tiring and frustrating. Although we want students to be independent thinkers and have as much autonomy as possible, learning to follow instructions is an important life skill for everyone. Failure to learn this skill can have lasting effects on children's social and academic opportunities as well as their success across a range of life domains (Bulotsky-Shearer et al., 2011; Donaldson & Austin, 2017).

When students consistently do not do what their teachers ask of them or fail to follow classroom rules, it is understandable that teachers feel disrespected. Failure to effectively address the behaviors that evoke these feelings can lead to increased teacher stress and eventual burnout (Hastings & Bham, 2003). Therefore, implementing strategies that support students to follow instructions and classroom routines are not only a matter of order and control but also of creating an environment that is conducive to learning and in which both teachers and their students feel respected.

Like the disruptive behaviors described in the previous challenge, noncompliance can occur for a number of reasons. Sometimes, it occurs because a student wants to avoid the task they are being asked to do. For other students, noncompliance is an effective way of accessing lengthy social interactions with their teachers. For some, noncompliance is a way of feeling in control. Although it is important to consider the reasons why noncompliance might occur when designing solutions to these problems, having some general, whole-class strategies also can be helpful.

Noncompliant Behavior: Scenario 1

You love being a teacher, but this year has been a struggle. Until now, you felt you had good classroom management skills, your students were learning, and you liked coming to school every day. However, you increasingly feel demotivated and demoralized by the sheer number of disrespectful students in your class. Although you have some well-behaved pupils, there are also many who refuse to follow even the most basic instructions to stay in their seats and pay attention to lessons. When you scan your class, you find students looking at their phones, chatting with peers, or doing anything other than what they are supposed to be doing. Repeated reminders are met with laughter or, worse yet, simply ignoring you. You are beginning to feel like you spend more time redirecting students to the lesson than you spend teaching the lesson itself. This isn't what you signed on for when you became a teacher. What can you do?

Scenario 1 Solution: Make It a Game!

When the same types of problem behaviors occur across several different students, individualized strategies are not a practical solution. Instead, a group-based approach is typically a more efficient and effective approach. Although there are a number of whole-class management strategies for teachers to choose from, one essential consideration is the degree to which that strategy is supported by evidence. One strategy with decades of research supporting its effectiveness is the Good Behavior Game (Barrish et al., 1969; Flower et al., 2014; Tingstrom et al., 2006).

The Good Behavior Game involves applying core elements of classroom management, including clear expectations for behavior, consistent feedback, and positive reinforcement for meeting expectations. Further, it is structured to foster teamwork and cooperation. The first step to playing the game is to set three to four clear, positively stated expectations for behavior. Although you might have a multitude of problems to address, focusing on the most important behaviors is the best place to begin. For example, you might choose expectations such as (1) follow instructions, (2) stay in your work space, and (3) do good work. The expectations are the rules of the game and should be listed on the board or on a poster that is visible to the entire class. During the game, teams will receive a point if *anyone* on the team breaks a rule, so the object of the game is to *avoid* points. Prior to playing the first game, teachers should decide on the maximum number of points teams can earn and still win the game. To do this, it is helpful to think about how many rule violations currently occur during a typical lesson so that the goal is reasonable and achievable. The number of points can always be made more stringent as student behavior improves. For example, for a 40-minute lesson, a teacher might decide that each team can receive a maximum of five points and still win the game. It is important to note that *any* team that does not exceed the point criterion is a winner; students are competing against the criterion and not against each other. This allows more students to access reinforcement and be successful.

The next step is to divide the class into two or more teams. The most important considerations in setting the teams are that you can easily see the team together (e.g., they all sit at the same table or at multiple tables near each other) and that there is a mixture of different types of students in the team. This means that each team comprises some (or at least one!) students who typically behave well, one (or more) students who struggle with behavior, and some students who are in between. Although it is tempting to put the most problematic students on the same team, doing so will defeat the purpose of the game.

The final step is to decide on some rewards that can be used when teams win the game. Rewards that are inexpensive (or free) and can be delivered quickly are the best choices. For example, teams might win a small piece of fruit or a special coloring sheet to take home. Activity rewards also are good choices. You might consider things like allowing winning teams a few minutes to draw with felt-tip markers, allowing them to go outside for break 5 minutes early, giving some computer time or free time, or hosting an impromptu dance party. Naturally, rewards should be grade or age appropriate.

To play the game, tell the students which teams they are on, ask them to choose a team name (or assign one), and write the team names on the board. Next, explain the rules of the game (i.e., the behavior expectations), and tell students that if anyone on the team breaks a rule, the whole team will earn a point. Reveal the criterion for winning the game and explain that any team with *less than or equal to* the maximum number of points can win a reward. It is up to you whether you announce what the reward is; some students find it more motivating if the reward is not revealed until the end of the game.

In the beginning, it is better to start with short games that result in most (or all) teams winning. This helps create a positive atmosphere by linking compliance with rules to positive outcomes. It also reinforces working as a team to meet a goal. As student behavior begins to improve, games can be longer and the point criteria can be reduced.

The information provided in this chapter (and in Chapter 3) will help get you started on playing the Good Behavior Game in your classroom. For additional information and tips on playing the game, as well as adapting it to different age groups and troubleshooting problems, you might find the article by Joslyn et al. (2020) helpful.

Noncompliant Behavior: Scenario 2

Hannah and Susana are best friends with a similar problem: they prefer to do what they want to do rather than what you ask them to do. It seems they can find a million things to do other that the work that has been assigned, such as trying to find a pencil, going to the bathroom, or rummaging around in their backpacks. Earlier in the school year, the girls were seated next to each other and constantly chatting during lessons. Naturally, you moved them to different tables, which reduced chatting but increased text and instant messaging. You then implemented a rule that students were not allowed to have their phones during class, which both Hannah and Susana ignored, sneaking their phones in a variety of relatively creative ways. Your patience is wearing thin, and you are genuinely concerned about how their lack of engagement with lessons is going to affect their learning. Hannah and Susana seem to follow rules in other areas of the school, so why are they being so disrespectful to you? What do you do?

Scenario 2 Solution: Find the Source of the Problem!

When students behave in ways that seem intentionally disrespectful, it is easy to focus on the behavior itself rather than on the reasons why the behavior might be occurring. As we noted at the start of this chapter, noncompliance can occur for a number of reasons. Even though Hannah and Susana seem to be engaging in the same disrespectful behavior, the causes of that behavior might be different.

Before we move onto what is different about Hannah and Susana, let's consider what is the same. It is clear they enjoy each other's company. The fact that they prefer chatting and texting to doing work means that they find those behaviors highly reinforcing, so we know that one reason those behaviors occur is because they allow the girls to get attention from one another. However, there could be other reasons why they refuse to do work that is assigned. Finding the reasons why behaviors occur involves a process called *functional behavior assessment* (You can read more about functional behavior assessment in Chapter 3.) Functional behavior assessment can be used for a range of behavior problems, including academic issues (Daly et al., 1997).

Let's consider the reasons why Hannah and Susana refuse work. In the section on our students, you learned that Hannah's academic performance is on grade level, which likely means that Hannah's issue has more to do with motivation to work rather than her ability to do the work; thus, we need to give Hannah a good reason to *want* to do her work. It would be great if all students wanted to do their work for the love of learning, but unfortunately that is not a sufficient motivator for some students. Providing other types of reinforcers can help them contact success, which over time can maintain behavior without the use of external rewards.

Susana, in contrast, has substantially lower academic achievement, and this probably factors into her refusal to do work. Her problem is not only about motivation but also about the ability to do the work that is assigned to her. Therefore, part of a solution for her would be to ensure that the work she is expected to do is set at the right level for her ability, alongside providing specialist support to address any academic issues. Work that is too difficult can exacerbate motivation issues because students learn that even when they try, they fail. Adapting work so that students can complete it to a good standard is sometimes sufficient for them to allocate more time to working and less time to refusal. However, in Susana's case, that might not be enough to solve the problem because she has a long history of both refusing work *and* accessing a valuable reinforcer: interactions with Hannah. Therefore, incorporating some function-based motivation strategies probably will be helpful.

We know that Hannah and Susana enjoy each other's company, but we also know that they can access these interactions even without their teacher's permission. In fact, they have been known to ignore their teacher in favor of talking to one another. Therefore, a strategy whereby the teacher solely allows Hannah and Susana time to chat once they finish their work is not likely to succeed. The key is to enhance the value of the reinforcer. For example, the teacher might allow the girls to both go out into the corridor to talk or play a game when they both have finished their work. Allowing them to earn the privilege of sitting at the same table might also be a way to enhance the reinforcer. The strategy of arranging reinforcement for the appropriate behavior (and reducing the reinforcing value of the problem behavior) is referred to as *differential reinforcement* (see Chapter 3 for more information). For differential reinforcement to be maximally effective, understanding the functions of behavior is critical.

Noncompliant Behavior: Scenario 3

Your significant other is probably getting tired of hearing you say "My students don't follow directions!" day in and day out. You are even tired of saying it. You've been kind to students, practically begging them to do what you've asked, and you've played "bad cop" as well, raising your voice and demanding they fall in line. Nothing seems to work consistently. At wit's end, you asked a colleague to come in, observe your class, and see if they could give you some tips that might help. After a particularly difficult class period, you debrief with your colleague. "See? I told them what to do, and they refused to do it!" you start. Your colleague pauses before saying, "I'm not sure that's what I saw happening. I think many of the students were confused as to what they were being asked to do and may have chosen to do something else rather than admitting they were confused." This surprises you, and you think about that for a moment. Your directions weren't clear? What can you do to ensure students know what is expected of them?

Scenario 3 Solution: Break It Down!

In an ideal classroom, students will raise their hands and ask cogent questions anytime they are the least bit confused or will even problem-solve with their peers to determine what the expectations are for an assignment; in the real world however, students complain, get off task, and mask their confusion with noncompliant and distractive behavior. A key strategy for ensuring that directions and expectations are clear and understood is to break them down into chunks or steps and to present them in multiple ways.

Many teachers simply state directions orally one time and expect their students to not only hear them and comprehend what is being asked of them but also to retain the information to follow instructions in the near future. This one-time auditory instruction often includes multiple steps and infers expectations rather than stating them explicitly. There are so many potential barriers in this type of direction (Mitchell et al., 2017)! Students with auditory processing deficits may not understand what is being asked of them, whereas students who are second language learners may not understand the vocabulary. Students who have attention deficits can miss part of the instruction, whereas students with memory deficits can quickly forget all the steps. Even the most gifted of students may find this type of direction difficult if they are explaining one part of the directions to a peer only to miss out on the following parts.

To ensure students understand what is being asked of them, both in directions and overall expectations, a good rule of thumb is to provide explicit, clear instruction in multiple formats (Mitchell et al., 2017). For example, when orally reviewing the directions, also have them projected on the screen for students to see. Break multistep directions down into sizable chunks or steps. Create a checklist for students to follow, and even check off as they complete different parts. Consider using a graphic organizer to help students see how different aspects of a longer assignment fit together. For more complex or multistep assignments, have the steps printed and posted on the classroom wall or uploaded to the class website for frequent access. After introducing each step orally and visually, ask a student in class to restate what the expectations are and, for more complicated steps, ask a second student to repeat or restate what the first said. When possible, provide visual exemplars of work that was completed and met all expectations or even videos of students completing the task or videos that could provide additional supports for those who need it. Taking the time to ensure directions and expectations are clear and accessible by all improves work engagement, which naturally increases compliance to instructions (Närhi et al., 2017). Finding multiple means to represent the directions and expectations to students is a key aspect of Universal Design for Learning (UDL), which is described in more detail in Chapter 6.

DEALING WITH STUDENTS' LACK OF MOTIVATION

Defining the Problem and Finding Solutions

· ·

When you were training to be a teacher, you might have envisioned a classroom of smiling faces where all students were well behaved and eager to learn. When you became a teacher, you likely found that the reality was quite different. In addition to a raft of behavior issues, teachers often find that some students do not seem motivated to engage with lessons or to learn. Lack of motivation can take many forms. Some students might be described as lazy or disinterested in learning, whereas others might seem overly negative about their abilities and therefore do not attempt tasks for fear of failure. Teachers of older students typically report motivation problems more frequently than those of younger children. One theory for why student motivation may decrease over time is that the focus on performance goals and grades overshadows goals related to learning new things and mastering important skills (Midgley et al., 1995; Scherrer & Preckel, 2019).

Motivation is a complex construct and can be affected by a number of factors (Martin, 2007). Although parental expectations and involvement are important in shaping a student's motivation to learn (Gonzalez-DeHass et al., 2005), the ways that teachers structure classrooms and activities also play a critical role (Urdan & Schoenfelder, 2006). Some teachers might become frustrated by lack of parental support and believe it is impossible to motivate students if parents are unwilling to help. Although it is true that most student problems are easier to solve with the support of families, teachers can still move forward with classroom-based interventions that can make a real difference to student motivation, learning, and achievement.

Another issue that often arises in discussions about motivating students is the difference between intrinsic and extrinsic motivation. Ideally, teachers would like students to engage with instruction because learning is motivating in and of itself. We want students' engagement to be maintained by acquisition of new skills, discovering things they did not know before, and feelings of competence and efficacy. We do not want them to be dependent on external rewards to engage in learning, such as stickers or certificates of achievement. However, we must be careful that our desire for intrinsically motivated students does not interfere with providing students what they need to be successful. Keep in mind that we as teachers, no matter how much we are motivated by our love of children and of learning, still do appreciate being paid for that work. Also, contrary to popular belief, providing extrinsic rewards does not necessarily undermine intrinsic motivation (Cerasoli et al., 2014). In fact, when extrinsic motivators are combined with verbal praise that functions as feedback, they can actually enhance intrinsic motivation (Cameron et al., 2001).

Lack of Motivation Scenario 1

Each morning, you start the day with a welcome to the class, a "bell ringer" or warm-up activity, a homework review, an overview of the objectives for today's lesson, and about 20 minutes of mini-lesson on the content focus of the day. You know your students like Lisa, Matteo, and Tom appreciate the structure, but you've been noticing that you seem to keep losing the attention of José, Kenneth, Flora, Kiernan, and Linda. After the first 10 minutes or so, José is up to sharpen his pencil, Linda is chatting to her peers, and the others do not appear motivated to listen or learn. You know Kenneth has already finished his homework, because he always does it, but then he does not appear motivated to go over the answers in class. This is so frustrating! You want to keep the attention and interest of this diverse class, but nothing is working. What do you do?

Scenario 1 Solution:
Mix It Up to Build Motivation!

Although structure is critical for every teacher—and most of their students—structure should not be the same thing as boring. Would you want to do the same thing every single day? We wouldn't. Consider instead identifying the tasks that need to be done, putting them on an agenda, but then mixing up how they are done to better include your students' voices and choices. For example, Linda is an extrovert and might appreciate being asked to be the "welcomer" for a week, meeting her peers at the door and saying "good morning." The warm-up activity might be done as a social, more engaging and motivating activity that can be done alone (for those students like Susana who prefers to work alone) or as a small group (for more extroverts like Linda and Isak). Let the students choose how they do the warm-up, provided the end result is that all participated, were engaged, and learned. In fact, you might even break the class into two groups, and while one group does the warm-up activity, the other could be reviewing the homework. Kenneth, Anna, and Kiernan might even be interested in walking around and supporting their peers in reviewing homework, which would play to their academic, social-emotional, and behavioral strengths.

When you are ready to begin the new lesson of the day, José (who needs to move often) can be the one to come to the board and point to today's objectives, while Flora or Linda read the objectives aloud to the class. Kiernan may even be asked to define some new terms or concepts that are part of the new objectives. Rather than moving straight into the mini-lesson, provide students the opportunity to do a Think–Pair–Share activity or an Elbow Partner activity, two cooperative learning strategies mentioned in Chapter 7, so they have a chance to move, talk, and reflect. Finally, when moving into the content of the lesson, remember that those 20 minutes do not have to always be done in a straight-forward direct instruction by the teacher format. Students may learn in co-taught groups (see Chapter 5), might learn cooperatively in stations (see Chapter 7), and will certainly benefit from having multiple ways that the material can be represented to them (Chapter 6). Structure is important, for sure, but strong teachers build flexibility into that structure to continually engage and motivate their diverse learners!

Lack of Motivation: Scenario 2

If you watched Matteo on the soccer pitch, you would never imagine he has any issues with confidence. He is the top scorer on the team and was recently named team captain. He is encouraging to teammates and often can be seen practicing with them after matches or during physical education. In the classroom, however, Matteo seems like a completely different person. When given work, he needs multiple reminders to get started and continue working. He rarely completes his homework. His performance is at least 1 year below grade level in both reading and

(Continued)

(Continued)

mathematics, so he receives specialized tutoring two times per week. His class assignments have been adapted so that they are set at an appropriate academic level and allow him to learn alongside his peers. However, the work he hands in is often incomplete, sloppy, and well below the standard he is capable of achieving. When asked why he doesn't try harder, Matteo's response is "I don't really care." What can you do?

Scenario 2 Solution: Get Him to the Goal!

Although tempting, it would be a mistake to automatically assume that Matteo does not care about the quality of his work. Although his behavior suggests a lack of concern about his performance, we probably need to dig a bit deeper to understand Matteo's perspective. Given that his achievement is 1–2 years below grade level, it is likely that Matteo is no stranger to failure in the classroom. Students who struggle with academics early in their school careers often fail to learn effective strategies for overcoming these struggles. Without these strategies, they learn that even when they try, they fail (Maier & Seligman, 1976). Therefore, it is not surprising that instead of trying to learn better strategies, students like Matteo simply try to avoid failure.

One effective way of avoiding failure is not to attempt things in the first place or intentionally do them poorly (which in turn, confirms that they "don't care"). For students like Matteo, motivating them to start trying again is paramount to getting them back on the right track. Matteo is already receiving specialized tutoring to help address his skill deficits in reading and mathematics. (You will read more about interventions for reading in Chapter 8.) Your role is to motivate him to apply those strategies when doing his work in the classroom.

Most people like the feeling of achievement and meeting goals. Setting goals can motivate us, provided those goals are challenging yet achievable (Morisano et al., 2010). When big changes in behavior are required, it is usually better to set smaller goals that set us up for attaining bigger goals. For example, if we rarely leave the sofa in the evenings and set a goal to go to the gym five evenings a week, most of us would not be successful. However, starting with a goal of one night per week (and then moving the goal to two nights, three nights, etc.) would be more likely to generate success. Over time, you could also incorporate goals about how much time you spend at the gym and what types of activities you do. In the same way, setting a goal for Matteo to do *all* his in-class and homework assignments with quality would likely be more demotivating than motivating. Instead, start with one feature of the work and set a goal around that. Note that the feature you start with might not ultimately be the most important feature.

The key here is to start with something that Matteo is likely to attain so that he can contact success quickly. For instance, you might set a goal for Matteo to bring back his homework each day with at least one thing completed. Or you might set a goal that his in-class work needs to be completed neatly (regardless of accuracy). Each day, Matteo should be provided feedback on how well he met the goal, including praise for what he did right and suggestions for doing better the next day (if appropriate). Graphing Matteo's goal attainment (or having him graph it) also is a powerful feedback tool. Using a soccer theme when graphing Matteo's performance might make it more engaging for him. Although seeing performance on a graph is often highly motivating, incorporating small rewards for meeting performance goals can further support motivation. For example, if Matteo met the homework goal for 4 out of 5 days in a week, you might allow him 10 minutes to read a soccer magazine on Friday afternoon. If he met the goal 5 out of 5 days, you might allow him 20 minutes to practice penalty shots with a classmate.

The strategies described here include both goal setting and a process called *shaping*. You can read more about these behavior analytic strategies in Chapter 3 on applied behavior analysis. Over time, it is likely that Matteo will no longer need the goal graph or the rewards to sustain better performance in class. As we build his success, we also will be building his skills and his self-efficacy, so he can feel as confident in the classroom as he does on the soccer pitch.

Lack of Motivation: Scenario 3

Over your career as a teacher, you have had every type of class imaginable. Some years you have had the dream classroom with the majority of students being eager to learn and without any substantial behavior problems. Most years have been a bit more challenging but never anything you could not handle. You are reflective about your teaching practices, so if your students do not seem interested in learning, you first try to change the instruction to spark their interests. You are a master at creating innovative activities that engage students with the learning process. However, this year, none of your strategies seem to be working. Despite incorporating a range of activities and assessment options into

(Continued)

(Continued)

your teaching, at least half your students demonstrate no interest in learning. Their heads are on their desks, and they look bored. What do you do?

Scenario 3 Solution: Give Them a Reason to Work!

Earlier in the chapter we noted that some students might not have developed an intrinsic motivation to engage with work. When students seem bored and disinterested, it certainly is good practice to ensure that the instruction is engaging and varied. However, if changing instruction does not seem to be enough to get the heads off the desks, adding some extrinsic reinforcers might help encourage participation so that students can access the natural reinforcers for engaging in learning. Using a token economy often is a good strategy for doing this.

Token economies involve setting expectations and then awarding tokens (e.g., points, stamps, stickers) for meeting those expectations. Earned tokens are then exchanged for activities or items at a later date. Token economies have been implemented across a range of settings and populations and have a substantial body of research to support their effectiveness (Soares et al., 2016). Many teachers have used variations of token economies in their classrooms. The degree to which these systems are effective, however, depends largely on the ways in which they are delivered. For maximum success, there are a number of principles derived from applied behavior analysis (see Chapter 3) that should be considered when developing and implementing token economies.

The first step in developing a token economy is to decide what behavior you want to change. For the class described in the scenario, you might start with only one expectation: participation in class. However, if there are other behavioral issues, like arriving on time and staying for the entire lesson, those also could be included in your expectations.

Once you have defined the behaviors you want to change, you can decide what types of tokens to use. The simplest way to deliver tokens is to have each student's name on a sheet of paper in your gradebook and to put a mark by their name each time they engage in the target behavior. However, teachers can be a bit more creative in their token delivery. For instance, the teacher might design class bucks, or have a marble jar, or use an electronic interface, like

ClassDojo®, to award tokens. Regardless of which approach you use, the most important factors in the effectiveness of your system are how frequently you award tokens and how often you allow students to trade their tokens for rewards. It is important to remember the more reinforcement you provide, the faster behavior will begin to change.

When you begin your token economy, you should try to catch each instance of the target behavior and award a token for it as quickly as you can. Be sure to deliver specific praise when delivering the token (e.g., "Anna, thanks for answering that question. That's a point for you."). To make token delivery easier, you might consider using the token economy during parts of the day (e.g., during particularly problematic lessons) rather than throughout the whole day. Once you are more comfortable with using the system, you can extend it to other parts of the day. It is also important not to wait too long before allowing students to trade their tokens for rewards. If there are long delays between earning tokens and trading them in, the tokens will lose their value and not be motivating. For young children, tokens should usually be traded at least once per day. For older students, tokens should be traded at least weekly and can lead to monthly reinforcers.

There are a few considerations when deciding what rewards students can "buy" with their tokens. Rewards should be things that can be delivered quickly and are inexpensive. For instance, students might be able buy access to special activities (playing a board game, extra time on class computers, being a class helper, eating outdoors) or access to small items like stickers or party favors. Occasionally incorporating new activities or items into the available options helps maintain interest and motivation to earn tokens. Typically, rewards are priced differently so that the more popular activities or items are more expensive. However, for the first few trade-in opportunities, teachers should ensure that everyone can buy *something*, even if some students have earned few tokens. This increases buy-in to the system and reinforces to students that following expectations will lead to positive outcomes. Teachers should never require students to trade tokens to access activities or items that would typically be available to them, like scheduled playtimes or school- or home-provided snacks.

One question that arises in using token systems is whether "fines" should be implemented; for example, if a student is late to class, should they lose some of their tokens? The simple answer is no. The risk with using fines is that some students will lose all their tokens before the time to trade them in. Usually, those at greatest risk for losing all their tokens are the very ones you are trying to motivate with the system; therefore, using fines will undermine what you are trying to accomplish. It also goes against what we know regarding Positive Behavior Intervention and Supports (PBIS, described further in Chapter 3). Therefore, you should think carefully about whether the potential risks incorporating fines into a token economy system outweighs the benefits of an earn only system. We think they don't.

As students begin to more frequently engage in the behaviors targeted by the token economy, be sure to point out some of the natural reinforcers for doing so (e.g., becoming more competent at a skill, learning more, having a more positive classroom environment, having your teacher nag you less frequently, making someone else proud of you). As behavior improves, you can *gradually* reduce the number of tokens you deliver. For instance, you might award a token for every other instance of participation rather than every time (other instances should still be acknowledged, however). If behavior improvements maintain, then you can reduce the token delivery a bit more. It is important to remember that token economies are not intended to be long-term strategies for maintaining motivation. Rather, their purpose is to get behavior started by providing a more motivating reason to do the behavior.

SUPPORTING LITERACY FOR ALL LEARNERS

Defining the Problem and Finding Solutions

No one needs to tell you that teaching literacy skills is one of the most important objectives in education. Those without good reading, writing, listening, and speaking skills are at a specific disadvantage in numerous aspects of their lives, including access to further education, employment, and some leisure activities. Children's development of literacy skills begins in infancy, when their parents or caregivers speak, read, or play with them. In fact, the number of words children hear from birth to three years old can have a profound impact on their later success at school (Hart & Risley, 1995). Although literacy begins at home, teachers obviously play an essential role in the further development of children's literacy skills, which will be critical in promoting their future success across a range of domains.

As you likely know from your own experience, many students struggle with different aspects of literacy. These difficulties can stem from lack of experience with language (either as a child from a family that doesn't communicate well or as a second language learner), cognitive processing difficulties, or early failure in literacy tasks. As you will read in Chapter 8, there is no one-size-fits-all approach to supporting literacy development. Therefore, having several strategies for promoting different aspects of literacy will help you better meet the needs of a diverse group of learners.

You have a class with a range of reading abilities, but luckily, most of your students are relatively good decoders. When asked to read aloud in class, most can read a passage with relatively few errors, although some are clearly more fluent decoders than others. You know you can work on decoding skills, so that doesn't worry you. What is worrying is that when you ask students a question about what they have read, they either stare at you blankly or look down at their book to try to find the answer. You want them to think about and process what they have read so that you can have meaningful discussions that spark their interest in reading more. What do you do?

Scenario 1 Solution: Be Brainy! by Adrienne Gear

There are many strategies to encourage children to think about what they read. For young readers, children can be introduced to "book reading" and "brain reading." Remind students that good readers learn to "book read" when they read the words in the book, but then they also learn to "brain read" by thinking in their brain about what those words mean. Although emergent readers may not be able to decode all the words, they can still practice brain reading. Modeling book reading and brain reading when reading aloud helps students identify the differences. As you read a few pages aloud, note to students that you are book reading, and then pause on a page and model brain reading by telling the students what you are thinking about as you read. Using a thinking bubble cutout, which you can hold up to show when brain reading is taking place, can be a positive use of a visual cue to support understanding.

The One Word activity is a simple, yet powerful exercise that you can use in both reading lessons and in content area instruction from the early years to upper grades. It is an excellent way of showing students visibly how thinking changes and evolves as individuals construct deeper meaning (Gear, 2018). In preparation for this activity, teachers are encouraged to choose a book that focuses on a particular theme: inclusion, poverty, homelessness, kindness, and so on. Note how this activity can also be linked to work on social-emotional learning (described in more detail in Chapter 9). Select one word that connects with this theme. The lesson starts by writing this one word on the board or screen. Invite students to think about the word and silently focus on a connection, a visual image, and a feeling that come to mind when they see the word. After a few moments, ask students to share their ideas with a partner then to share with a small group. Students record their responses on the board around the one word, creating a class web. Depending on the age and ability of the students, you can do this with various levels of support.

After you create the class web, explain that the class will be reading a story connected to the word but that students should pay attention while reading the story (either aloud or to themselves) and notice if their thoughts change or shift in any way. At the end of the story, invite the class to think about the word again, and share any new thinking that the story has presented for them. Using different colors, add the new thinking to the web, creating a new layer around the web. Reflect on the fact that sometimes, when people read, something in the story can start to shift the way they see or think about something. This new thinking doesn't replace the previous idea but "stretches" it, helping learners to have a new perspective.

This One Word activity also works well when focusing on a new topic of study or theme in a science or Social Studies class. Write the word on the board before beginning the unit, and invite students to share their initial thoughts and connections. After the unit of study is complete, revisit the word and see how much more information and new insights you can add to the web.

Promoting Literacy: Scenario 2

You want your students to be knowledgeable about current events, so you often bring passages from online, newspapers, or magazines to share with your students. You try to bring things that cover a range of topics, from climate change, to world politics, to human rights, and even to the latest controversies in professional sports. However, you find class discussions a bit discouraging. Although students seem to enjoy hearing about or reading the articles, when you lead a discussion, they seem to only focus on the facts of the news item rather than processing what they have read. You want them to be critical thinkers and sophisticated consumers of information, but it's clear your students aren't quite there yet. What do you do?

Scenario 2 Solution: So Now What? by Adrienne Gear

Helping students move from the literal content into a deeper, transformed understanding can be challenging. Scaffolding students' thinking and helping them move between one level of understanding to the next can provide the context for their understanding to move to that next level. The What/So What/Now What strategy provides clear stages for students to be able to experience these shifts in thinking (Gear, 2018).

Create a large, three-column table on the board or screen (see Table 1). Choose a short passage of text, preferably connected to a unit of study the students are already working on. Read the passage aloud twice, and invite students to focus on the three most important points. These are literal facts extracted directly from the text. After sharing their facts with a partner, invite a few students to share the facts and record them in the first column under the "What" heading. Consider multiple ways for students to share and record their facts (e.g., pictures, speech to text, oral explanations). Explain that these are the literal facts from the text but that good readers don't only extract facts and move on; they take time to think.

Explain that the next column on the chart is for them to add their thinking: questions, connections, visual images, and inferences. Invite them to share their thinking with a partner (orally, through text messages or videos, face-to-face, or online) and then invite students to share with the class. Have their responses recorded in the "So What?" column. Finally, tell students that you want them to stretch their thinking even more and move into the last column. This is for what is sometimes called "transformed" thinking, or the "Now What?" section. Invite them to think about how the information may have shifted the way they are thinking. "What are you thinking now that you may not have ever considered before?" Scaffolding students thinking in this way provides them with the tools and language to deepen their understanding with any topic or subject area. An example appears in Table 1.

Table 1

Example of a What/So What/Now What Chart

WHAT?	SO WHAT?	NOW WHAT?
What does the book tell us?	*So what am I thinking about? (connections, questions, inferences)*	*Now what am I thinking that I hadn't thought about before?*
• Starfish arms grow back when they get cut off	• How long does it take? • That reminds me of worms.	• Too bad that doesn't happen to soldiers. If it did, maybe they wouldn't be so scared to go to war.

"I have nothing to write about!" You have lost count of the number of times you hear your students say this. You remind them that they all have unique experiences, cultures, and hobbies, but still: nothing. Even when they do find something to write about, their ideas are underdeveloped and disjointed. You are not so worried about spelling, punctuation, and grammar at this point because you feel more confident about how to fix that. But how do you get your students to write with *meaning*? What do you do?

Scenario 3 Solution: Put Something in Your Pocket! by Adrienne Gear

When we teach writing, we often place our focus on the product, process, or genre. Paran and Wallace find that the "most prevalent approach .... is still the product approach with teachers and textbooks providing linguistic models which students are encouraged to work from and base their own writing on" (2016, p. 452). Although this provides a type of scaffold for the student, it neglects to honor their individual contexts, cultures, or needs. Paran and Wallace have suggested that the genre-focused approach teaches new writers to consider *why* texts are produced the way they are, what the purpose of the writer was, and how certain linguistic elements display the writer's choices. Obviously, recognizing a student's culture or background knowledge or context can help support them as a growing writer. (More strategies for culturally responsive instruction are provided in Chapter 6.)

Teachers need to consider if they are trying to teach their students to "learn to write" or to "write to learn" (similar to the same question for reading). Students might be taught to focus on the writer (what are their thoughts as they work?), the text (what words are they selecting to communicate?), or the reader (what might someone glean from the writing?) (Hyland, 2011). Note how this considers so much more than simply focusing on grammar, spelling, or punctuation!

Writing involves many different skills to include working memory, short-term memory, long-term memory, graphomotor skills, language, higher-order cognition, processing, and organizing (Anderson et al., 2001). No wonder it is so daunting to many students! Developing an awareness of thinking as a writer is one of the best ways to reduce the stress of deciding on a topic and helping young writers feel more confident as they work on their specific writing skills.

Many teachers incorporate some time in their week for students to free write or have unstructured writing time. This often involves time in the weekly schedule when students have the freedom to explore their own topics and choose what medium to use, what tool to write with, where they want to write, and who they want to read their writing. Some use journals for this unstructured time, or provide writing prompts, or ask for QuickWrites. Too often, though, these responses are rather superficial and even boring—both for the writer and the reader.

Brain Pocket Writing (Gear, 2020) is an alternative to journal writing, providing students the freedom to choose their own writing topics while at the same time helping them develop a more metacognitive stance about generating independent topics for writing. Making the shift from journal writing to Brain Pocket writing can result in writing that is more focused, interesting, and enjoyable to read.

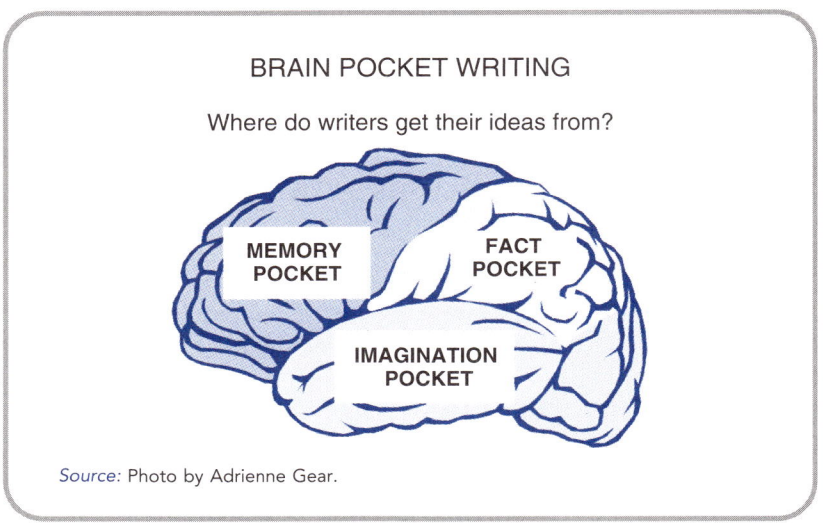

Source: Photo by Adrienne Gear.

To start, ask students, "Where do writers get their ideas?" Explain that most writers write from ideas they already have stored in their head. Explain that each person's brain organizes thinking into three different storage "pockets": memories and experiences are stored in a Memory Pocket, facts and information are stored in a Fact Pocket, and creative ideas are stored in an Imagination Pocket. When a writer begins writing, they usually focus on one of these pockets to find their ideas.

Draw a large Brain Pocket image on the board or screen, and model specific topics one might find in each of the Brain Pockets (see sample). Explain that each person's Brain Pockets are unique, particularly the Memory Pocket because no one shares the same memories. Invite students to create a similar image in their Brain Pocket notebook (or using technology). Explain that although students won't necessarily be writing on all of these topics, they can now use this as a source for ideas.

Brain Pockets—Teacher Model

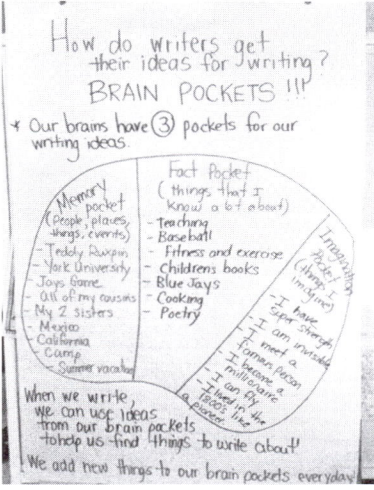

Source: Photo by Adrienne Gear.

Brain Pockets—Student Sample

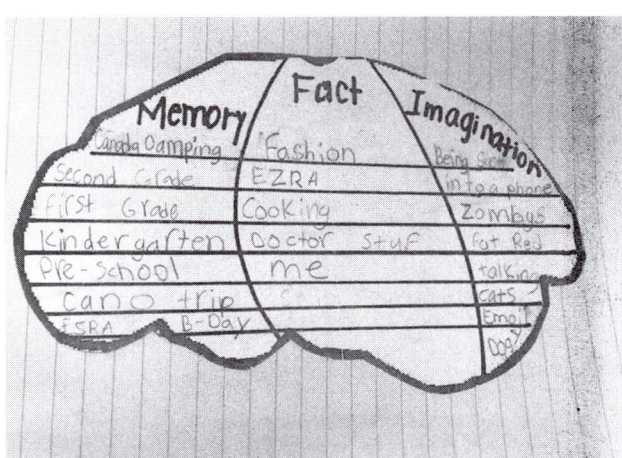

Source: Photo by Adrienne Gear.

Like most journal writing, students usually do Brain Pocket writing once a week. It is an activity that teachers can easily integrated into center time, or the large group can be working on their Brain Pocket Writing while other students are receiving additional reteaching or guided instruction on their writing. Encourage students to look over ideas from their Brain Pocket plan and choose one pocket they would like to access from that day. When assessing or conferencing with students about their writing, make sure to include their Brain Pocket writing.

TEACHING IN CULTURALLY DIVERSE CLASSROOMS

Defining the Problem and Finding Solutions

The past decades have seen the composition of classrooms change dramatically. Consistent with growth in immigration (United Nations, 2019), teachers regularly teach students from a range of cultural, ethnic, and religious backgrounds. Although some of these students will have been born and raised in the countries where they are being educated, others will be new to the educational systems in which they currently find themselves. Not only may the language be foreign to them, but school practices, rules, and routines might also be new and potentially unusual.

Cultural diversity provides a wealth of opportunities for students to learn from one another and broaden their knowledge of different nations, cultures, and religions. In general, teachers should adopt approaches that both acknowledge and appreciate cultural diversity. Although all students will be expected to abide by the norms and procedures used at the school, allowing both native and immigrant students to share their cultural practices and customs can create opportunities not only to see what is unique about our respective cultures but also to appreciate what is shared.

Despite the many benefits, teaching a class of diverse learners is not without its challenges. In addition to language barriers, students may struggle with acclimating to both educational and social systems within the school. Teachers might also have to negotiate issues regarding stereotypes and prejudices as they attempt to create a positive and inclusive classroom environment.

Cultural Diversity: Scenario 1

You knew when you entered the teaching profession that your students would have different academic skills. You expected some students to read better than others or some students to struggle in math. You were ready to explain concepts a second time or pair students with their peers to provide additional support. However, you never considered what you'd do if those students did not even understand your language! How do you teach math or reading or writing when there are students who don't even speak English? Worse yet, not all of these students speak the *same* first language. Susana speaks German; José, Matteo, Camila, and Luis speak Spanish; Ivan speaks Russian; Fatima is Syrian and speaks Arabic; Linda speaks Swedish; Mohammad and Isak are Iranian and speak Persian; whereas Kiernan speaks Irish Gaelic and Hassan speaks Somali as their primary languages, although both have strong English skills. There is no way you can learn all of these languages. What can you do?

Scenario 1 Solution:
Use Alternative Teaching!

Alternative Teaching is one model used when co-teaching. Alternative Teaching is when one educator works with a larger group of students as the other educator works with a smaller group (Karten & Murawski, 2020). Typically, teachers use Alternative Teaching when a small subset of students could benefit from reteaching, pre-teaching, or even enrichment (Murawski & Ricci, 2019). In Scenario 1, many of the students do not speak English as their primary language and therefore would definitely benefit from both pre- and reteaching at times.

Consider having one co-teacher start the lesson with a warm-up activity or homework review for the first 10 minutes. During this time, the other educator in the room would be able to pull Susana, José, Matteo, Fatima, Mohammad, John, Flora, and Amy to a small group (physically when in a brick-and-mortar classroom or to a breakout room online when working through distance learning). The first six students are second language learners who are struggling the most with the language; Amy and Flora are your American students who have an intellectual disability. All eight of these students would benefit from a co-teacher proactively presenting key vocabulary for the day's lesson. Pre-teaching the vocabulary will help all of these students access the instruction from the lesson by removing one of the major barriers to understanding. Once the lesson is done, they might work in a small group again to reinforce the instruction, while their peers begin some homework or independent activity (Karten & Murawski, 2020).

Students can be strategically clustered for Alternative Teaching groups based on their needs and strengths. For example, Mohammad and Isak are both Iranian, but Mohammad is struggling, whereas Isak is more advanced. Therefore, you could allow the two to work together so that Isak can help support Mohammad's language acquisition and understanding. (You'll read more about peer tutoring in Scenario 3.) You can bring together small groups to provide additional supports throughout the week and vary their arrangement depending on what you are trying to accomplish (Murawski & Ricci, 2019). Although this small group of eight may need to work together more often to help scaffold the instruction for them, you might also create a group of students who need help due to behavioral or attention needs or even a group of the strongest learners like Kenneth, Anna, Linda, Kiernan, and Isak who, although a few of them are English language learners, could still be grouped together and given a challenge to solve collaboratively.

Working with another teacher, specialist, or pedagogue can provide a variety of options for helping meet the diverse needs of an inclusive class. Alternative Teaching is only one model for co-instructing students when co-teaching. Check out Chapter 5 for more information on using co-teaching as a solid instructional strategy to support diverse learners.

Cultural Diversity: Scenario 2

Even though you have great academic diversity in your class, and most of the students show strong academic development, Fatima and Mohammad are struggling in most subjects. Both arrived to the United States around 2 years ago, but they have been at your school only since last year. During the time in your class, you have invested a lot in supporting their development. They are both studying English as a second language (ESL). They are both struggling with the English language, and you feel they are getting less motivated to study despite all the support you have offered. You have provided support with extra ESL lessons together with another teacher, but so far that hasn't made the difference you were hoping for. You need to help them start succeeding more with their studies and let them experience learning and development, but how?

Scenario 2 Solution: Use Familiar Contexts and Students' Own Interests

Although we try to individualize strategies to student needs, sometimes the best solutions are aimed at the entire group. For almost everyone, different subject-specific concepts can be difficult to understand if one is not familiar with the content. For instance, much of the content we use in our teaching can be focused on American culture and norms; for those who are new to that culture, the concepts might be difficult to understand or cause confusion. To understand the content, it helps to have a context (Garten et al., 2019). Therefore, integrate more context into lessons.

Part of your strategy will be to make your learning environment more accessible and to ensure that the content has meaning for your students. Therefore, you will need to find out more about Fatima and Mohammad's interests, so you can engage them as much as possible. Obviously, students are typically quite familiar with the things they are interested in. That familiarity will facilitate their understanding even when they don't know every word they hear or read. Although Fatima and Mohammad are the only two who are struggling at the moment, given that many of your students can benefit from this approach, you should integrate context in whole-class instruction. Alternatives can be offered so that everyone can have a context that provides meaning for them (Murawski & Scott, 2019). Providing choice also fits nicely with the concept of UDL, which you will learn more about in Chapter 6.

Another whole-class approach that will support myriad learners is the language development approach, which can be used in all the subjects that you teach. This means preparing explanations of key words and concepts that your students need to learn and understand, including synonyms for key words and explanations of what they mean. Again, it is important to remember the importance of context, and try to provide definitions, explanations, and examples within a context that is familiar to Fatima and Mohammad. You can read more in Chapter 8 about how you can support your students more specific in the area of literacy.

This suggested solution is based on UDL. When you have a diverse class, creating adaptations for each of them can prove too challenging and resource intensive. By designing your learning environment to fit many different needs, you'll have fewer students who need intensive, individualized support. You can read more about strategies related to integrating UDL in Chapter 6.

Hassan is from Somalia and has attended your school since the start of the school year. His family immigrated to the United States when he was 2 years old. Hassan is skilled at drawing and likes to write storybooks that he can illustrate. He is a capable reader, reading at about grade level, and he seems to do well in mathematics. Although he seemed to enjoy participating in lessons earlier in the year, he now seems more reserved. If you call on him to answer a question or solve a problem on the board, he almost always has the correct answer; however, you can hear some of the other students whispering and giggling. Last week, you heard Hassan shouting at some of the other students on the playground. When you asked the children what happened, Hassan said that the other kids were saying that his father was a taxi driver and his mother cleaned houses (despite them both being skilled professionals). The other boys said they didn't do anything wrong. What do you do?

Scenario 3 Solution:
Let Him Share His Strengths!

There are a number of issues that need to be addressed in this situation, including reflection on the degree to which the current curriculum and classroom practices actively encourage respect for cultural diversity and individual differences. Although there are a range of strategies for addressing cultural stereotypes and biases (e.g., Derman-Sparks, 1989), arranging situations that allow students to challenge implicit beliefs about others can be particularly helpful.

Given that Hassan is good at academics and art, allowing him to tutor other students would provide an opportunity for students to work supportively together while allowing Hassan to share his knowledge and skills with others. Although designating Hassan as a peer tutor to a less academically competent student is one option, another evidence-based strategy is to use class-wide peer tutoring (Maheady et al., 2006; Simonsen et al., 2008). Because class-wide peer tutoring allows everyone in the class to serve as both a tutor and tutee, it increases the variability in peer pairings and allows students to be paired with different peers across tutoring sessions. In a diverse classroom, this means that students will have more opportunities to work with peers who might be viewed as different from them, thus providing more opportunities to disconfirm negative stereotypes and to encourage positive interactions among peers (Bowman-Perrott et al., 2014).

To use class-wide peer tutoring, you will need to select a skill that requires a distinct correct answer (such as spelling words, sight words, math facts, capitals of countries, etc.). You will then need to prepare lists or flash cards of the content to be taught as well as a sheet for recording correct and incorrect answers during the tutoring sessions. Different lists or flash cards can be created to suit academic abilities and distributed accordingly during the tutoring sessions. For example, you might have different spelling or sight-word lists for different students.

Once you've prepared your materials, you then need to train students how to be good tutors. Explain that they will be trading roles as teacher and student. When they are the teacher, they will ask the question (or present the flash card) and silently count to five. If their tutoring partner gives the correct answer before they finish counting, they should tell them their answer is correct (e.g., "That's right! Good job!") and record it as a "first try" on the scorecard. If their partner doesn't get it right (or doesn't answer), they should say, "The answer is __. Let's do it again." They should then present the item again, allow the student to answer, and record it as a "second try" on the scorecard. This process is called *active error correction* (Barbetta et al., 1993; Simonsen et al., 2008). It guarantees that the student will get the answer correct on the second try and allows them to practice the correct answer in the presence of the question. At the end of the session, students will need to tally the number of first-try answers and second-try answers. The pairs get two points for every first-try answer and one point for every second-try answer.

During class-wide peer tutoring sessions, the teacher divides the class into two teams, and then each of those teams in divided into pairs. To ensure that students work with different peers across sessions, the teacher should designate the pairs rather than allowing the students to choose. Tutoring sessions are usually about 10 minutes, during which each student spends 5 minutes as the teacher and 5 minutes as the learner. At the end of the session, the pairs add up their points, and those points are added into a team total. The team with the most points wins. Although teachers can offer a small reward to winning teams, being designated the winner often is sufficient to motivate students to earn as many points as possible during the tutoring sessions. It is important to vary not only the composition of tutoring pairs but also of the two teams to ensure that all students experience being on a winning team and that no one student is identified as always bringing down the team.

In addition to supporting the growth of academic skills, class-wide peer tutoring has been shown to increase positive peer interactions and decrease negative interactions (Simonsen et al., 2008). Within a culturally diverse classrooms, it can provide opportunities to meaningfully engage with peers with whom students might not typically include in their peer groups, such as Hassan, and to work cooperatively toward a shared goal. Although class-wide peer tutoring is typically considered a strategy rooted in applied behavior analysis (Chapter 3), it also is a great example of a cooperative learning strategy. You'll find more information about these types of strategies in Chapter 7.

DEALING WITH AN ACADEMICALLY DIVERSE CLASS

Defining the Problem and Finding Solutions

Every teacher has experienced classrooms comprised of students with a range of academic abilities. However, regardless of what academic strengths and challenges those students bring to the classroom, teachers are still expected to deliver the curriculum in a way that is meaningful and effective for all students. This is a tall order for any teacher because the reasons why children may academically excel or fall behind are as varied as the children themselves. Children's early experiences at home have a significant impact on school readiness skills, including their abilities to follow classroom routines, their pre-academic skills, and their vocabularies (Belsky et al., 2007; Hart & Risley, 1995). Some children might also have special education needs or physical or mental health issues that may affect their academic performance.

Without effective skills and strategies to meet the needs of diverse learners, teachers may find themselves "teaching to the middle." In other words, they aim their teaching strategies at those students whose academic abilities are on grade level without sufficient adaptations for those who fall at the ends of the distribution, sometimes called "in the margins" (Meyer & Rose, 2005). Quite obviously, this tactic can potentially result in more academically able students becoming bored and disengaged from learning. Likewise, students who are below grade level may find themselves confused, frustrated, and unable to keep up—ultimately resulting in a similar disengagement from learning as their more advanced peers. For both groups, instruction that fails to adequately engage students in the learning process risks not only preventing them from reaching their academic potential but also increases the likelihood of disruptive behavior (Meyer & Rose, 2005).

Special education provision can offer support for both students and their teachers, but this often is not enough to ensure positive outcomes (McIntosh et al., 2008). In addition, not all students at the lower or upper ends of the academic spectrum will qualify for these services. Even if they do, there is a growing expectation that general education classroom teachers will play active roles in supporting these students in inclusive general education classrooms and settings. Now more than ever, it is imperative that all teachers have access to a range of strategies that can effectively engage all students in the learning process and help them acquire essential academic skills that reflect their true capabilities and prepare them for a brighter future.

Academic Diversity: Scenario 1

Given your students' range of academic abilities, sometimes you think you are teaching four different grades at the same time. Mathematics instruction is particularly difficult. You have grouped the students in your class according to their abilities and have attempted to set work that is appropriately challenging for them, but you feel like you keep missing the target. Whole-group instruction seems impossible; the high achievers either answer all the questions before the other students have a chance, or they sit there looking painfully bored. Your lower-achieving students never attempt to participate during lessons, and many won't even make eye contact when you ask questions. You also have noticed more disruptive behavior, particularly with students chatting to one another or finding other things to occupy their time (staring out the window, playing with things in their desks, bothering other students). You need a strategy to get everyone engaged in instruction, but you also need to quickly identify those who are struggling during the lesson, so you can calibrate your teaching accordingly. What do you do?

Scenario 1 Solution: Play Cards!

All teachers know that more engagement leads to better learning (Lochner et al., 2019). However, regardless of the range of academic activities in a classroom, getting everyone actively engaged can be difficult for any teacher. Unfortunately, some of the strategies we use for evoking participation naturally limit students' opportunities to respond. For instance, asking a question and then calling on a student to answer is a common practice. However, once the teacher hears a correct answer, the opportunity to respond (OTR) ends for all the other students who raised their hands (and it is impossible to know how many of those students actually would have given the correct answer). Although there are some high-tech strategies for promoting more participation in classes, such as electronic response clickers, the resources required to implement these strategies might be out of reach for some teachers. Luckily, response cards offer a low-tech option that any teacher can implement. Response cards are essentially small dry-erase boards that allow students to write their responses to the teacher's questions. There is a wealth of research demonstrating positive effects of response cards on both academic achievement and reduction of problem behavior (Morgan et al., 2010). Further, the strategy is appropriate for students with and without special education needs (Berrong et al., 2007; George, 2010; Randolph, 2007). A particularly important feature of using response cards is that they provide immediate feedback to the teacher regarding who is "getting it" and who isn't.

Using response cards requires that each student have access to a small dry erase board, a dry erase marker, and an eraser. You can make your own dry erase boards by purchasing a sheet of shower panel from a local building supply store and having it cut into multiple boards. You can also create response cards on paper, such as the one in the side box (True-Daley, 2021), and laminate the paper for students to use with dry erase markers over and over again. You can further reduce costs by asking students to bring a sock or flannel from home to serve as their eraser.

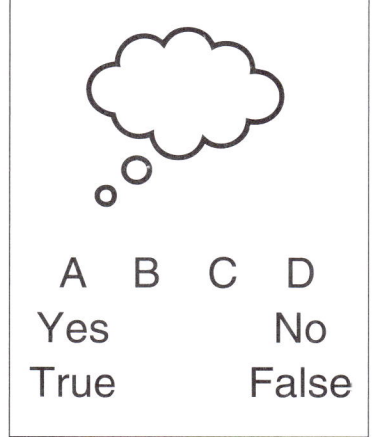

Source: Jaime True-Daley. Used with permission.

Prior to sessions in which response cards will be used, you should prepare several questions you plan to ask during the lesson. (Remember, the more response opportunities, the more learning.) With groups of academically diverse learners, you will probably need different versions of each question to allow everyone the opportunity to confidently participate. If different academic groups have different names (e.g., blue group, purple group, red group), you can easily designate the questions for each group. Preparing two sets of questions that assess the same skill or concept is a good idea because it gives you an opportunity to reassess students' understanding if there are many incorrect answers to the first question.

When using response cards, it is important to cue simultaneous responding so that everyone raises their cards at the same time. This reduces the pressure on students who may need longer to answer. Some teachers use a countdown once they've determined that most students have written their answers or are close to completing their responses (e.g., "OK, three, two, one, cards up!"). Immediately after the students raise their cards, you should scan the class to determine how many students have answered correctly. This provides important feedback regarding how well students have understood the concept being taught and can tell you whether you need to go back and explain the concept again or if it is safe to move forward. It also might help you identify particular students who consistently answer incorrectly, so you can provide some additional support. (You can read more about other types of formative assessment in Chapter 2.)

After you have scanned the classroom, it is time to immediately provide the correct answer for the question(s) and explain why the answer is correct. This can be the perfect opportunity to address the diversity of the class. Groups can be quickly formed by the responses. You can ask students who answered correctly to explain their answers to peers in their groups who didn't answer correctly. If you are a special educator, or co-teaching with one, you might have one group get some specially designed instruction to support those who are truly struggling. Test students' understanding of the concept by following up with a similar question.

In addition to helping increase active participation and learning, using response cards is fun. Most students report that they prefer response cards over hand raising and that they feel like they learn more when they use response cards (Clarke et al., 2016). Some teachers worry that using response cards will evoke more off-task behavior, and it is true that some students would rather doodle on their white boards than pay attention to instruction. However, as response cards become integrated into classroom activities, the novelty of drawing on them typically wears off. Teachers can further address students' desires to doodle by allowing them some time to draw on the boards at the end of the lesson.

Academic Diversity: Scenario 2

You're teaching both English and Social Studies to an inclusive class of 23 incredibly diverse learners. You are committed to helping them all succeed, but doing so is stressing you out! Students with disabilities have some different needs from the other students in your class, plus you have some gifted students who you suspect are often quite bored with the instruction you've prepared. You've tried arranging seating arrangements according to curricula and abilities so that you have the students with the biggest academic challenges near you at the front of the class. It hasn't escaped your attention that you are unintentionally leaving some students to get on with learning on their own—or letting them sit and do little—as well as potentially stigmatizing those you have moved to the front of the room. Plus, you find yourself running around the class to attend to those who are more likely to ask for help rather than helping those who are most in need. After all, you are only one person! To make matters worse, your school doesn't provide resources for another teacher or assistant in the classroom, so all the pressure is on you. What do you do?

Scenario 2 Solution: Give Them a Choice!

Because you have such academic diversity in your class, you need to make the learning environment as accessible as possible. Therefore, you give your students different opportunities or ways to learn the academic content. Since you have two curricula to manage (English and Social Studies), you can compare them, looking for similarities. Those similarities will help you plan for some whole-class activities that can work for all the students. To both challenge the quick learners and those who have more difficulties in such a way that they get an opportunity to study in their proximal zone of development, you will need to offer options. Thus, you can plan tasks at different levels that train the same abilities.

In the classroom, try to present the learning goals in different ways. Some students need visual support, some prefer to have instructions in writing, and some prefer to listen to instructions. The students have different capacities in working memory, so you will also want to provide your students memory support so that they can go back to the lesson when they feel a need for it. Without a doubt, you also have students who would benefit from being able to prepare themselves even before the lesson.

If you use some sort of digital learning platform at your school, as most do post-pandemic, make sure that your lesson content, learning goals, and learning tasks are available online *before* you introduce the content in the classroom. With such a platform, all homework—if you give your students homework—should be available there. That will also be helpful for students who miss a lesson, so they have a chance of not falling behind. Some of your students might also receive support from a special education teacher, paraprofessional, educational therapist, or classroom assistant outside of your classes; having materials uploaded proactively ensures that those individuals have access to those materials as well.

There are many possible ways to reach a goal as well as ways to show that the goal has been reached. Talk to your students. Ask them about their ideas regarding how they would like to learn the academic content, and offer alternative ways to demonstrate their learning. Although it is not feasible to offer 23 different ways, you can let your students come up with ideas and have an influence on the process; in the end, they will have some options to choose from that they helped develop, thereby increasing student buy-in. Similarly, you can develop a process with your students wherein they can identify different options to demonstrate for you what they have learned and that they have reached the learning goals. One student might do it in writing, another student might record a short video, and yet another student might organize a role-play to show what was learned. There are many ways to demonstrate learning and different abilities (Meyer & Rose, 2005).

Consider embedding choice and different options in your instruction. For example, if you start your lesson with an introduction, you may find that many of your students can manage only short introduction times, whereas others prefer longer, more in-depth introductions. Those who prefer the longer introductions can often manage to have the introduction divided in two parts. In that way, you can start with a short instruction to the whole class and then give more instruction to those who need it a little later during the lesson.

It is difficult to manage a class with great diversity alone if you primarily use whole-class instruction. Therefore, consider making a shift. Start to use a station system in your classroom more frequently, and spend only short moments of your lessons with whole-class instruction. To facilitate this, you should organize the seating for your students into groups. That will also facilitate meeting sensory-motor needs and increase student collaboration. You can read more about those strategies in Chapter 1 on sensory-motor development and in Chapter 7 on cooperative learning. For example, you might create four groups with six students in each group. Then you can organize a system with four stations: one station might be watching video clips about the content, the second can involve skills training that would be easy to do individually, the third could be a practically oriented station, and the fourth station might be a station where you would facilitate a student-driven discussion and interaction.

When you initiate a system with working stations, do not expect it to work perfectly and smoothly from the beginning. Students need to be taught the model, and they will require some time to learn and get support in their learning process. In the beginning, it can be wise to select three stations with activities you know that your students enjoy doing and with which they are already familiar. Every station doesn't even have to be on the academic content for the lesson. That can develop over time. Initially, it is more important to teach the system to your students, let them get familiar working in stations, and help them learn that some of the stations involve independent work without teacher support (or at least a minimum of that). The students still have support from each other, and that can be a great asset both for you and your students. The strategy used in this solution involves UDL, which you can read more about in Chapter 6, and cooperative learning, which is described in more detail in Chapter 7.

Academic Diversity: Scenario 3

You look out at the beautiful faces of the children in your class and take a deep breath. Flora, who has an intellectual disability and Down syndrome, is happily chatting to Eva about her favorite TV show; Eva appears amused and is sitting listening quietly. As usual, it appears that Fatima is doodling on her paper as she sits in a chair she has continuously and slowly moved daily a little farther away from her peers; you know she is uncomfortable because she speaks so little English. Luis is also doodling before class begins, sharing his pictures of types of fish with Tom, who is sitting next to him. There is so much diversity in this class—not only academically but also in terms of language, culture, gender, interests, behaviors, skills, and social-emotional intelligence. Every time you do an activity that you think will be fun and motivating, you still have a few children who appear uninterested, bored, or even actively disengaged. You know that your job is to teach them all, not only those who are academically at grade level, but how can you do that? What else can you try?

Scenario 3 Solution: Calling All Kids!

As was mentioned in the scenario, there is only one of you. But that does not mean you are alone! Although another adult in the room would certainly make teaching and grouping easier, you should not give up on grouping because you do not have additional adult support. You already know that your students are diverse—why not use that diversity to your advantage? Some of your students are strong academically, whereas others have their strengths in appropriate classroom behavior or in language or even in leadership skills. Cooperative learning techniques are ones in which teachers get students in small groups to emphasize those strengths.

During times when you need to teach academic information at different levels, you can divide and conquer. Create small groups in which there are different roles for each student. A student who may not be as strong academically but is strong in leadership skills, such as Linda, might be an excellent "Facilitator" Oscar likes to be helpful but can be the class clown if he doesn't have a specific task to do, so he can be the "Materials Manager." Someone like Camila, who speaks multiple languages, can help support her peers who are English language learners as the "Interpreter," whereas Flora, who is far behind her peers academically but loves to participate and can be supported by her friends, can be the group "Reporter." As someone who likes to write, Hassan can be the "Recorder" for the group, and Amy, another student with significant academic needs, can be the group's "Cheerleader," whose goal is to keep the group upbeat, working, and positive. Students like Anna, Kenneth, and Kiernan might be bored with the content or their peers, so making them the group "Consultants" (i.e., the people with a lot of knowledge whose job it is to help others gain that knowledge while continuing to learn more on their own) would be perfect for them. Having specific roles when working in heterogeneous and diverse groups will help students play to their strengths, supporting one another to learn the content at different levels.

Cooperative learning techniques (described further in Chapter 7) can also help address diverse academic levels by allowing students to occasionally work with more homogeneously grouped peer activities. Although you need to be sure not to overuse academically homogeneous groups, so that students do not feel they are in the "smart" or "dumb" group, using them occasionally based on formative assessment data (such as that you may have identified using the response card strategy mentioned earlier) can be helpful. Based on data, create small groups of students who have similar academic or background knowledge on a topic. Again, use the cooperative learning strategies described in Chapter 7 to encourage students to support one another's learning as you circulate, question, and facilitate.

Different levels of questions or work on the same topic can enable all groups to address the same topic where they are rather than where the curriculum says the grade level should be. By preparing different levels of work around the same topic, students can work collaboratively with their peers on solving problems, answering questions, watching videos, and learning more content that engages them at their level, all while avoiding the need for you to run around like a chicken with its head cut off!

SOCIAL-EMOTIONAL CHALLENGES

Defining the Problem and Finding Solutions

Emotions, emotions, emotions—think back to when something emotionally charged happened during recess or lunch. When you try to start teaching, all the students can think about is what happened during that time. Or consider when you are about to give an assessment. Some of your students will be anticipating an unfavorable outcome, and unfortunately, they will then probably think only about that. Their attention will not be where it needs to be for learning even though they, like you, may want it to. As the teacher, you too can experience negative emotions, like anxiety or frustration, during class, which will hamper your teaching and your students' learning. Strong positive emotions can equally distract from learning tasks. For instance, consider the distraction in the classroom after one of your students does something positively overwhelming (such as score an amazing goal) during leisure time. All of this demonstrates that the ability to regulate emotions is important and affects school success, especially as they relate to achievements and social interactions (Brackett, 2019; Ivcevic & Brackett, 2014).

One strategy to help students manage their emotions so they will benefit, instead of hamper, their learning focuses on teaching social-emotional learning (SEL). You can read more about SEL in Chapter 9. Worth noting is that SEL works well in combination with other strategies presented in this book.

Linking emotions to learning in your teaching can be an effective way to both engage your students more during class as well as enhance their academic achievement. Emotions have a great impact both on attention and on memory. Learning activities that are emotionally charged will be remembered both for longer, and more accurately, compared to more neutral activities during a lesson (Brackett, 2019; Medina, 2014).

One way to regulate emotions is to teach students how to talk about them. That means that students should learn to label their emotions. "If you can name it, you can tame it. Labeling an emotion is itself a form of regulation" (Brackett, 2019).

Developing strong peer and adult relationships is also an important factor related to SEL. Most effective educators recognize that good teacher–student relationships typically lead to positive outcomes like improved academic results, improved social skills, and fewer behavioral challenges. Strong and positive teacher–student relationships have positive effects, especially for students with the most need (Sabol & Pianta, 2012).

Social-Emotional Challenges: Scenario 1

The physical education (PE) teacher who, together with paraprofessionals and volunteers, organizes activities during recess has come to talk to you about two students from your class: Ivan and Anna. The school has a physical activity profile, and different ball games are usually organized during recess. The PE teacher says that he always tries to include everyone but that Ivan almost always stays outside the games and tends to alone during recess. He says that this trend worries him because the other students are building relationships, and Ivan is at risk of being isolated. Anna, in contrast, loves participating in ball games, but she often gets into conflicts with her peers during the games. She is not coordinated when playing, and she often misses the ball and instead hits her peers. They think this is done intentionally and, at times, a conflict is initiated if someone supervising recess isn't close or quick enough to prevent it. These two students have been on your mind recently as well. You wonder how Ivan is feeling since he has become quieter over time, and it seems like his attention and thoughts are often elsewhere rather than on what's going on in the classroom. Anna is frequently almost hyperactive, and you were hoping that the recess activities would help her reduce her need to move around during class. To some extent that has worked, but you often have to start your classes by resolving conflicts before any academic teaching can start. Sometimes, the students seem to continue to have their attention on what happened during recess, even though you have tried to sort it out. You and your colleagues are worried about how your students feel and about what you should do to make the class function well together with everyone included. You are also worried about how this will affect the academic achievement for these two students—even though Anna is a fast learner. You are increasingly feeling that you are gradually losing time on task for more students in the class. What can you do?

Scenario 1 Solution:
Adaptive Games and Skills Training

These described challenges can have many causes, and there are often several ways to reach a goal or resolve problems. Because the challenges during recess might be connected to ball activities, you and your colleague decide that you will try a sensory-motor approach. You consult with the PE teacher. He says that Ivan hasn't yet developed and automated the skills to catch and throw balls or bounce balls. Thus, it is natural and understandable that he tries to avoid ball games. Such games would cause him stress since he hasn't yet developed the skills needed to succeed.

During PE lessons, the PE teacher has taught both balance and ball skills. During these activities, he observed that Anna had good balance as long as she could have her eyes focused on a spot, but as soon as she shut her eyes, she lost balance. When bouncing a ball, Anna was skilled on her own when she was able to have her eyes on the ball. She is actually also skilled with both hands and feet when handling a ball. However, any time she is asked to handle, bounce, or throw a ball with her eyes closed, all skill ceases. Based on this information, you and your colleagues decide on a strategy to both get Ivan and Anna included in the recess activities immediately and try to also resolve the challenges long term.

During recess, there are always several activities. To include Ivan, you can organize some activities with balls that move slower, and for some activities, you can create rule adaptations that de-emphasize ball skills. To include Anna, you might organize both individual ball skill games and games in pairs or small groups that have less demand on the skills she needs to develop. At the same time, those adaptations can require high intensity for Anna, which will help her focus in the following lesson in the classroom. So, during recess, you simply adapt the activities so they become more inclusive. Those adaptations will possibly also benefit more students.

Another strategy is to organize skills training for Ivan and Anna during PE lessons and at recess. These skills training activities may also be used as pause or brain break activities during more theoretical lessons in the classroom. Ivan would train on ball skills with balls that give him a manageable challenge. At the same time, he might work on training his eye-hand coordination and body knowledge. Anna would work on her balance both with her eyes shut and when focusing on another activity. She might also train how to bounce and dribble a ball with her eyes shut. When these activities work, she would then progress to combining skills—bouncing a ball (or two balls) while standing on a balance plate (or on one leg) first with eyes open and then with her eyes shut.

The more your students develop the skills needed, the less the need for adaptations during PE and recess games. By collaborating with other educational professionals, such as the PE teacher, teachers can learn additional techniques and continue to use them as needed in the classroom environment (Chavez & Lahav, 2023). You can read more about the strategy applied here and the importance of sensory-motor development and its impact on the classroom in Chapter 1.

Social-Emotional Challenges: Scenario 2

You have implemented formative assessments in your teaching for several years. Now you experience that your class has a slower academic progress than you would expect. You know your students well and believe that you have good relationships with them. You try to give every student feedback that they can use to improve their learning. To know where your students are so that you can adapt your teaching and for training and learning purposes, you use tests and quizzes often, providing your students both a score or grade, as well as your formative comments. But it hasn't helped. Even worse is that two of your students—Monica and Linda—have told you recently that they often feel stressed and anxious. They are ambitious and eager to succeed, but they say that they are afraid of failing. You have tried to make them feel more relaxed and assured them they can be calm and are performing well, but it doesn't seem to be helping. What can you do?

Scenario 2 Solution:
Pure Formative Assessment

You can probably help Monica and Linda with a solution created for the whole class. In fact, this same solution may help many students in your class toward better academic progression. Sometimes rather small changes in one's current teaching methodology can have great positive impact. For example, reducing the number of tests or formal assessments you give your class on a regular basis can make a big difference.

Tests and quizzes, which are summative assessments as opposed to formative ones, tend to cause the most anxiety and result in the least amount of learning. Monica and Linda (and their peers!) won't experience as much stress and anxiety if formal assessments are minimized.

Avoid mixing formative and summative assessments because that hampers the effect of formative assessment. By focusing on pure formative assessment, you can both contribute to less anxiety about possible failure and at the same time contribute to better academic progress. It can also be beneficial to offer opportunities for your students to be successful, which is especially important for students like Monica and Linda, who are anxious they will fail. As most of us know, failure does not typically act as a motivator but rather a discourager (Lauvås & Jönsson, 2019).

Instead of giving frequent tests as summative assessments, repeat instruction of the same academic content together with formative feedback. Complementary to doing more pure formative assessment, this will also support students' declarative memory (Bjork & Bjork, 2019). You can read more about the strategy used in this scenario in Chapter 2 on formative assessment. To learn more about pure formative assessment, check out the book *Embedded Formative Assessment* (2nd edition) by Dylan Wiliam (2017).

Social-Emotional Challenges: Scenario 3

In every class, there is simply so much to do and so little time to do it! In addition to the academics that need to be mastered, and the sheer diversity of students who vary in their academic abilities, your school leader recently called together a faculty meeting and let everyone know that there is also an expectation that this will be a "trauma-informed school." She explained that that meant that all faculty, staff, and leaders will be informed about and sensitive to the trauma their students may be experiencing. After all of the negative fallout during the COVID-19 pandemic, students and their families were still experiencing issues related to physical and mental health, and social and financial well-being, and students needed a safe, stable environment to come to daily. Although you recognize that many of your students do indeed bring a variety of emotions to the class every day, you aren't sure how you can support them in a meaningful way while also teaching math. What can you do?

Scenario 3 Solution:
Teach Them to Ask for Help

In Chapter 7 on cooperative learning, we emphasize how important it is for students to learn how to ask for help from the teachers and from each other. We cite Altun as saying, "learning together and asking for help is considered among the best strategies for learning how to learn" (2015, p. 451). That is certainly easier said than done, especially when applied to emotional needs. Although students may ask one another how to do a particular math problem, they will likely be far less willing or able to share that they feel left out, or anxious, or other deep feelings that are affecting their learning. While some cultures may actively embrace supporting one another as a community, others may expect individuals to take care of their own social-emotional issues, eschewing the idea of talking with others about their needs (Rothstein-Fisch & Trumbull, 2008).

After setting up clear guidelines of what is and is not acceptable when sharing sensitive information with peers, teachers can use cooperative learning techniques to help create a trauma-informed class. By talking with students about critical issues happening in the news (e.g., pandemic, racism, political turmoil) and giving them the chance to talk with one another about particular topics in small groups, you can provide your students the opportunity to open up about their feelings in safe and brave spaces. In small groups, such as stations, most groups can be focused on academic tasks, but one group might be tasked with talking about topics related to SEL. As students rotate, they all have time to share feelings with their peers related to burning topics or difficult conversations when they get to the Safe SEL Station. The questions in the side box provide opportunities for students to begin to engage with one another about courageous conversations and open up the classroom to be a place for support and a recognition that we are all going through something. Groups can be created based on cultural backgrounds, gender, interests, topics, language, or other similarities to show students they are not alone.

QUESTIONS FOR AN SEL SAFE STATION

- How are you feeling today? Why?
- What is bothering you this week?
- Is anything causing you stress right now? What is it?
- What kinds of things can we do as your classmates to support you better right now?

- What kinds of things do we as your classmates do that add to your stress? How can we stop them, if possible?
- We all feel down or anxious at times. Are you feeling down or anxious?
- What makes you happiest?
- What kinds of things do you think about that worry you?
- Is there any information you need to help relieve your stress or anxiety?
- What things do you like to do that make you happy or feel good?
- What are things we can do as your classmates to make you feel happier or safer?

To encourage more interaction, students can be allowed to respond to questions on anonymous cards, electronically through questions on PollEverywhere or MentiMeter, or with a self-selected and trusted peer. In addition, students can be partnered with peers who have been trained in supportive strategies. Students who already appear to have strong emotional intelligence (EQ; Bradberry & Greaves, 2009), like Oscar, Hannah, Eva, Amy, and Isak, may be prime candidates to get additional training and then act as peer facilitators of conversations regarding social or emotional issues. To be clear, these students would not be acting as mini-therapists but merely supportive friends who are there to listen and encourage others to share how they are doing. If any major issues arise, they would know to share that information with a trusted adult.

MANAGING OUT-OF-CLASS ACTIVITIES

Defining the Problem and Finding Solutions

· ·

Any teacher can tell you that teaching doesn't happen only in the classroom. They can equally confirm confidently that not all problem behaviors occur in the classroom—and not all problem behaviors are *student* behaviors. In addition to effective curriculum delivery, meaningful assessment, and classroom management, teachers also are expected to handle a range of issues that occur across the school. Although some of these issues might be student related, others might involve working with families or coworkers. Whether it is ensuring good communication between home and school, making sure that students use good manners while eating, or supporting colleagues to work collaboratively, educators have a range of responsibilities that extend well beyond their own classrooms. Luckily, applying some of the same strategies for dealing with in-class behavior can also be effective in other settings. Teachers can even adapt some of these strategies for use with parents and colleagues. The aim of these strategies is to help teachers think about how they can generalize evidence-based classroom practices to other issues that might occur across the school.

You look forward to recess every day. While the students are outside, it is your chance do a quick tidy-up of the classroom, take a deep breath, and collect your thoughts. However, now it is beginning to feel like recess (and other breaks from teaching, such as lunchtime) is the calm before the storm. When your students return to class, you often think someone has replaced them with a pack of wild animals. Your moment of peace is replaced with absolute chaos. Some students are chatting with friends and loudly laughing, some are play wrestling, and others are still lingering in the hallway. You have to tell students to return to their seats at least four times before anyone even hears you. You pride yourself on getting students engaged with instruction and learning, but you are worried about how long it takes to get everyone back on task after a break. You know these lengthy transitions are eating into precious instructional time. What do you do?

Scenario 1 Solution: Competition Time!

Many teachers struggle with transitions, and they are right to be worried about the amount of instructional time lost when students do not settle back into lessons quickly. In fact, some research estimates that 25% or more of the time allocated for instruction can be lost due to lengthy transitions (Codding & Smythe, 2008). Transitions from more preferred to less preferred activities can be particularly problematic because students often are reluctant to stop something they would prefer to keep doing. Moving from less structured to more structured activities can create similar problems. When student attention is diverted to what has just happened (e.g., lunch) or what is currently happening (e.g., play wrestling with a peer), getting students to focus on the upcoming activity can be a difficult task.

Seamless and timely transitions require procedures that help students focus quickly on what they need to do and where they need to be. One evidence-based strategy for accomplishing this is the Timely Transitions Game (TTG; Hawkins et al., 2015; Yarbrough et al., 2004). Like the Good Behavior Game (GBG; described in more detail in Chapter 3), packaging effective strategies into a game format makes them easy for both students and teachers to remember. To play the game, you first need to define what students must do to demonstrate they are prepared for the next activity. For example, older students might be required to be sitting quietly in their seats with book, paper, and pencil on their desks. If the transition involves leaving the classroom, the requirement for younger students might be for everyone to be in a single line beside the door, quiet, and keeping their hands and feet to themselves. Often it is helpful to display the definitions of successful transitions on a poster, using words, pictures, or a combination of both.

Once you have defined what a good transition looks like, you need to decide how long you would like it to take. Think about what would constitute a reasonable amount of time for all of your students to do what they need to do to be ready for the next activity. Timing some of your students who transition quickly and easily can be a good indicator of how long the transition should take. For most activities, transition times of 90 seconds or less are reasonable and attainable, although more complex transitions (e.g., those requiring students to gather materials or move a greater distance) might take longer. Be sure to set a reasonable goal for each transition students must complete in a school day. If you have students with physical or developmental disabilities that make quick transitions difficult, you will need to adjust your expectations accordingly.

To play the TTG, you will need to prepare a few materials. The first is a poster with transition expectations. The second is note cards (or slips of paper) with the goal completion time for each transition plus four more cards. You will use the cards to choose the "winning" transition time during each game. Each card should have a different time goal, each within 5-second increments of the target goal. For instance, if your ideal transition time is 90 seconds, your cards might include 85, 90, 95, 100, and 105 seconds. When first starting the game, it is better to have more cards above the goal than below the goal because it increases the chances that students will win, which maintains interest in playing the game. The third requirement for the game is a scoreboard where you can record the number of points the class earns, and the fourth is a list of rewards that the class can earn. Chapter 3 provides some ideas regarding rewards that are effective, efficient, and inexpensive.

Like the GBG, the TTG operates on an interdependent group contingency. This means that for anyone to win, everyone has to meet the goal. The best time to explain how the game works is before a transition. Tell students that you will be timing how long it takes to get ready for the next activity. Next, explain what "getting ready" means by pointing to the poster and explaining the definition of a good transition. All the time cards for the transition should be in an envelope, which you should show to the class. Explain that you will draw a card from the envelope once everyone is ready and that if the time on the stopwatch is less than the time on the card, the class will get a point. Once the class earns a certain number of points (determined by you), the class will earn a reward.

Unlike the GBG, rewards are delivered after several TTGs rather than after each game. This is because reward delivery after each transition would further delay the lesson or activity, thus defeating the purpose of the game. The simplest strategy for delivering rewards is to set the point goal and provide the reward once the goal is met (e.g., after five points have been earned). However, when setting the point goal, it is important to ensure that students aren't required to wait too long before earning the reward. In the beginning, it is helpful to set the goal so that students can potentially earn a reward at least once (and preferably twice) per day. Once students are successfully transitioning, you can gradually increase the number of points required to earn the reward.

There also are more creative ways that teachers might set the point goal. For instance, the prize could be spelled out (e.g., D-A-N-C-E, P-O-P-C-O-R-N), whereby students earn a letter for each transition they win. The reward is provided once students have earned all the letters needed to spell the reward. Another strategy is to have a teacher-versus-students game, whereby each time student transition in less than the target time, the students earn a point. If the transition exceeds the goal, the teacher gets a point. At the end of the day, the teacher tallies the points, and the students earn a small reward if their points are greater than those earned by the teacher.

Managing Out-of-Class Activities: Scenario 2

It's a common complaint among teachers, and you are no exception: how can you get students to do all their homework? It seems like the students who need it least are the ones who are the most consistent in getting it completed, whereas those students who struggle and need the academic review are the ones who don't do it or at least don't complete it consistently. You've done everything you can think of. You have students copy the homework into their planners from the board where you write it up each day. You have the due date on the board with the homework. You remind students to do the homework as they walk out of the room, and you check homework and assign points when they get to class. You've even been posting the homework on the class website and explained your policies to parents when they came to Back to School Night. Still, there are so many students who don't do their homework! What do you do?

Scenario 2 Solution: Universally Design Your Homework

Homework is an oft-debated topic. There are so many questions related to it: Should teachers give homework? If so, how much? What makes homework effective? What techniques can teachers use to get students to do their homework? Do those techniques work with all children? Even as researchers continue to debate the homework conundrum, most concur that—if you are giving homework at all—children at younger grades should not get more than 10 minutes per grade level (Cooper, 2007; Redding, 2000), and homework is more beneficial for students in the upper grades than lower grades (Protheroe, 2009), although more does certainly not equal better. Consider the five fundamental characteristics of effective homework: purpose, efficiency, ownership, competence, and aesthetic appeal (Vatterott, 2010). Universally designed homework can help with each of these areas.

Using a UDL lens, teachers can provide more options for students regarding homework completion. First, as the teacher, you must clearly identify the objective of the homework; different objectives might include homework for review, for additional practice, for more information, or simply to provide students with tasks that reinforce self-regulation, time management, managing distractions, goal setting, and maintaining attention (Bembenutty, 2011), all valid practices in and of themselves. Once you've clarified the objective for yourself, it is time to share that objective with your students in a manner that is appropriate to their age, grade, and developmental level.

MENU OF HOMEWORK OPTIONS

Feeling wobbly on fractions?

Watch the YouTube video and the teacher video linked in our class Google Drive, and answer the questions asked on the Video Worksheet.

Feeling pretty good about fractions?

Complete every other problem on pages 87–88 in our math textbook. Show your work at least five times. You can choose which problems to show your work on.

Feeling super confident about fractions?

Complete the four challenge problems offered on page 89 of the math textbook. Show your work on at least two of the problems.

"When teachers design homework to meet specific purposes and goals, more students complete their homework and benefit from the results" (Epstein & Van Voorhis, 2001, p. 191). Giving children more say in what homework they do and how they accomplish it will increase buy-in and motivation (Carr, 2013). Provide them with choices that match their strengths and interests as well as different options that might address any learning or socioeconomic barriers they may be experiencing (e.g., homework can be done at lunch, in the classroom, after school, online, in the library, or during teacher office hours to provide supports). Students with disabilities often struggle more with homework than their nondisabled peers, so offering additional scaffolds for all students will ensure their needs can be met as well (Bryan et al., 2001). Because of the diversity of abilities in your class, it will behoove you to have a range of options for homework that provide both more supports and more challenge; let students know about the diversity in options, so they can work to challenge themselves, again tying into the need for some students to learn to set goals and to take ownership of their learning as they get older. Check out the menu of options offered as an example on page 65.

Managing Out-of-Class Activities: Scenario 3

Ask most students what their favorite part of school is and you'll hear "Lunch!" or "Break!" or "Recess!" No matter how engaging teachers try to make their lessons, nothing is as engaging for students as being around their friends in social activities. Although you recognize how important this social engagement time is, you are also racking your brain for ways to make your lessons come to life for your kids. You seem to constantly run out of time in the classroom to make those real-world connections that will resonate with your students. You want them to understand how certain material will be needed in the real world, but you feel stifled by time and the pacing plan required to address all of the required curriculum. What can you do?

Scenario 3 Solution: Make Friends!

As the students make friends during breaks and lunch, you can make friends with the paraprofessionals and additional service providers who have different relationships with the students. While new friendships are in and of themselves a wonderful benefit to any stressed teacher, the plan to communicate with those adults who interact with students outside of the classroom is a strategic one. PE teachers get students moving and interacting; what better place for them to make concrete connections with something you have taught in the classroom recently? Think about it. If you recently taught a geography lesson about the United States, the PE teacher could use chalk to draw an outline of the country on the blacktop and have students kick a ball to San Francisco or New York or San Antonio, getting points if they are able to hit the target. If you taught a lesson on division, the PE teacher could challenge students to dribble the soccer ball 20 divided by 4 times up and back. If you taught a lesson on vocabulary, verbs, or adjectives, the PE teacher could engage students in a funny story-building game where they toss a Hacky Sack ball to one another in a large circle, adding words as the ball goes around. One or two students could stand on the outside of the circle yelling out what type of word (e.g., adjective, noun, verb) the next ball receiver needs to give.

What does it take to embed this type of fun practice into other parts of the day? It takes communication and collaboration! These topics are covered in more detail in Chapter 4, but essentially teachers need to reach out to their educational colleagues and talk about how to accomplish both fun and practice. Chavez and Lahav (2023) have recommended that teachers get to know other educational professionals' *traits*, consider the *application* of their jobs (e.g., what the intentionality is of their profession as it relates to students), and then consider *goals* for collaboration; they call this the TAG (traits, application, goals) Framework.

Individuals with whom teachers can collaborate include PE, art, music, and dance teachers; occupational, physical, and educational therapists; school counselors and psychologists; behavioral, academic, and athletic coaches; and classroom and special education paraprofessionals. Each of these individuals can describe the types of activities they do with students, while classroom teachers can share their content goals. On a regular basis, classroom teachers can also let their colleagues know which students are struggling and need either extra academic practice on a topic or might need some behavioral supports or even help making friendships. Together, colleagues can collaborate to problem-solve and even try to come up with fun, kinesthetic, and engaging ways for students to practice skills while still having lots of fun. That's a real win-win!

MANAGING LACK OF COLLABORATION AND COMMUNICATION

Defining the Problem and Finding Solutions

We teach even the youngest of children how to communicate—through words, gestures, and pictures. We teach them that they should collaborate with others by sharing their toys, sandbox, and snacks. Yet both communication and collaboration are skills that can be difficult for even the most professional of adults to master. Even someone strong in both oral and written communication can struggle with those skills when faced with a new, difficult, or awkward situation. However, strong communication skills are necessary to engage in collaborative relationships in the educational field, such as co-teaching, which has often been referred to as a professional marriage (Murawski, 2010). Collaboration itself may seem simple; certainly, to share responsibilities, resources, and accountability with someone who has the same goals should be relatively easy - shouldn't it? Yet, it is the collaboration among adults in schools that is more often the difficulty as opposed to the collaboration among students or even adults and students.

Getting teachers to "play nicely" with one another takes work (Murawski & Ricci, 2019). To begin, most teachers are taught how to teach in a classroom on their own and may have the expectation, based on their own experiences in classes, that they will be a solo act. They may also feel that there is an expectation for them to demonstrate competency by merely keeping their classroom door shut and handling any student issues on their own. Interestingly, however, although teachers may think that the expectation is for them to manage on their own, researchers have reported that, especially when working with students with disabilities, "collaboration is not merely a suggestion; it is a professional imperative" (Gajda & Koliba, 2007).

Working in isolation carries its own issues. The increased diversity of students' academic abilities is compounded by their diversity in terms of language, cultural backgrounds, gender roles, behavioral needs, socioeconomic status, interests, motivation, and social-emotional skills. Teachers frequently lament that they are no longer asked to focus on academics but instead to also serve as coach, police, counselor, therapist, nurse, and even parent. So much is asked of each individual educator that it is ludicrous to think that we can accomplish all that needs doing alone and without the benefit of collaborating with other experts. This can be easier said than done. Major barriers to interprofessional collaboration include time to connect, communication skills, ego and control issues, logistics, and administrative support (Murawski, 2010). For schools to embrace inclusive education and meet the diverse requirements of their learners, teachers and specialists need to be able to use and improve upon their own communication and collaboration skills.

Managing Lack of Collaboration and Communication: Scenario 1

You always wanted to be a teacher, but now you are wondering how much longer you can continue like you have been. You are super stressed out, and every day you feel like you are giving 110%. It is simply not sustainable. You look at your colleagues, and it feels like they are doing the same thing. Everyone shuts their classroom door and tries to do it all by themselves. Currently, the special education teachers and paraprofessionals are pulling students out of your class for different supports. Although that might be helpful, it actually adds to your stress because then there are many times when the students pulled from your class miss out on critical information you are teaching. In addition, while there are times that teaching assistants are in your classroom, they seem to wait to be told what to do; you don't have time to teach the students and the assistants as well! Ultimately, you don't know how long you can keep this all up. You are getting seriously burned out. What do you do?

Scenario 1 Solution: Create a Village!

There is a famous African proverb that says, "It takes a village to raise a child." This is so true! Teachers tend to think they are solely responsible for the students in their care, but when they think that, they are neglecting the myriad other adults who are available for consultation and collaboration. When we shut our classroom doors and try to address the diverse academic, behavioral, physical, and social needs of our extremely unique (and often needy) students, we do them a disservice. Collaboration to the rescue!

Reach out to the school nurse to do a mini-lesson on the importance of handwashing during a unit on health at the elementary level. When you introduce a unit on new vocabulary, invite the school psychologist to co-teach with you. As you introduce new terms and their meaning, your colleague can teach about how words can affect others and how to avoid hurting others' feelings by being careful with your words, adapted of course to fit the grade level and maturity of the class. A paraprofessional might teach a short lesson on how to make friendships or how to use a new piece of technology while using stations in your class, whereas a speech teacher might come in and help all students learn techniques to help with active listening. Invite the PE teacher to have lunch with you and get some ideas as to how to incorporate more active and kinesthetic activities into your lessons. Have coffee with the special education teacher, and ask for strategies for ways to better include your students who have more extensive support needs; better yet, invite them to co-teach with you! Each of these strategies is doable. They simply require teachers to recognize that they cannot—nor should they—do it all alone. It takes a village to raise a child, and you have 23 children, so start to build your village!

Managing Lack of Collaboration and Communication: Scenario 2

You are committed to the idea of creating a village to support your diverse group of 23 students. But now you are faced with how to actually implement that idea. To co-plan or communicate with others requires time, and you simply have none! Every time you feel like you might have the opportunity to meet and connect with colleagues, it seems like your school leaders schedule more formal meetings or professional development. You know these professional development trainings are useful, but you are feeling desperate for some additional time to connect with others. What do you do?

Scenario 2 Solution: Ask for What You Want

Although the answer seems simplistic, teachers do not tend to ask their school leaders for what they need. In one research study, 70% of new teachers reported needing support, yet 25% of those educators did not ask for help because they thought it was incumbent upon them to figure it out on their own (White & Mason, 2006). There is a culture in many schools that leads teachers to think they are on their own, as opposed to a more collaborative culture that supports reaching out and asking for help. Yet, research has found that a collaborative culture among educators results in better teaching quality, which results in improved student outcomes (Ronfeldt et al., 2015); if that is the case, why wouldn't school leaders want to support more collaboration and communication?

That leads us to the solution: ask for what you want.

Go to your school leaders and clarify your needs. Explain that you want to collaborate with colleagues, either through consultation or co-teaching, but that you will need some time to do this. Be prepared with a concrete request of how much time you need, the individuals with whom you would like to collaborate, and the goals for that collaboration. Karten and Murawski (2020) have shared a variety of ways for teachers to find time to communicate and collaborate from scheduled meetings to summer planning days to professional learning community (PLC) meetings. When school leaders recognize the need for additional time for their teachers to meet and plan with other educators, they can help with the creative brainstorming of ways to support that collaboration. Some of these ideas might include letting teachers plan during other whole-school events, providing them with substitute teachers for a specified amount of time, supporting their classes themselves, or creating a PLC for those individuals who are co-teaching (Karten & Murawski, 2020).

Managing Lack of Collaboration and Communication: Scenario 3

Isak is a student in your class who has high academic achievement. Often everything works well with him in the classroom, but you experience that he is increasingly challenging you. Sometimes he questions what you are teaching, and sometimes he even questions how you are doing it. You know your subjects well, and your stress is growing as he continues to question you. Most often you simply have to end the discussion, and when he still doesn't want to give up, the interaction sometimes results in you having to reprimand him. A few times you have even asked him to leave the classroom—a technique you know is not a good one. In the last few weeks, you have sometimes also had to argue with Isak in front of the whole class; for instance, once he wouldn't put away his laptop even though you asked him to repeatedly. Now you often feel stressed when you interact with him, and you have experienced that you have less patience with him. You know that you shouldn't "compete" with your student, but you feel that Isak is constantly challenging your authority in the classroom. You can't lose your authority with the rest of the class, so you have to find a way to make Isak stop challenging you the way he does now. You don't like to abuse your power as a teacher, and you don't like being so reactive to his challenges. You need a solution, another strategy. What can you do?

Scenario 3 Solution: Understand and Regulate Emotions

There can be many reasons for the situations that occur, but it is quite clear they include many emotionally charged moments both for you as Isak's teacher and for Isak himself. Emotions can both be part of the challenge and part of the possible solution. A viable first step would be to reflect on your own emotions to recognize them. Next, you should talk to Isak about how these situations make him feel, sharing with him one-on-one and at his level how these interactions are affecting you and your feelings. If you are not used to talking about feelings, you can consult with and get help from the student health team at your school (e.g., school counselor, nurse, psychologist, social worker, educational therapist). It is important for you to try to understand your own feelings and why they occur. We as educators frequently believe we have to manage our own emotions and treat all of our students equally, but it is unreasonable to think that students' behaviors or words won't affect us. It is healthier to acknowledge their impact, name those feelings, and then identify ways to address them in a way that supports both you and the student.

Once you have acknowledged the impact of Isak's actions on your own emotions, you can begin to talk to Isak too. You (or a person from your student health team if you think it would be better) can help Isak understand his feelings and why he gets them. Depending on age, maturity, and ability with language,

Isak may not have sufficient words for his feelings, so you can help him label them. To label his feelings will be necessary for him to be able to regulate them.

When you together understand your feelings and why you have them, this will help you both begin to alter the situations and react differently. By regulating your feelings, you can avoid or at least minimize and control these challenging situations. You and your student will then both be able to express your feelings in a way that works for you and that won't interfere with the lessons. Being able to communicate to oneself, one's colleagues, and even one's students can significantly help situations where emotions play an important role.

MANAGING TIME, STRESS, AND OTHER TEACHING CHALLENGES

Defining the Problem and Finding Solutions

No one needs to tell you that teaching is an incredibly rewarding, but also incredibly difficult, profession. Teachers set high expectations for themselves, as do many of those around them—school leadership teams, colleagues, parents, and most important, students. However, those outside the teaching profession often do not realize how difficult an educator's job is or how many roles and responsibilities they have to juggle, often with limited resources. Contrary to popular belief, the teaching day does not end when students leave the classroom. There are lessons to plan, papers to grade, parents to call, committees and trainings to attend, reports to write—the list could go on for pages. During and after the COVID-19 pandemic, some social media posts summed up how little most people know about what teachers deal with on a day-to-day basis. For instance, one parent wrote on Twitter: "I have homeschooled my two children for 20 minutes, and now I think teacher salaries should be $1,000,000 per year."

Teacher stress and burnout can be a function of a number of factors, including demands to adopt new curricula and teaching strategies, preparing students for high-stakes tests, dealing with pervasive problem behavior, coping with difficult parents, or increased job expectations in the face of ever-dwindling resources (Richards, 2012). However, our own behaviors, such as procrastination, inefficient time management, and resistance to change can exacerbate stress and make an already stressful situation unbearable. Learning to manage our own behavior, along with that of our students, can help us feel more effective and efficacious, which helps us combat stress and better enjoy the work we do (Beltman et al., 2011).

Managing Time, Stress, and Other Challenges: Scenario 1

You've been a teacher for a few years and have been amazed (and frustrated) at the number of new initiatives and curricula that have been introduced during the time you have been in the profession. Last week you attended a staff meeting where yet another external consultant was giving a training on a new way of approaching behavior management across the school. The principal said that the school is invested in this approach, and he wants all teachers fully on board. You feel like these strategies sound like a lot of work. You already have so many other things to do, and your students' behavior is not all that bad, so you're wondering why you need to change what you're doing—especially when you feel confident you'll be asked to do something different next year. What do you do?

Scenario 1 Solution: Embrace Evidence-Based Change!

School leaders are often under enormous pressure to be new and innovative, which means that they (or someone above them) make decisions to change things that don't appear to need changing. All educators want to make sure they are using the most up-to-date and effective strategies for their students, but change for the sake of change can wear staff down and affect motivation. It is hard to fully get behind a new curriculum, teaching approach, or classroom management strategy if you know you will be asked to do something completely different in a year's time. This is a pervasive problem in education and not one that you'll be able to fully control. However, there are things you can do to feel more confident that the changes you are being asked to make are going to change things for the better.

One of the most important considerations in determining whether a particular strategy will be effective is the degree of evidence that supports it. The best type of evidence is experimental research. Although there are many ways to do experimental research, one common approach is to measure the effects of a strategy on one group and compare those effects to a group that *didn't* get the strategy. For instance, researchers might ask 10 primary schools to implement a new reading program. They would also select an additional 10 primary schools to use their existing reading programs. The first group would be called the "treatment group," and the second would be called the "control group." The researchers would need to ensure that both groups were roughly equal in terms of number of students, teacher-to-student ratios, socioeconomic status, and other demographic variables so that they could rule out any factors that might account for differences in reading performance between the groups. Across all 20 schools, they would measure students' reading skills at the beginning of the study and again at the end. If the school that used the new program had higher reading scores (or greater improvement in scores) at the end of the study, the researchers could safely conclude that the new reading program was better at improving reading skills than other approaches schools were currently using.

All of this is a long-winded way of saying that research is important, but many teachers don't learn about research strategies or the importance of research in their teacher education programs. Not everything that gets printed in a teacher magazine or website represents stringent research findings. And not everything that is popular in schools necessarily has evidence to show that it works. Unfortunately, there are many examples of intervention programs that have been implemented nationally (and cost lots and lots of money) that turned out to do little to improve outcomes for students or their teachers (Spaulding et al., 2010; West & O'Neal, 2004). Therefore, one of the best things that teachers can do is to ask about the evidence for particular programs or strategies they are asked to implement and to be savvy about interpreting the answers they receive. Anyone can say "The research says this is effective!" but it is quite another thing to be able to point to where that research is published in a respectable research journal.

Educators should always be cautious about claims for a particular strategy or approach that doesn't clearly define what is intended to change or improve. For instance, consider a claim like "This program helps students capture the joy of reading.'" What does that mean? Findings based on solid research typically are more specific, pointing to the precise things that will change. For example, "This program showed that students improved comprehension skills by 1.5 levels within one academic year." That claim might not be as catchy as capturing joy, but it certainly tells you more about what the program is likely to do. Another red flag is claims that there is evidence to support a strategy but not being able to identify the source of that research. Any program based on solid evidence will display that research loudly and proudly (you'll see that the authors of this book have a list of research evidence at the end of the book and that we cite our sources as we go!). Testimonials, theories, anecdotes, and people with strong opinions do not constitute credible evidence.

So, where does that leave you? The main takeaway message is that all educators need to ask the tough questions when asked to implement something new. If there is good evidence that the strategy has produced meaningful, measurable outcomes in a school similar to yours, it is probably worth giving it a go. However, teachers (and the school leadership team) need to be diligent and brave about pushing back on requests to make changes or implement new things without any evidence that those things will make a difference. Getting a bit more comfortable with educational research might help build your confidence in asking questions and evaluating evidence. If your school decides that there is enough evidence to proceed, then the success of the new strategy, program, or curriculum will largely be based on the integrity with which it is implemented. That means it will need everyone on board and all hands on deck to implement the strategy well. Change is often uncomfortable and inconvenient, but if it is based on solid research indicating it will improve outcomes for you and your students, it is likely worth the effort.

Managing Time, Stress, and Other Challenges: Scenario 2

From the minute you arrive to school until you leave for home in the late afternoon, you are constantly busy. Even during your lunch break, you resolve student issues together with colleagues while eating. Your teaching schedule this year is good so that you actually have blocks of time to use for planning and assessments. But it seems like that time disappears every day. Colleagues frequently come and talk to you about things they find urgent. You receive many phone calls every day, and when you can't take them, you then have voice messages to take care of later instead. Parents often try to call you during the school day and expect quick replies. If you don't reply ASAP, they continue trying to reach you when you are at home at night. Because you are far away from being able to do everything you need during the school day, you are trying to simply do more at the same time. The reality is that you end up doing almost all of your planning and assessments at home at late hours. You are ambitious, but the time isn't enough, and you are already doing way more hours a week than you should. It is frustrating and stressful. Your home life is suffering, and you have no balance. Your situation must change. What can you do?

Scenario 2 Solution: Do One Thing at a Time and Schedule Your Priorities!

Your day is now full of workflow interruptions, and that is one of the reasons why your time for planning disappears. These interruptions take your attention away from what you were doing, and you will end up having to start over again. When you are able to work with full focus and without interruptions, you feel the difference. You accomplish so much more when you have workflow. When someone else wants your attention, it might be urgent and perhaps also important for that person, but that does not mean it is equally urgent and important for you. If you stopped to analyze the interruptions, you might find that you could actually avoid many of them by diplomatically apologizing, stating that you are not available, or deferring your assistance to another time in the future.

You need to make time for those things that are important to you. This will require that you schedule your priorities. That also means that you need to schedule limited times when you are available at your phone and when you will respond to e-mails and other messages. If you communicate that both to parents and to colleagues, most will respect that and not expect immediate replies. Communicating your need for structure will validate that structure.

In addition, consider the inefficiency of multitasking. In a nutshell, multitasking is not effective. It is more effective to do one thing at a time. Thus, when you have scheduled things that you find important, you will focus on *monotasking*; put your cell phone on silent, with no notifications, and focus on the task at hand. Find a place to sit and work at your school or home where few people might approach you.

Finally, recognize that no one can do everything. Prioritizing will become key. In Chapter 10 on time management, you will learn more about how to manage yourself for balance and to develop strategies to make the best use of your time. In that chapter, you will also be introduced to a tool called "the teacher's time management matrix" that can be helpful. With all of these strategies, you may find yourself able to drink a cup of coffee, pet the dog, and even enjoy a show on Netflix occasionally.

When you are in front of your students, you shine. You know the content, you can identify their needs, and you love problem-solving to figure out how to better get the content through to them. The school day you can deal with— it's all the time when you are not in front of students that is overwhelming you! There are so many to-dos on your list that you tend to simply avoid doing them altogether; it is too much to face. In addition, you have to remember to do all of your household chores (e.g., dinner, child and pet care, laundry, cleaning), your own schoolwork as you work on your master's degree, and not neglect your family. It's embarrassing how often you find yourself saying, "I'm sorry," "I forgot," or "I'll do that now." You completely acknowledge that you put things off until the last minute mainly because there is so much to do, but you are pretty tired of feeling like a chicken with its head cut off. What do you do?

Scenario 3 Solution: Bullet It!

Feeling overwhelmed is a result of trying to constantly react to all of the many requests, actions, and to dos coming at you on a regular basis. It is natural to put work off when you are stressed, but we all realize that this ends up resulting in more stress in the long run. In addition, there are so many other things that come up in the day of a teacher—from lesson plan ideas, to notes from parent conferences, to grocery lists, to general thoughts about the day. One great way to address all of this mental chaos is to use a bullet journal.

WANT TO LEARN MORE ABOUT BULLET JOURNALING?

Watch this 4-minute video and see how you can use one notebook to pull your tasks all together.

https://bit.ly/3tuVlhz

Bullet journals are a way to help organize all of this information into one book you keep with you at all times. Although they were originally designed to have little dots, or bullets, instead of lines, to encourage doodling, drawing, listing, and creating your own system of organizing, you can use any notebook you like. Ryder Carroll, the originator of the bullet journal system, describes it as an analog system to "track the past, organize the present, and plan for the future" (Carroll, 2018). It's perfect for the busy teacher! Lists can seem overwhelming as they grow and grow; also, lists don't help you identify priorities. Sticky notes are great for short memos, but they can become unwieldy, hard to find, and difficult to document information for the future. Carroll's bullet journal system of creating bulleted tasks, notes, and events all in one place can help educators identify priorities and even capture great lesson ideas or allow for mental health journaling. As Carroll says, "It is the difference between being busy and being productive" (2018).

By identifying tasks and events, it is less likely you will forget important items. The most critical tasks can be starred to emphasize them, helping ensure you don't forget the most crucial or time-sensitive items. Spend 5 minutes in the morning looking over your tasks and planning your day. Keep notes during the day as you go, quickly jotting them down as needed. When the school day ends, sit down again for another 5 minutes to look at your tasks and determine what you are going to do and when. Decide what needs to be done right then, do it, and cross it off the list. Go to sleep every night knowing you are on top of things. In fact, you may even be able to bullet in, and prioritize, that good night's sleep!

PART II

RESEARCH AND STRATEGIES
DEVELOPING YOUR TEACHER'S TOOL KIT

SENSORY-MOTOR DEVELOPMENT

Defining Sensory-Motor Development

Motor development is a widely used term and can be briefly defined as "adaptive change toward competence" (Sugden & Wade, 2013). Physical education (PE) teachers might think of the development of gross motor skills (e.g., throwing a ball), whereas classroom and special education teachers will probably think more of a student's fine motor skills (e.g., writing). Both these examples are natural parts of motor development.

How children handle their own bodies—their different motor skills—is important both for their ability to participate in social activities during school breaks and their ability to perform different academic tasks in the classroom. We will describe and exemplify this later in the chapter.

Given the importance of motor development, why then is the focus of this chapter sensory-motor development and not only simply motor development? As most readers know, when you train your motor skills, you will most likely become better at performing those motor tasks. Consider, however, if those improvements are because you have improved your ability to interpret the sensory input you have received or if perhaps you have improved your ability to give your body more accurate orders on how to execute the action. Either way, our view on this is that it is not that important if your improvement is in the area of receiving and interpreting signals or in the area of sending the correct signals. What matters is that the motor development is improving! Because it all is both about sensory *input* and about motor *output*, this area of focus is called sensory-motor development.

There are more reasons to focus on strategies related to sensory-motor interaction and not only the motor aspect of the

Sensory-Motor Development involves the sensory input and motor output required for actions to occur. If there is a delay in either part, students can struggle.

equation. When motor development is brought up in schools, there is the immediate impression that is the responsibility primarily of the PE teacher or perhaps, to some extent, the special education teacher or occupational or physical therapists. The reality however is that motor development—or preferably *sensory-motor development*—is an important concern for every teacher. More importantly, by the end of this chapter, you will recognize that strategies for improving sensory-motor development are great assets or tools that you as a teacher can benefit from in the process of managing your classroom and supporting your students.

MAKING CONNECTIONS

Chapter 3 on applied behavior analysis provides more information about how learning can be impeded when children try to meet their own sensory needs.

The potential benefits of investing time in training sensory-motor development are enormous. However, this is not a quick fix but rather a long-term process. It is important and beneficial to invest time in training for the long-term effects. Most teachers want tools that can have a positive impact instantly. We completely understand wanting a quick fix strategy, and there are elements of this work that will have immediate impact in the classroom. Many students, in more or less every classroom, have different sensory needs to be met. These needs include sensory needs of students with disabilities like attention-deficit hyperactivity disorder (ADHD) or autism. When certain needs aren't met, students can't concentrate. When that occurs, students with these needs try to find ways to meet their own needs, often resulting in disturbing other students and challenging behavior in the classroom.

What are some of those sensory needs? Sensory needs can be about high sensitivity to noise or smell or visual inputs, but often it is about the need to move. The sensory need connected to physical activity is connected to the student's vestibular system, but the key is that it is connected to the need for movement. We can't imagine any teacher who doesn't have students, with and without identified disabilities, who need to move! We are convinced that, every day, teachers have students with these needs and can experience them as quite challenging to meet—especially if they are requiring students to sit for the full day. These sensory needs can be met to a high extent directly in the classroom via both the physical environment and teaching strategies employed by the teacher. Because these common sensory needs are something that concerns every teacher, we naturally recognized the need to offer inclusive strategies to address this need.

Historical Perspective on Sensory-Motor Development

The literature on sensory-motor and learning falls in the area of neuroscience. The basic area of motor development research has its origin in a combination of psychology and biology. Piaget could be considered one of the early researchers in psychology connecting motor development and learning. An area that is part of sensory-motor development is Ayres Sensory Integration (ASI) that to some extent is a part of this inclusive strategy. ASI has its origin in the work of Jean Ayres that began around 50 years ago (Ayres, 1972; Schaaf et al., 2018; Schoen et al., 2019). The evidence base behind the ASI tool is mostly focused on its application to children with autism, but it has interesting implications for many general school settings. Because students with autism are among the student population who many teachers feel the least prepared to teach and have the most difficulties in meeting their needs within the classroom setting, knowing more about ASI is worthwhile.

Jean Ayres developed her ASI tool starting in the early 1970s. At the same time much work was done in Europe, especially in Germany, in an area called psycho-motor training. This was also closely connected with motor development. One of the key persons in the development of that area was Professor Kiphard from Germany (Kiphard, 2009). The work of both Ayres and Kiphard became popular in Europe in the 1980s. Another individual, a Danish physiotherapist and PE teacher—Britta Holle—also had a significant impact on the way motor development was viewed and addressed in Europe. Quite a lot of that work was done on an individual basis (one-on-one). In the 1990s, the trend in Europe moved toward integrating play in schools, and the focus became doing everything in group settings as opposed to more individual work.

In 2003, Swedish researcher Ingegerd Ericsson presented her PhD thesis about motor development, concentration, and school performances. Her work presented an intervention study done in first through third grades (Ericsson, 2003). In her research, she demonstrated how daily physical activity and training for motor development had a positive impact on school performance in basic theoretical subjects (math, language, Social Studies, science).

In Sweden, the 2010s led to more of a focus on the importance of motor development in schools or at least of the importance of physical activity. Substantial support in that regard was a book published in 2016 about physical activity and effects on the brain. This book was "Brain Power" (in Swedish: "Hjärnstark") by the Swedish psychiatrist Anders Hansen (2016). That book had a great impact within Sweden and showed, among other things, how physical activity can be useful for students in schools. Hansen's book focused on effects on the brain from physical activities that raise the heart rate. Based on his research, there is now a connection to different kinds of cardiovascular exercise that now is popular among Swedish schools, often resulting in positive outcomes on academic school performance.

The current needs of schools to improve academic engaged time for students and to have calmer classrooms will probably lead to the next step in the history of sensory-motor development. We hope that part of the next step will be to apply the inclusive strategies focused on sensory-motor development that we present here. To finalize this short summary of the history and to aim forward toward making new history, it may be of interest to mention a German study from 2016 (Koutsandréou et al., 2016). Researchers looked at working memory among children 9–10 years of age. They implemented two interventions. One program was with cardiovascular exercise, and the other was a special motor-demanding intervention. The cardiovascular exercise had a good effect on working memory, whereas the motor development training had a significantly larger positive effect. Interesting. So, why not include and combine them both in your own teaching environment? Continue to read, and we will share how to do that successfully.

Benefits to Sensory-Motor Development

When you want to support your students through sensory-motor development training, it is obviously helpful to know exactly what each student needs to develop, but fear not! You don't have to be an expert in sensory-motor development. By doing any training in general, you will still experience positive outcomes. Every teacher—no matter what type of teaching area—can include a sensory-motor development perspective in their own classroom. You can choose to support your students with some physical and sensory-motor activities on a group level. If you have a specialist in this area at your school, that is of course helpful, and we hope you will collaborate with that individual, but you can realize many positive effects for your students on your own or together with your colleagues. Consider these areas for development:

Working memory. Both cardiovascular training and motor-demanding training are good for building one's working memory (Koutsandréou et al., 2016). Please note that there is also a positive correlation between fine and gross motor skills with several other aspects of cognitive functions to include academic performance in both mathematics and reading comprehension (Geertsen et al., 2016). Sensory-motor development can possibly also play a role for working memory from another perspective. If a student is not well developed from a motor perspective, that student will probably use much of their working memory capacity for motor control and activity. Thus, that student may be having to put focus and attention on their motor activity, if it is not well automated, instead of on the academic learning during the lessons.

In an American study, researchers included physical activity within math and language lessons for third graders (Read et al., 2010). The students who participated in the groups with physical activity achieved significantly improved outcomes in mathematics and spelling performance compared to the students in the control groups. In addition, results from a 2017 review of the literature looking at effects of classroom-based physical activity interventions on academic and physical activity outcomes showed increased on-task and reduced off-task classroom behavior in addition to improved academic performance (Watson et al., 2017).

Some of these desired effects might be reached by implementing activities outside the classroom, but consider how much better it would be to engage students in the classroom as well if you want to improve their working memory. Remember that it is always wise to take baby steps. Teachers don't need to do everything at once. Motivation is a good factor for success for teachers as well as for students. Begin by trying out one or some of the recommendations that you find interesting and relatively easy to start, and make additional sensory-motor activities a reality in your classroom.

Concentration and focus. Today every teacher has a diverse classroom. Of course, there are big differences in diversity among students in different classes and at different schools. However, in every classroom there are students with different needs from many perspectives. One of those perspectives is a sensory-motor perspective. Adding more physical activity to the learning environment can have long-term effects on concentration, attention, and time on task (Buchele Harris et al., 2018; de Greeff et al., 2017). Some students need to move to be able to concentrate and learn well. Other students may need to move around every 20 minutes or so, whereas others need some sort of movement much more often. Some students can't focus when they move, and other students have difficulties concentrating on the academic work because they need their full attention on remaining in their seat and being quiet.

"Kids do well if they can" wrote the American researcher and psychologist Ross Greene (2017). What a positive perspective! We are convinced that students do indeed want to succeed. Our task is to give them good opportunities to do that. To handle all the different needs that you have among your students in a classroom can sound like *Mission Impossible*. However, by recognizing the need for movement and by embedding it in various ways throughout the day—to include allowing students to choose when, where, and how they move (within limits, of course)—will help address that diversity.

MAKING CONNECTIONS
....................●

Read more about strategies for supporting reading skills and literacy in Chapter 8.

Reading. There are many factors that influence a student's reading ability, and sensory-motor development is one of them. Eye movements, including visual perception and visual-motor integration, can affect reading ability (Bellocchi et al., 2017; Clifton et al., 2016). Eyes have muscles that need to be properly trained. Although that happens naturally for most people, some children may need intentional training to support their eye tracking. Teachers can support such training in many ways. For example, one technique is to develop tracking skills using racket sport activities using balls that give an adequate challenge. Sometimes a child's reading ability can also be hampered by vestibular needs (Braswell & Rine, 2006; Franco & Panhoca, 2008; Grabherr et al., 2015; Lane et al., 2019). Students with such needs might benefit from vestibular-stimulating activities like jumping on a trampoline, spinning on a board, or using a swing. This is why some classes offer bouncing balls for students to sit on. For some, it is supportive of their vestibular needs; for others it helps with a need for movement; and for the rest it may simply be fun and different.

Writing. When teachers have students who are struggling with writing when using paper and pencil, the teachers might want to consider a connection to a need for sensory-motor training. Writing ability is closely connected to sensory-motor development and motor memory (Palmis et al., 2017). Although most students have strong fine motor skills and know how to hold a pencil, some still struggle. For those individuals, training their motor skills will help.

Watch those students who appear to struggle with writing. You may see some students get tired quickly while writing; others may appear to be using their whole arm rather than the wrist while moving the pencil. For these individuals, you can teach them to master isolated movements in each joint starting with the shoulder, followed by the elbow, and finally the wrist. Feel free to bring in some rhythmic gymnastics bands with sticks or skipping ropes to make this type of instruction fun. Rope skipping is good training for learning how to focus movement to the wrists, and the whole class can use it as a brain break or movement activity, thereby removing any stigma from those students who need it to support their physical writing skills. During the time in which students are in this motor training period to support handwriting, allow students to compose their work using a computer, iPad, speech to text, or other tools that can facilitate composition without requiring the handwriting skill.

Social development. An important part of the school curriculum is social development. An important part of that development will occur during recess, nutrition breaks, lunch, sports and after-school activities. Many common social activities include the use of different balls (e.g., tennis balls, footballs, basketballs, soccer balls). To be able to enjoy participating in activities including balls, students need some aspect of coordination to manage to bounce, catch, and throw. If they have not mastered these skills, students tend to avoid these activities with the risk of missing out on important social development. Thus, training in the mentioned skills, adapted to the ability of each student, can be useful. Training can, of course, be included in PE lessons, but educators shouldn't forget about the opportunities to work on these skills elsewhere. For example, in the classroom, co-teachers might gently throw a ball to students as they ask questions, encouraging students to throw the ball back to them.

Behavior. When a student behaves in a certain way, there is always a function serving that behavior (Karlsson, 2018). The student might gain something (e.g., attention or a tangible) or manage to escape something (e.g., a person or the situation) or a combination thereof. However, behavior can also have another purpose, namely, a sensory-motor reason. Students may simply have an internal need to act in a particular way. This is acutely evident in some students with autism, who may rock or "self-stim" (Kapp et al., 2019). Their behavior is not meant to be intrusive or distracting to the class; it is merely what their bodies need to feel secure. Identifying appropriate alternative behaviors for them that still serve the sensory-motor need is important. For example, for a student who needs to flap their hands, giving them a fidget spinner might serve the same sensory-motor need and yet be less distracting to the other students in the classroom. Many teachers have found that putting heavy-duty rubber bands at the bottom of students' chairs allows them to move their feet and bounce without making noise or disrupting the class. This strategy also frees students' hands for academic tasks.

For students with ADHD, the needs for sensory-motor adaptations in the classroom can be great. These needs may be reduced by cardiovascular exercise, which has also been found to enhance executive functioning skills in this population (Benzing et al., 2018). For example, students may be allowed to show their answers to a math problem through doing that number of push-ups. Or, provided a door to outside is close at hand, they may be allowed to run around the school building during a 3-minute brain break activity. This type of physical activity will not only result in a calmer, more focused student in the short-term, but it can also result in positive acute and long-term effects (Den Heijer et al., 2017).

Barriers to
Sensory-Motor Development

Think you can't find the time to include sensory-motor activities in your classroom? Consider this: most teachers who have included sensory-motor activities in their classroom for a while actually experience that they get *more* time to focus on teaching their subject and that their students have *more* time on task. Is your mind blown? Perhaps you as a teacher don't feel comfortable in leading different physical activities. In that case, you can focus more on trying to organize your teaching so it naturally includes some movement and physical activity. For example, ask students questions and have them move to different parts of the room to show their answers. ("If you think the answer is A, go to this corner. If you think the answer is B, go to this other corner.")

It is not that difficult to implement sensory-regulating activities and use of equipment in the classroom. One small area in the classroom could be set up to have activity cards available; students can earn or be provided with opportunities to visit that area during the lesson. If your class is organized into groups, using a station system provides students with activity simply through the transition between stations. You can add to that by having one station where students are asked to work while standing (or/and use bicycle chairs).

Implementing sensory-motor training designed for more long-term results can be a bit more difficult and/or intimidating. That can also be more challenging to fit in to the school day when there is only one teacher in the classroom. If one is co-teaching or has other adults in the room with whom to collaborate, they can accomplish more complex sensory-motor training. Implementing long-term sensory-motor training is much easier to do if it becomes part of a school initiative or something that all teachers in a grade will do together as a team-oriented school development activity. Why not bring this concept to your principal?

School Leader Spotlight

Establishing an inclusive sensory-motor environment both indoors and outdoors is your responsibility. Indoors: set a standard concerning the physical environment of each class by ensuring there are seating and movement options for students. Outdoors: develop an environment that the students find stimulating to move around in, that has activities that increase heart rate (cardiovascular effects), and that is completely accessible for all your students. Organize the outdoor environment so that it includes motor challenges at all levels. Create a truly inclusive sensory-motor environment. An important key for this recommended type of environment is that it is organized so that students can move and play without needing instructions from the teachers or other staff. Although this may require initial financial outlay, the outcomes will be well worth it in the long run—behaviorally, socially, academically, and physically.

Strategies for Effective Sensory-Motor Development

It is more or less impossible to manage a diverse classroom by having many individual solutions. Teachers simply do not have the time to individualize for every single need or every single student. Let's be "street smart" here. Being street smart in this situation means to apply something that we all know: the buffet! Want to address the varied sensory needs in your classroom? Organize your classroom like a buffet. Choice is key to teachers' sanity and to students' success. Choice is also a major component to universally designing your lessons, which you'll learn more about in Chapter 6.

One important perspective you need as a teacher when you start organizing your buffet-style classroom is that your focus must be that every student shall have the most possible time on task. Contrary to how many classrooms appear, the goal is *not* merely to have students sitting still in their chairs for the most time possible. Be clear on your true goals for this to be successful.

The buffet-style classroom physical environment might include the following:

1. **Bicycle chair.** The student can be cycling at the same time as focusing on academic tasks and learning. This type of equipment makes a huge difference for many students and especially those with great needs in the area of movement or physical activity. It doesn't tend to disturb other students, and for some students, this is a key to being able to stay in the classroom and to also get time on task.

2. **Desk where you can adjust the height,** including working while standing. If your school will buy new equipment, why not have adjustable desks for every student? However, if that is not possible, you can most often meet the needs in

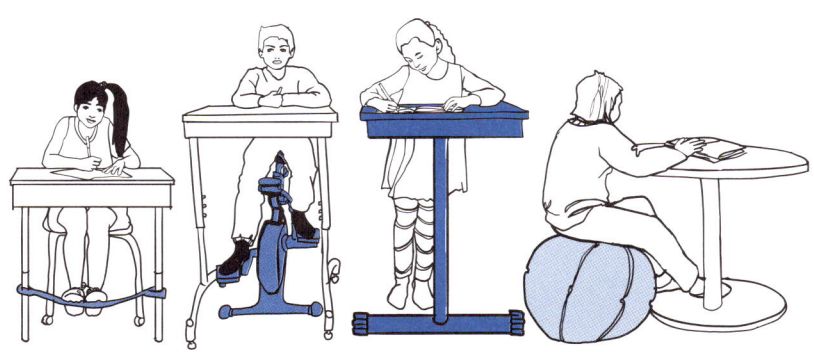

Source: Madelene Egerfält. Used with permission.

your classroom with only a few such desks. That can be sufficient as part of your buffet offerings.

3. **Balance chair.** For some students, having to manage their balance while sitting helps them focus. Other students will certainly want to try these chairs when you introduce them, but after a while only those who need them will use them. There will also be students in your classroom who absolutely cannot use these chairs and focus on academic tasks at the same time. That is one of the beauties of the diverse classroom and the buffet-style arrangement. Students can pick what they need.

4. **Seating ball.** These are large balls that students can use instead of a chair. Our experience is that both students and teachers appreciate using these for sitting; the same goes for the balance chairs. These balls are also a relatively low expense for the school. At least a few of these balls will be a good part of your buffet.

5. **Portable computer table.** There are many types, but one we are familiar with is called Ztool. With this type of table, your students can choose to work more or less anywhere, and your available learning environment will be even more flexible. These tables are relatively inexpensive, about the same as seating balls.

6. **Trampoline.** Get a small one, nothing massive. This is useful equipment especially in K–3 classrooms but can also be used in upper grades. These trampolines help

regulate sensory needs and can raise students' heart rates for short moments. We admit that students jumping on a trampoline in class is not completely silent, but the students normally acclimate to the small sound quickly. Teachers may need to work to ignore the bouncing, but if students can, we can too!

7. **Spinning board.** There are different types of boards available, but the important function is that it is easy for the student to independently, and without the need of support, sit and spin around on it. The spinning gives an intensive sensory regulation connected to a sensory system called the vestibular system. Students who truly benefit from spinning will often spontaneously use the board as needed. Without a board, student with such needs will find another way of cater for their needs, which often results in moving around in the classroom or spinning on their own. With less need to move around in the classroom or self-stim, students are more likely to spend more time on task. One example of this spinning board that works well is called Gonge Karusell.

8. **Bouncy bands** on chair or desk. This is a type of rubber band that the students will have instead of a footrest so that they can move their feet without noise. At the same time, this caters to their sensory needs. The students have their hands free for schoolwork at the same time as regulating their sensory needs.

9. **Fidget tools.** Have a variety of fidget tools for use in the classroom. Like with the rest of your classroom buffet, these tools are available for everyone, not merely for a specific student. It is simply part of your offerings. Although you may think you know which student will benefit from what, by offering everything to your whole class, many more students will benefit. This is also a key aspect of Universal Design for Learning, which you can read about in Chapter 6. After an initial period, when everyone wants to try everything, the result will gradually be that students will use what they benefit from; this definitely establishes a win-win situation.

10. **Desk and floor screens.** At times, some students may need less visual stimulation input, a smaller environment, or simply some time alone; offering an option to meet these needs, without leaving the classroom and missing out on content, is doable if your buffet includes some desk and floor screens. The smaller desk screens, which you can also create through the use of manila folders if necessary, can reduce visual input for students who need that and should be easily accessible for any student who feels the need to use one. The larger floor screens can create a room within the room for a group of students or for an individual.

11. **Desk pods.** Consider organizing your classroom so that students have the opportunity to put their desks in groups of four to six. Compared to seating individually or in pairs, this helps free up more space in the classroom. More space makes it easier to include different kinds of activities during lessons. When students are in groups, it also tends to motivate them to talk to and interact with the others in the same group rather than speaking out loud to the whole classroom. This will also help facilitate another of the strategies presented in this book in Chapter 7 called cooperative learning.

Instructional strategies to help with sensory-motor development include the following:

1. **Organize activities** where you offer both inclusive motor activities and activities that raise the heart rate without totally exhausting students. Such activities will both be beneficial for time on task during the following lesson and in the long term have a positive impact on working memory capacity (e.g., Geertsen et al., 2016; Koutsandréou et al., 2016). Morning activities tend to have a positive outcome on students' cognitive functioning for the rest of the day (Tilp et al., 2020). Intensive physical activities for even as short as 4 minutes can have an immediate positive effect on attention and impulse control in students with ADHD (Silva et al., 2015).

2. **Use short activity breaks in the form of rewards for the students.** Consider the Good Behavior Game and Timely Transitions Game we mentioned in Part I. Students can earn rewards through appropriate behavior. Offering activity breaks as a reward also serves a dual purpose: you will be able to meet the movement needs that many students have. Although most activities need to be only 20–30 seconds, longer activities can be used as well (Ghaderi et al., 2017). In addition to being used as class-wide or individual behavioral rewards, short physical activity is also perfect for when students need a brain break, when teachers need a few minutes to work on something, or as a transition between topics. Examples of activities may include: (a) walk around the classroom, give a high 10 with as many of your peers as possible for 30 seconds, and do a vertical jump while doing it; (b) stand in pairs and do rock paper scissors with your whole body for 30 seconds; (c) similar to rock/paper/scissors, both peers show a number of their fingers at the same time, using addition or multiplication, and the one who wins is the one who is the quickest to summarize the fingers correctly, (d) walk like a gorilla, and sound like a sheep for 20 seconds (teachers should participate also); (e) stand in pairs and

mirror each other for 20 seconds each; and (f) student choice on how they want to stretch for 30 seconds. Before starting each activity always let the students know exactly what they will do, for how long, and with whom; it is also useful that they know what they are supposed to do when the activity is finished. A timer is a good tool during these activities. Every time you reward your students with an activity break, be sure to tell them what they have done well. That means that you will give your students positive specific feedback (you can read more about functional forms of feedback in Chapter 2 cn formative assessment). These activities both support students in meeting their need to move and at the same time reinforce appropriate student behavior. This type of activity also works well when combined with Positive Behavior Interventions and Support that you will read about in Chapter 3 on applied behavior analysis.

3. **Include movement and physical activity as part of your regular teaching in the classroom.** As stated, students who struggle with attention benefit significantly from increased movement (Mahar, 2011). Although the prior bullet emphasized the use of movement as a reward for appropriate behaviors, integrating activities where the students use their bodies, work standing, or move around as part of the regular pedagogy is also recommended. Groups can work while standing at a large board. Movement is even more effective on learning if the physical activities are relevant for and connected to the content you are teaching, as opposed to movement for movement's sake (Bartholomew et al., 2018; Mavilidi et al., 2018). For example, an elementary teacher might line up 10 students and ask the remaining students to move half of them away, whereas a high school teacher might have students use a graph on the floor to demonstrate longitude and latitude or solve algebraic equations and move themselves on the graph accordingly. Simply using Station Teaching, wherein students move from station to station to complete academic tasks, may not integrate the movement into the curriculum, but stations do at least offer movement.

4. **Teach outside of your classroom.** A natural way of including movement and physical activity is to teach in a different environment. Go outside if you can! Use a hallway, another teacher's room, or an empty theater space. If you have the opportunity, build lessons around nature. From an academic perspective, being able to help your students apply their learning into different contexts helps with generalization. Another potential effect suggested in research is that this generalization into a different environment may strengthen students' memory and thereby enhance their learning (Bjork & Bjork, 2019; Smith & Vela, 2001).

Getting Started With
Sensory-Motor Development

Teachers don't need to be experts in sensory-motor development to organize their classroom sensory-motor buffet offerings or to include more physical activity in the learning environment. This chapter, in combination with one's own competencies and experiences, will enable every teacher to make a positive impact that will benefit students.

Get started in your classroom right away by starting small. Become more aware of how often students are able to get up and move; try to ensure it happens at least once every 20 minutes. Consult with a PE teacher or occupational or physical therapist for additional kinesthetic ideas, or ask around to see which teachers are known for creative movement in their classes. If you start talking and reflecting about this with your colleagues, you may find that there are a lot of expertise and creative ideas out there.

In your own classroom, start organizing your buffet. Depending on what material and equipment already exists at your school, you might need talk to your principal. Explain what a wise investment it would be to buy some of the equipment your school will need, and offer to collect data on how it affects student learning. Naturally, you can always start on your own and focus only on your personal learning environment, but if you can include your colleagues and your principal, this could evolve into a whole school initiative. Get 'em moving and learning!

FORMATIVE ASSESSMENT

Defining Formative Assessment

Formative assessment typically refers to those strategies aimed at assessing and supporting learning *as learning occurs.* One of the most valuable features of formative assessment in classrooms is that it allows teachers to adjust teaching strategies in a more timely and effective manner because they are actively assessing their students' understanding as part of the teaching process rather than finding out what students know or have understood *after* teaching has occurred. Formative assessment can be contrasted with summative assessment, which typically occurs after instruction has ended and is usually aimed at assessing performance or achievement. Formative assessment is typically referred to as *assessment for learning,* whereas summative assessment is referred to as *assessment of learning.*

Black and Wiliam have defined formative assessment as "the extent that evidence about student achievement is elicited, interpreted, and used by teachers, learners, or their peers, to make decisions about the next steps in instruction that are likely to be better, or better founded, than the decisions they would have taken in the absence of the evidence that was elicited" (2009, p. 9). In his book *Creating the Schools Our Children Need*, Wiliam (2018) described five key principles for formative assessment:

1. ensure that students know what they are meant to be learning;

2. find out what students have learned;

3. provide feedback that improves student learning;

Formative assessment is referred to as *assessment for learning.*

Summative assessment is referred to as *assessment of learning.*

4. have students help each other learn; and

5. develop students' ability to monitor and assess their own learning.

In this chapter, we describe these five key elements from a practical perspective. We also describe how formative assessment helps both students and their teachers learn more effectively together and how you can learn to adapt and continuously develop your own classroom practices around the use of formative assessment.

Historical Perspective on Formative Assessment

Michael Scriven (1967) and Benjamin Bloom (1968) are two key figures in the early history of assessment and evaluation. Their early work—more than 50 years ago—led educators to use assessment as a tool to increase learning and improve teaching; however, it was not yet called formative assessment. In their 1986 seminal article, Lynn and Douglas Fuchs published an analysis on the effects of systematic formative evaluation in special education. Their work was among the first directly connected to the area today called formative assessment. More recently, Paul Black and Dylan Wiliam (1998, 2009) are other key persons who have continued to make contributions to both theory and practice in the area of formative assessment.

Benefits and Barriers to Formative Assessment

Benefits. Formative assessment is a strategy that, when well applied, has a positive impact on academic performance. It provides a structure for the teaching and learning processes in schools. It offers teachers ongoing information to help them structure their teaching in real time. Using data to drive instruction helps ensure a continuous improvement process (Murawski & Lochner, 2018) while also offering teachers an unbiased overview of how each of their students is understanding the content. When all students are struggling with a concept, teachers are able to step back and recognize there might be an issue with the way in which they are presenting the concept. When a group of students is struggling, teachers can determine if that group needs additional scaffolding or a different way to approach the concept. A major advantage of formative assessment is that it also works well when combined with the other evidence-based inclusion strategies presented in this book. These strategies will be helpful to support you as a teacher in successfully managing your diverse classroom.

Barriers. One barrier to formative assessment is actually the frequent use of summative assessments often required of or by teachers. In fact, the more summative assessments provided, the less instructional time teachers have with students; this then results in less time for educators to use formative assessment techniques to course correct when students are floundering.

In their book *Pure Formative Assessment*, Lauvås and Jönsson (2019) wrote that "a lot indicates that the following conditions need to be met for assessment to have positive effects on the students' learning and motivation:

MAKING CONNECTIONS

Working with a teacher who is skilled at formative assessments can help you more seamlessly integrate them into your classroom. Check out Chapter 5 on how co-teaching can help you develop this skill.

- Summative assessment shall preferably not be used more than absolutely necessary.

- The summative assessment shall as much as possible be separated from the formative assessment, so that...

- the formative assessment is *pure formative assessment.*" (p. 12)

Key Components of Formative Assessment

In today's classroom, teachers are likely to have a diverse group of students with many different learning needs. However, the underlying principles of formative assessment are common across learners. In the next sections, we discuss how you can apply those principles in different ways so that each student in your class has the opportunity to benefit from the formative assessment process.

Principle 1: Ensure that Students Know What They Are Meant to Be Learning

Students need to know what is expected from them, including what they are supposed to be learning. This information must be communicated in ways that work for every student, so teachers must have multiple ways of defining expectations. For example, teachers can communicate expectations in writing, with visual support, orally for the group, and even individually to a particular student before a lesson. Teachers can display expectations on a board or a screen in the classroom, and they can also be on the learning platform used by the school. Some schools require teachers to write or post their daily objectives in student-friendly language; the key is not only to post the objectives but to ensure that students recognize and understand those objectives. When communicated clearly, knowing the purpose of the lesson will help students engage and focus on their learning. It also offers a helpful base as students work on tasks so that teachers can offer coaching via functional feedback.

Principle 2: Find Out What Students Have Learned

"To teach well, we have to find out what students already know. But students do not always learn what we teach. That's why finding out what students do know is essential to good teaching" (Wiliam & Leahy, 2015, p. 63). Essentially, this boils down to knowing where your students are and then teaching to that level. This can be easier said than done, especially when students will be at a variety of levels. Yet it is imperative that teachers view the feedback that they receive from students as a valuable tool for moving forward with instruction. "The most important factor at the start of a lesson is that the teacher must be open for feedback from the students about what they already know or don't know" (Hattie & Clarke, 2019). Both feedback about individual students and about the group will give you valuable information that you can use to continuously improve your instruction in the classroom.

For example, suppose a teacher delivered a lesson on how to divide fractions. They might see students attentively watch them demonstrate how to solve the equations, and some might even ask questions about the process. They might also see that students worked through the practice problems and said they understood their errors. The teacher might go home feeling like they had taught an effective lesson. What happens if the students' homework or test scores tell a different story? The teacher taught; the students did not learn. What now?

By using formative assessment throughout the lesson, the teacher would have had a better grasp on which of the students actually did and did not understand parts of the lesson. They would have been better able to catch the students before they practiced doing things incorrectly or experienced failure on homework and tests. Individual mini-whiteboards are an example of a practical tool teachers can use to get the feedback they need from students to adjust teaching. There are also many digital tools (e.g., Socrative, NearPod, PearDeck, Kahoot!) and analog tools (e.g., Plickers, Opportunities to Respond [OTR] cards, popsicle sticks) that provide teachers with immediate feedback from their students. Often, students can also use these tools for their own self-regulation. In several digital applications, students can adapt their challenge, monitor their own progress, and receive immediate feedback at the same time; in addition, teachers have access to their students' data to determine groupings, identify the need for group or individual review, and so on. Being able to offer students timely and specific feedback is key to their improvement. Researchers have suggested that "the most important takeaway from the research is that the shorter the time interval between eliciting the evidence and using it to improve instruction, the bigger the likely impact on learning" (Wiliam & Leahy, 2015, p. 9).

Principle 3: Provide Feedback That Improves Student Learning

In 2007, Hattie and Timperley did an analysis related to the impact feedback has on learning and achievement. They identified four areas as the focus of feedback: (1) about the task, (2) about the processing of the task, (3) about self-regulation, and (4) about the self as a person. They noted that feedback about processing the task and feedback about self-regulation are the more powerful forms for learning. Although feedback about the task itself is a common approach, it is not as powerful as feedback that focuses on processing or self-regulation. Further, feedback aimed at the person can actually be counterproductive. Feedback on the self as a person typically does not provide information that a student can use for learning. Saying things like "good job" or "you're doing great" when a student isn't performing well can be make the student feel as though the teacher has low expectations for them. This low expectation might lead students to identify themselves as students with low ability (Hattie & Timperley, 2007).

Stone and Heen (2014) described three purposes of feedback and how they satisfy our need for appreciation, coaching, and evaluation. Most of us need to feel appreciated, but the way that feedback is delivered can affect how much appreciation we feel. Feedback that is specific, authentic, and delivered in a form that the receiver values is much more likely to make us feel appreciated. For academic achievement, coaching and evaluation are critical. When combined with Hattie and Timberley's research, we recognize that offering feedback about the processing of learning tasks or about self-regulation is the most productive for student growth.

Stone and Heen (2014) also described three types of feedback triggers that can block or hamper the effect of feedback. If we feel feedback is wrong, unfair, or unhelpful, we are likely to become defensive and to reject or ignore the feedback. This is referred to as a *truth trigger*. How we receive feedback is also strongly influenced by who is giving us feedback. The relationship between teacher and student can greatly influence how the student will receive and react to the feedback provided. Feedback is more likely to be heard if both parties feel respected and appreciated by one another. Thus, the relationship between feedback giver and feedback receiver is called a *relation trigger*. Note that both what the student thinks about the teacher as the feedback giver and how the student feels treated by their teacher can influence how they receive feedback. If feedback feels threatening or is critical, the receiver is likely to become defensive; such feedback includes what is called an *identity trigger*. Think about how some students react when a teacher says, "You've been talking too much today. If you talk out again, I'm sending you to the office." Instead of being quiet and considering the teacher's statement as feedback that they have been too chatty, some students may see the comment as a threat and respond by jumping up and saying, "I'm going to the office then!" Why would they do that? Haidt wrote, "Responses to threats and unpleasantness are about 10 times faster plus they are stronger and harder to inhibit than responses to opportunities and pleasure" (2006, p. 29). Clearly, feedback that might include an identity trigger may result in a strong response but not one we would want in the classroom.

PRACTICAL RECOMMENDATIONS FOR IMPLEMENTING FEEDBACK

- ***Develop strong relationships with your students.*** When teachers have good relationships with their students, feedback is more easily received and more effective. The better you know your students, the more you will know about how to adapt your feedback delivery and what types of feedback work best for each of your individual students.
- ***Use feedback that makes your students think.*** This means that task-oriented feedback with the purpose of coaching is often a strong choice. When coaching, try to ensure that the feedback offered has its focus on the processing of the task. As always, it is best to word feedback so that it is positive in nature.
- ***Offer think time.*** When asking a question to the class, always wait some seconds before selecting a student to answer. Consider asking students to wait to raise their hands or call out answers. This allows more students a chance to think about the question and their response. Use the same strategy when students ask you a question; wait some seconds before you answer so that students also have a chance to think about the question and potentially help with the answer.

- *Use positive specific feedback (PSF).* This type of feedback should answer the questions *what is the student is doing well* and *why that is good.* Feedback that is nonspecific (e.g., "Well done!" or "Good job!") is less likely to be effective because it doesn't specify the behavior on which you are providing feedback. In addition, vague praise can potentially be misinterpreted; in other words, the student might think you are providing feedback on one behavior, but you actually attempting to praise another behavior. Also, ensure that feedback is focused on what the student is doing (e.g., "Your drawing shows a good understanding of perspective") rather than the student as a person (e.g., "You are so creative"). Because most of us prefer positive feedback, PSF can help build good relationships with your students. PSF often functions as a positive reinforcer, meaning that it makes the behavior you provided feedback on more likely to occur in the future (see Chapter 3 on applied behavior analysis).
- *Avoid negative or threatening feedback.* Although there are times when teachers may feel compelled to provide negative feedback (e.g., "When you color with the black marker, I can't tell what you are drawing"), this does not tend to be the most effective for changing student behavior. The use of negative feedback makes it more likely that the feedback will not be well received. Furthermore, you may even hamper or block the effect of other feedback you give. Practice turning the feedback around to be positive when possible.
- *Focus on progress rather than results.* Recognizing and acknowledging progress toward a goal, rather than only goal attainment, can improve motivation and enhance performance. This strategy also allows those students who tend to meet goals more slowly than others to access frequent positive feedback. Instead of comparing themselves to other students, when focusing on progress, every student has the opportunity to compare their work in relation to their own performance or personal best (Liem et al., 2012; Martin & Elliot, 2016).
- *Let the students succeed.* To help students learn as much as possible, each one of them should be engaged in investing efforts and time on their studies. The way students plan and execute learning tasks is often based on their personal experiences. If a student has experienced lots of failure academically, they will frequently—and

(Continued)

(Continued)

understandably—lack the motivation to take on new challenges. Lauvås and Jönsson summarize this well: "A student who has failed earlier and received poor assessments will probably put less effort on the tasks to not risk experiencing more failure. After repeated failures, most students will completely give up and instead avoid or make sure to get attention in other (often less constructive) ways. The only way to break this downward spiral is to let the students manage their tasks. As soon as they have succeeded with a task, the probability that they will take on more similar tasks will increase" (2019, pp. 24–25). To give every student a good chance of success, teachers need to offer different ways or approaches to each task that involve a variety of abilities, interests, and actions. A strategy called Universal Design for Learning (UDL) will help in this regard; you can read all about UDL in Chapter 6.

- ***Make sure the feedback is useful.*** This quote from Wiliam and Leahy sums it up: "The only thing that matters with feedback is the reaction of the recipient. That's it. Feedback – no matter how well designed – that the student does not act upon is a waste of time" (2015, p. 107). Restated, feedback that students use for their learning is time well invested. School tasks revolve around both academic and social development. Thus, feedback that leads toward improved academic development, social development, or both is worthwhile.

Principle 4: Have Students Help Each Other Learn

This fourth principle for educators creating their formative assessment strategy is about engaging students to assess and support each other, which in turn provides support for the teacher and complements the teacher's feedback. It is critical, however, that students receive training on how to appropriately and supportively provide feedback to their peers. This can be based on the same principles and advice related to what to focus on and what is important for giving and receiving feedback. Teachers should not assume that students know how to appropriately provide positive feedback to their peers.

According to Lauvås and Jönsson (2019), peer feedback can even be the most effective form of formative assessment. They note that it is pure formative assessment because no assessment from the teacher is involved. Other than time invested for training, it means no extra work for the teacher and can be easily incorporated into each class session.

Hattie and Clarke (2019) recommend a specific form of peer feedback called "cooperative feedback," where students work in pairs. Both students read and discuss one student's work, and then the student who has done the work decides what revisions need to be made. The process is then repeated for the other student in the pair. As with most strategies, cooperative feedback requires time for students to be trained, but once they have learned the skills, it can be applied to any subject or task. It is also important to consider how to pair students and ensure that no student will be embarrassed or humiliated in any way in front of their peers. Given the fact that inclusive classrooms have students with various abilities and disabilities, teachers need to strategically pair students and teach them appropriate ways to provide feedback. This principle of students helping their peers is closely aligned with the concept of cooperative learning, which is described in more detail in Chapter 7.

Principle 5: Develop Students' Abilities to Monitor and Assess Their Own Learning

This fifth principle deals with how educators encourage students to take ownership of their own learning as well as how students come to understand *how* they learn. The term referring to knowing how one learns is called *metacognition*. When students learn how to self-monitor their own actions and self-assess their own work, they begin to understand more about what they know, don't know, and how they learn best. This also helps students become better prepared to take appropriate action to set and meet their own learning goals. Being able to self-monitor and self-assess are important life skills. Consider how we as adults frequently consider our own actions and make changes accordingly. These are skills that need to be explicitly taught and practiced by students. "Most of what our students need to know hasn't been discovered or invented yet. *Learning how to learn* used to be an optional extra in education; today it's a survivor skill" (Wiliam & Leahy, 2015, p. 169).

Peer feedback can help students develop their self-monitoring and self-assessment skills because the peer feedback process allows them opportunities to both give and receive feedback. Hearing a peer's assessment of their work can help them more objectively assess their own strengths and potential areas for improvement. The better they become at this skill, the better their capacity for taking responsibility and ownership over their own learning. Like other strategies, training students to self-monitor and self-assess takes time, but it is time well spent on developing an important life skill.

Professional Development

As in all development processes, it is important to take small steps initially to give time to get used to and implement new actions in your practice. There are a number of resources for learning more about formative assessment, including the book *Embedding Formative Assessment* by Dylan Wiliam and Siobhan Leahy (2015). Consider creating a reading group so that you and your colleagues can discuss the book together. Another professional development activity that could support the use of formative assessment techniques is for teachers to share their ideas, strategies, and tools with one another. Although forums exist online (e.g., TeachersPayTeachers, Facebook groups, etc.), often there is a wealth of expertise at one's own school. An additional strategy is to identify a number of different formative assessment tools (e.g., GoogleForms, EdPuzzle, Quizizz, Flip-Grid, Explain Everything, Edulastic, Formative, Jamboard, Kahoot!, Mentimeter, Padlet, and the list goes on) and have different teachers try a different one for a specified period of time. Then teachers can come together and share their experiences, barriers, and outcomes. Move over Book Club; we have a Formative Assessment Club!

School Leader Spotlight

As a school leader, promoting pure formative assessment will help maximize teacher resources and student learning. It is important to remember that pure formative assessment means avoiding mixing formative and summative assessment. This can be challenging initially, but encouraging teachers to use peer feedback in their classrooms is an excellent first step toward this goal. Consider working toward a school culture where you optimize formative assessment and minimize summative assessments. Remember that you will need to give teachers time for proactive planning for the diverse classroom; however, the more teachers use formative assessment, the less time they will need to spend on summative assessment. In other words, if most of the feedback your teachers are giving to students is *during* the lessons rather than *after*, then after-lesson tasks will naturally be reduced. Your teachers can then allocate more time for proactive planning. To implement effective formative assessment based on all the five key strategies outlined in this chapter will take time and need continuous updates and further development. Therefore, you might consider devoting some time to formative assessment at monthly staff meetings, which includes working in small groups to discuss strategies, share success stories and good examples, and problem-solve any obstacles together. Consider modeling formative assessment strategies as you give feedback to your faculty regarding the ways in which they are using formative assessment with their students.

APPLIED BEHAVIOR ANALYSIS

Defining Applied Behavior Analysis

In this day and age of evidence-based practice, using educational strategies that are grounded in science is more important than ever. Behavior analysis is a scientific approach to understanding how people's interactions with their environments shape and maintain their behaviors. Applied behavior analysis (ABA) involves using the science of behavior analysis to solve important problems in the real world, like helping children acquire important social and academic skills or supporting teachers to manage their classrooms more effectively. Essentially, ABA is an approach to understanding how our environments teach us to behave in particular ways and then using that information to rearrange the environment to support behavior change that is important to the person. When educators learn how to apply an ABA lens to understanding the behavior of students, they quickly see that many behavior problems are actually environmental problems.

Although educators can use strategies based in ABA to address a range of issues in schools, it is important to note that ABA itself is not a technique or intervention. It is a science that underpins a range of educational and behavior support strategies. You might be using some of those strategies in your school now without even realizing that they are based in the science of ABA! For instance, token economies (Kazdin, 2012), Positive Behavior Interventions and Supports (PBIS; Sugai & Horner, 2020), and behavioral activation (Kanter et al., 2010) are all based on principles derived from ABA. Some ABA-based strategies might be in implemented for groups (e.g., classroom management strategies), whereas others might be specific to the needs of an individual (e.g., supporting a student to develop social skills). At their heart, ABA-based strategies seek to change

ABA is an approach to understanding how our environment teaches us to behave in certain ways and then how we can use that information to rearrange the environment to support desired behavioral change.

behavior so that individuals can more easily access opportunities and positive outcomes that are important to them. ABA approaches are person centered, meaning that they take individual strengths, choices, and goals into account when planning the best approach for supporting behavior change.

Historical Perspective on Applied Behavior Analysis

The science of behavior analysis has been around for more than 100 years. Its application to educational issues began in the 1950s with behavior analysts not only seeking to solve common behavior problems at school (e.g., Barrish et al., 1969) but also looking to improve academic teaching and learning (e.g., Skinner, 1968). Behavior analysis remains a thriving science with a number of scientific journals devoted to publishing behavior analytic research. Some of those journals focus exclusively on educational applications of ABA (e.g., *Journal of Behavioral Education, Education and Treatment of Children*). When educators use ABA-based strategies in their classrooms, they can be confident those strategies are based on a solid scientific footing.

As with any science, new innovations and refinements to existing strategies are constantly being developed. Behavior analysts are therefore expected to stay current with these developments in the same way that you would expect your medical doctor to stay current with advances in assessing and treating health problems as well as for promoting good health. Although there are a number of tried and trusted behavior analytic strategies that educators can employ in their classrooms, staying abreast of scientific advances can ensure those strategies are being used as effectively as possible. Consulting with a qualified behavior analyst can help schools ensure they are using the most effective and up-to-date ABA-based strategies. Don't have access currently to a qualified behavior analyst? That's not a problem. In this chapter, we'll introduce you to ABA benefits, barriers, basics, and strategies for beginning to implement ABA in your own classroom.

Benefits and Barriers to Using ABA-Based Strategies

Benefits. One of the most important benefits to using ABA-based strategies is that they are backed by decades of scientific evidence to show they are effective. In fact, there are few approaches to changing behavior that have the degree of scientific backing that ABA does.

A primary benefit of ABA-based strategies is that they are person centered. When we are trying to understand why a student may behave inappropriately or fail to meet school expectations, we examine what that student's environment has taught them and what their interactions with the environment mean to them. Not everyone views the same events as reinforcing; for example, some students love praise and public attention, and others will do anything they can to avoid being the center of attention. An ABA-based approach seeks to understand the student as an individual and create an environment that helps them access the things that are personally important to them while also meeting expectations that will set them up for success over the short and long term.

An additional benefit of ABA-based strategies is that they are optimistic. Inherent in the behaviorist philosophy that the majority of our behaviors are learned is the belief that anyone is capable of change. In other words, if problem behavior is learned, it can be unlearned and replaced with responses that increase the person's access to important social reinforcers.

Barriers. ABA is probably one of the most misunderstood social sciences, particularly as it is applied to education. There are a number of misconceptions about ABA that are still propagated across educational textbooks and websites. Some people believe that ABA equates to "bribing" students to behave well through the use of stickers, sweets, and other extrinsic rewards (Curwin et al., 2018). Although it is true that ABA-based strategies seek to make educational environments more reinforcing, using arbitrary rewards is likely to result in short-lived results and thus is not representative of good behavior analytic practice. Instead, behavior analysts seek to identify the reinforcers that occur naturally in the environment (i.e., functions) and then work to change the contingencies for the behaviors that interfere with a person's success. In other words, they use the reinforcers that once maintained problem behavior to increase behaviors that will support the student in developing better academic and prosocial skills. By supporting student success through changing the environment, we put students in contact with important intrinsic, self-mediated reinforcers (e.g., feeling good about what they have accomplished, being able to do something they could not do before), which are essential components in maintaining behavior change over the long term. There is a wealth of research showing that the use of extrinsic reinforcers can enhance intrinsic motivation (e.g., Cerasoli et al., 2014; LeGray et al., 2010).

Another barrier to implementation of ABA-based strategies is that they typically require behavior change on the part of the teacher. In other words, teachers usually have to do something differently in terms of how they respond to the student or how they arrange other parts of the classroom environment. This means that they cannot keep doing things exactly the way they are currently doing them and expect behavior to change. Although most educators understand this, those who are less open to adapting their interaction styles and classroom routines may struggle with ABA-based strategies. These teachers may need extra support for intervention implementation.

Understanding Behavior the ABA Way

We often find it difficult to understand why people behave in the ways that they do, but this does not mean that behavior is random. All behavior occurs for a reason. Although it is intuitively appealing to search for causes of behavior inside the person (e.g., a bad attitude, laziness, lack of respect for others), the causes of many problems reside in the environment. The key is understanding how our environments teach us (or fail to teach us) to behave in particular ways. Each of us has a learning history, which comprises all the lessons we have learned through our experiences with other people and events.

What we often refer to as personality traits or individual differences are actually behaviors that we have acquired through our learning histories. Over time, learning histories become so ingrained in us that we forget they were actually acquired through environmental experiences. Take a moment to think about a good (or bad!) part of your personality and how you might have learned to be that way. Are you kind because your parents told you it was good to be kind, modeled kindness, and praised you when you were kind to others? As you grew older, did it feel good to be kind? Or perhaps you had an experience of being bullied that made you more sensitive to the feelings of others. It is possible that being kind to others made you feel good because you knew you were preventing someone from feeling the way you felt. When we begin to examine the parts of us that make us who we are, we can begin to see the powerful influence our environments exert on us.

Can't-do and won't-do problems. One key distinction that we need to make when attempting to understand behavior is whether we are dealing with a *can't-do* or a *won't-do* problem (Mager & Pipe, 1997). Can't-do problems are those in which the person has not learned the skills necessary to do what needs to be done to be successful. Won't-do problems are problems in which the person could do the necessary behavior but chooses not to. Can't-do problems involve *skill deficits*, whereas won't-do problems are *motivation problems*. Unfortunately, the behaviors that occur because of can't-do and won't-do problems often look the same.

For instance, two students in your class might become disruptive when given a particular task, refuse to do the task, or even leave the classroom. However, the reasons why each student engages in these behaviors might be different. A student who is *unable* to do a task often behaves in problematic ways to avoid revealing to others that they are not competent. A student who *can* do a task but chooses not to might find that refusal not only prevents them from having to do the work but also results in a great deal more teacher attention than if they had sat quietly and completed the task. Given that these problems likely occur for different reasons, the approach to dealing with those behaviors naturally would also be different. Skill deficits require interventions focused on helping the student acquire the skill, whereas motivation problems require finding strategies that make doing the task more appealing than not doing it. We will discuss some of these strategies in more detail later in the chapter. The important takeaway message for now is that behavior change solutions need to be based on *why* behaviors occur rather than on what they look like.

Function. Although learning histories play a large role in making us who we are, educators rarely have access to a comprehensive account of a student's learning history. The good news is that regardless of learning history, many keys to understanding behavior can be found in the current environment. That means that the things we do on a day-to-day basis in our classrooms might be working to undo some of the faulty learning histories our students have encountered. However, sometimes the things we do can actually strengthen problem behavior and create an even longer history of problem behavior.

Understanding our everyday effect on behavior requires an understanding of the concept of function. *Function* refers to the purpose a behavior serves for the individual. Identifying the function of a behavior will help us understand what makes it continue to occur or what maintains it. In ABA, we say that behaviors are maintained by their consequences. A consequence is simply any event that follows behavior and influences the likelihood that the behavior will occur again. Those consequences that increase the likelihood of behavior are called reinforcers. If a behavior results in getting (+) something that you want, and that makes you more likely to do the behavior again, we say that behavior has been *positively reinforced* (R+). For example, a teacher might attend to a student when they shout answers but rarely calls on them when they raise their

The **function** of a behavior refers to the purpose a behavior serves for the individual. The four main functions of behavior are attention, escape, tangible, and sensory.

hand. The student will learn that shouting results in the attention they want, and they will continue to shout. The teacher's attention is a positive reinforcer. If a behavior results in removing (–) something that you did not want, and that makes you more likely to do the behavior again, we say that behavior has been *negatively reinforced* (R–). Consider the student who wants to escape from their math class so they continue to disrupt the teacher. If the teacher sends the student out of the class for their disruptive behavior, the teacher has inadvertently negatively reinforced the behavior and made the student more likely to do it again!

Although we can probably think of many reasons why we do the things we do, ABA research suggests there are four main categories of functions (Lewis et al., 2017). The first category is attention. You have probably had some students in your classroom who will do just about anything to get your attention. Some do not even seem to care if the attention is for good or bad behavior, and some even seem to enjoy negative attention more. Some students also might be highly motivated by the attention they receive from their peers. Attention is a positive reinforcer because it is added after behavior and increases the likelihood of behavior.

The second category of function is escape. You might have encountered students in your class who are experts at avoiding work. They are in constant need of materials that they need to locate, frequently get out of their seats, or take forever to begin a task. Essentially, their behaviors are aimed at avoiding or terminating an activity or situation they find unpleasant. Escape is a negative reinforcer because removal of the unpleasant event makes the behavior more likely to occur in the future.

The third category of function is tangible (which means something concrete). Tangible items are positive reinforcers because they are added after behavior and increase the future likelihood of behavior. Teachers often use things like stickers or time on the computer as tangible reinforcers for positive behavior. However, problem behaviors also can be strengthened by tangible reinforcers. Have you ever allowed a student in your class to do a preferred activity (like color or play a game) or to have something they wanted (like use of the iPad) to distract them from problem behavior? In these situations, students will quickly learn that doing the wrong thing pays off!

The fourth category of function is sensory stimulation. This is when there is something about doing the behavior that is reinforcing in and of itself (e.g., it feels good to do it, or doing it makes an unpleasant sensation go away). Behaviors maintained by sensory stimulation could include things such as students rocking in their chairs, drumming on the table, or spinning their pencil on the desk. More serious behaviors, like self-injury or self-harm, also could be maintained by sensory stimulation (either because the pain feels good or by doing the behavior some other sensation—like anxiety—goes away). Sometimes students do not notice that they are doing these behaviors; they aren't aimed at disrupting others, getting attention, or avoiding tasks. Sensory stimulation can be either a positive reinforcer or a negative reinforcer.

It is important to note that some behaviors might have more than one function. Imagine a student who protests and occasionally runs out of the class when asked to transition from a preferred task (time on the iPad) to a less preferred task (a group reading lesson). When they threaten to run out of the classroom, the teacher sometimes tries to entice them back by giving them five more minutes on the iPad. Although the teacher is trying to do the right thing by keeping the student in class, they are likely reinforcing the protesting and use of threats. But what is the function of that behavior? The iPad is clearly a tangible, but because the student is also avoiding the onset of the non-preferred task, there also might be an escape function.

It is also important to note that we sometimes misinterpret functions of behavior based on our casual observations. For instance, most problem behaviors recruit some kind of attention regardless of whether that is the consequence the individual is seeking. A student who gets angry and destroys property might get a great deal of attention from adults after the behavior, but the actual function of that behavior might be something else (like escaping from a difficult situation). Qualified behavior analysts are skilled at using systematic methods to identify functions of behavior and incorporating that information into student-centered behavior plans. The important takeaway message for educators is that *all* behaviors occur for a reason (i.e., they have a function) and that understanding function is essential to effective individualized intervention.

Triggers. In addition to understanding the functions that maintain behaviors, it is also important to consider the environmental events that set the occasion for or trigger problem behavior. These are referred to as the *antecedents* for behavior (antecedent means "to come before"). For example, you might know that when you seat two students next to one another, they are likely to talk and play instead of doing their work. Essentially, you know that the presence of a particular peer is an antecedent, or trigger, for problem behavior. Similarly, you might know that asking a student to write things on paper will result in a refusal to do work, but if you allow them to do the work on a tablet, they will happily comply. In this instance, written work is an antecedent for problem behavior, but a request to do work on a tablet is an antecedent for appropriate behavior. Understanding the antecedents that evoke problem behavior can help us understand the situations in which those behaviors are most likely to occur and how we might be able to modify situations so that appropriate behavior is more likely. There are some examples of how we might do this in the strategies section that follows.

The ABCs. When we consider the antecedents that evoke behavior and the consequences that maintain it, we are identifying contingencies of behavior. This is often referred to as an ABC (antecedent, behavior, consequence) *contingency*, or a three-term contingency, and is the simplest unit of analyzing behavior (see Figure 3.1 for an example). If educators are able to identify potential ABCs, it often allows them to see the causes of students' behavior more clearly. Because it puts the focus on events occurring outside the individual, it prevents us from making personal attributions or judgments about the student. In other words, it helps us understand behavior more objectively.

Figure 3.1

ABC Example

| Bob is given a difficult task. | Bob makes a rude comment to the teacher. | Bob is sent out of class. |
| A: Antecedent (unpleasant situation) | B: Behavior (behavior) | C: Consequence (escaped task) |

Basic ABA Strategies

Analyzing environmental factors that contribute to behavior and developing effective behavior change strategies can be complicated. However, there are some core ABA-based strategies that all educators can easily apply in their classrooms. All of these strategies are grounded in decades of research and have demonstrated effectiveness across a range of ages and educational settings. When you employ these strategies, you should first consider *why* the problem behavior is occurring or *why* the appropriate behavior is not occurring. In other words, think about the ABCs, and allow that to inform how you will implement the strategy. We offer some examples of how to do this in the sections that follow.

Differential reinforcement. Differential reinforcement means that we provide a different response to one behavior than we do to another. Another way of thinking about this strategy is that we are reinforcing something that is *different* from the problem behavior. You will recall that all behavior has a function (i.e., all behavior occurs for a reason). Let's imagine there is a student in your class who typically gets their work done, but they often disrupt the class by making silly noises and pretending to fall out of their chair. You notice that each time they do this, you tell them to stop and their peers laugh. You have also noticed that if other students have your attention, the noises and chair falling are more likely to occur. You could make a reasonably safe assumption that these behaviors are maintained by your attention and, probably to some degree, the attention of their peers. You might also have realized that you are reinforcing the problem behavior! Actually, that is good news because now you know you can fix the problem. Differential reinforcement would involve reinforcing something different from the problem behavior. Ideally, you would watch for occasions when the student was doing his work quietly and then provide praise, thus offering the student the teacher attention they craves but by doing a different, more classroom appropriate, behavior. As they get better at working quietly, you could increase the amount of time they must work or the amount of work they must complete before you provide praise. The full name of this procedure is "differential reinforcement of alternative behavior (DRA)" (LeGray et al., 2010).

When using DRA, it is important that you stop reinforcing the problem behavior and instead focus on reinforcing the alternative behavior. If the problem behavior continues to be reinforced, it will continue to occur, especially if it is easier to do than the appropriate behavior. Also, remember to make the reinforcer specific to the function of the problem behavior. For example, if you think the function of a challenging behavior might be escape, then you would reinforce instances of the alternative behavior with that reinforcer. As a case in point, you might ask the student if they wants to take a quick stretch break, go get a drink of water, or run a quick errand for you. Another helpful tip is to use instructions to tell students about what you are doing because it speeds the learning process. For example, you might say, "Oscar, if you work quietly for 10 minutes, I will come over and spend some time with you. However, if you make a lot of noise or do silly things, we won't get to spend time together." Using rules helps students understand what is expected of them, so they do not have to figure it out for themselves (Alter & Haydon, 2017).

When using DRA, remember that behavior change usually takes time. Think about your attempts to change your own behavior in the past. For example, you might have planned to exercise more or eat healthier. However, you would be unlikely to meet your goal if you said you would go to the gym 5 days per week for an hour and a half per day. In fact, you might give up and conclude that it is too difficult to build exercise into your daily routine. However, imagine if you set a goal of going to the gym 1 day per week for half an hour and then gradually added days to your exercise plan. You probably would be more successful. For most behavior change, if we expect too much too soon, then problem behaviors tend to come back quickly.

In ABA, we use a procedure called *shaping*. This means that we start out with small expectations and build those expectations slowly across time. If you are using DRA, and the student starts doing more of the problem behavior than the appropriate behavior, you might be moving too fast. Set the goal a bit lower, and move forward from there. Patience is a virtue, especially in the classroom.

Time-based reinforcement. As we have noted several times in this chapter, people do the things they do because their behaviors get reinforced. In other words, there is a reinforcer (attention, escape, tangible, sensory) that occurs when those behaviors occur. However, what would happen if the person received the reinforcer without having to do the behavior? For example, what if the teacher said that every 10 minutes, students could stand up and dance for 30 seconds. What if while students were independently working, the teacher spent their time going to each student to ask how they were doing or comment on how happy they were that the student was there? Research indicates that we would see a lot less problem behavior (Phillips et al., 2017)!

In time-based reinforcement, whatever reinforces the problem behavior is provided according to a schedule rather than providing it because a particular behavior has occurred (Austin & Soeda, 2008). For example, suppose you had a student who called out for your attention at least eight times during a 40-minute lesson. That means that, on average, the student calls out about every 5 minutes. If the teacher arranged to check in with the student every 4 minutes or so, they could probably prevent the call-outs. The check-ins provide the attention the student craves without the need to engage in problem behavior to get it. Small time-based breaks can prevent behavior that functions to access escape, as can brief access to tangible items. Chapter 1 identifies strategies for providing class access to different environmental items that may also address sensory-motor needs.

When using time-based reinforcement, it is important to ensure that the delivery of the reinforcer occurs frequently enough to prevent the problem behavior. If a student engages in a problem behavior frequently, then the schedule of reinforcer delivery needs to be even more frequent. For some teachers, this might be impractical within the constraints of a busy classroom. If so, they might find another strategy (such as DRA) a better fit for their classroom. Using a device to signal when it is time to deliver a reinforcer (e.g., a Motivaider®) can be helpful when implementing a time-based reinforcement because it allows the teacher to get on with other duties instead of looking at a watch.

Providing choices. Most teachers are familiar with the concept of providing choice. What they might not know is there is a wealth of research demonstrating that this strategy can be helpful for students who engage in escape-maintained behaviors, particularly if those behaviors tend to occur because of work demands (Shogren et al., 2004). When we give choices, we lessen the aversive features of the demand because the student has chosen the task. All of us will naturally choose things that appear more reinforcing to us, and the same is true for our students. It is also worth noting that the act of making a choice can be reinforcing in and of itself because it gives us a sense of autonomy and control. Chapter 6 shares more of the benefits of using choice in a universally designed classroom.

One of the biggest worries teachers raise about using choice making in their classroom is the time it might take to make two to three assignments that accomplish the same instructional goal. It seems like two to three times the work! However, that doesn't have to be the case. Consider allowing students to choose to do either the even- or odd-numbered questions on a mathematics worksheet, or allowing a choice between three different topics on an essay, or even allowing the student to demonstrate mastery of vocabulary by providing the definitions or using the work correctly in a sentence. Allowing students a choice of where they will complete an assignment (at the desk or on the floor) or how they complete it (on paper on or on the computer) is another simple way of incorporating choice into classroom activities. Again, providing choice is also an important part within the strategy of Universal Design for Learning addressed in Chapter 6.

If you choose this strategy specifically to address a problem behavior, remember that it works best with those students whose behaviors are maintained by escape (Romaniuk et al., 2002). If you think a challenging behavior is maintained by another function, then a different strategy likely would be more effective.

MAKING CONNECTIONS

Get additional strategies for meeting students' sensory needs in Chapter 1 on sensory-motor development and tips on providing choices in Chapter 6 on Universal Design for Learning.

Curricular revision. Recall that earlier in the chapter we made a distinction between can't-do and won't-do problems. These strategies assume that the primary problem is one of reinforcement or motivation (i.e., won't-do problems). Although the process of shaping is helpful for both types of problems, challenging behaviors that stem from an inability to do a particular skill will obviously involve increasing the student's repertoire so they are competent. Using curricular revision also can be helpful. This strategy involves setting work at a level that is better matched to the student's skill level, thus making the task of attempting work less aversive and more likely to result in success. Like providing choices, this strategy involves changing an antecedent so it is more likely to evoke appropriate behavior so that the behavior can then be reinforced. In this way, we are building a new reinforcement history for success at school.

ABA at the Classroom Level

Up to this point, we have discussed ABA-based strategies as they relate to dealing with the behavior issues of individual students. These approaches are particularly helpful when a teacher has one or two students in the classroom who seem to need some additional individualized behavior support. However, if a teacher finds that several (or most) of the students in the class display some sort of behavior that interferes with their success at school, then a group-based ABA strategy might be the first step to improve the learning environment for everyone.

Good Behavior Game. One of the strategies that has garnered the most empirical evidence over the past several decades is the Good Behavior Game (GBG; e.g., Bowman-Perrott et al., 2016; Flower et al., 2014). This classroom management strategy is easy for teachers to learn and, with just a bit of practice, easy to implement. The idea underpinning the GBG is that students must work as a team to follow classroom rules and win the game. Teachers first set three to four clear expectations about behavior (i.e., the rules for playing the game) and post the expectations in a visible place in the classroom. Next, the teacher divides the class into teams. Teachers can divide the class in half to form two teams or have multiple, smaller teams (e.g., four students per team). During the game, if anyone on the team fails to meet an expectation, the team earns a point. Teams with less than a certain number of points at the end of the game win and earn a small reward (e.g., 3-minute dance or brain break, 5 minutes for drawing, high-five from the teacher, small piece of fruit). Each game typically lasts for one lesson (20–40 minutes) so that multiple games can be played across the day.

A variation of the GBG is the Caught Being Good Game (Bohan et al., 2020). This version operates in the same way as the GBG, but teams earn points when all members of the team are meeting expectations. Teams must earn a certain number of points to win the game. This version is preferred by some teachers because it places the focus on meeting expectations rather than rule infractions. It can also be easily implemented with older students.

Although a comprehensive guide for playing the GBG is beyond the scope of this chapter, Joslyn and colleagues (2020) published step-by-step instructions for using the GBG as well as a troubleshooting guide. It is also important to note that although there are commercial GBG products available to schools (e.g., PAX; Johansson et al., 2020), these products are not imperative for implementing the GBG at your school. Using free, published guidance, teachers can effectively implement the GBG at little to no cost.

Positive Behavior Interventions and Supports. PBIS, also often just known as PBS for Positive Behavior Supports, is "a systems approach for creating a positive social culture and developing individualized behavior supports" (Walker & Hott, 2017). PBIS provides a tiered framework for delivering behavioral interventions so that schools can use their resources more effectively and efficiently. The first tier of support, often referred to as *universal intervention*, includes strategies that are implemented across all student and school settings to promote positive social and academic behavior. This level of support specifies the school's values regarding behavior (e.g., to be responsible, respectful, and safe) and the reinforcement strategies that will be used to promote those values (like the GBG or other reinforcement systems). The goal of Tier One supports is to take a proactive and preventative approach to behavior management.

However, some students will have behavior or academic needs that exceed the reach of Tier One strategies; those who are nonresponders to Tier One are offered Tier Two strategies, which are aimed at providing evidence-based supports for specific types of problems, such as engagement with lessons, social skills, disruptive classroom behavior, or school attendance. Student with the most complex needs, whose behavioral needs require more intensive support, receive Tier Three supports. These supports tend to require sophisticated assessment of the student's needs (e.g., functional behavior assessment) followed by highly individualized intention planning to ensure those needs are adequately met. Some schools have students in Tier Three evaluated for special education services. Research shows that if schools arrange effective Tier One and Two supports, only about 5% of the student population will require Tier Three (Walker & Hott, 2017).

A major aspect of PBIS, as you might have gleaned from its name, is that it emphasizes the need for proactive positive support, as opposed to simply reacting to behavioral or academic issues when they occur. Reactive approaches might increase the likelihood of punitive strategies, which rarely work over the long term and have a range of negative side effects to argue against their use (e.g., people tend to avoid situations where they are punished, thus creating an environment where students don't want to be). Many excellent texts on behavior management (such as that by Walker & Barry, 2022) now use the ABA concepts taught in this chapter and apply them to the PBIS tiers; they emphasize building relationships with students, creating class-wide structures and learning environments, and implementing individualized interventions for specific students that are positive, data-based, and focused on function.

COMMUNICATION AND COLLABORATION STRATEGIES

Defining Terms

Both communication and collaboration are integral aspects of any school, classroom, or teacher's day. They are both integral and ubiquitous, so ubiquitous in fact that the terms are often used without a true understanding of what they entail. Despite the obvious need for both communication and collaboration in schools, there is often little professional development or consistent training on their use (Glazier et al., 2017). In this chapter, we define both terms and provide concrete strategies for helping teachers to use both.

Communication involves "exchanging information in a form that is mutually understandable. [It] may include listening, speaking, signing, use of a communication board, writing, or any other format in which two or more people can interact to share information" (Murawski & Spencer, 2011, p. 46). General communication might focus on sharing needs, such as physical, social, identity, or practical needs (Adler et al., 2020). In education, our needs may be more specific, such as the need to share information, problem-solve, make requests, or identify or achieve educational goals. There are different ways to communicate and different individuals with whom to communicate. Teachers need to communicate with colleagues, students, parents, specialists, and administrators. Each of these interactions may require different forms, techniques, or strategies related to communication. Clearly then, communication is not straightforward nor often easy.

Communication involves exchanging information.

Collaboration is a style of interaction.

Collaboration is a general term as well and one used to describe many situations. Friend and Cook (2021) defined collaboration as a *style of interaction* wherein two or more people work cooperatively toward a shared goal. Murawski and Spencer (2011) clarified that "collaboration can be done with *any* activity where you work together toward a goal; you can collaborate to bake cookies, plan a school dance, or create an Individualized Education Program" (p. 19). Thus, although a meeting may result in multiple educators coming together to discuss a student or situation, if the participants are not sharing a goal or working cooperatively, that meeting will lack collaboration. Collaboration does not always happen; it requires a commitment to a common goal, a willingness to work with others, and the sharing of resources and accountability; good communication skills can help with this. In strong inclusive schools, teachers do not teach in isolation. They collaborate on both horizontal (across classes) and vertical (across grades) levels and work interdependently (Dieker, 2007). They embrace the concept that *together everyone achieves more* (or TEAM).

In the first part of this chapter, we focus on strategies to bolster communication skills. Because communication is such an integral part of strong collaboration, the majority of the chapter provides strategies for strong communication. In the second part, we pivot to techniques that will enhance school collaboration. Both skills are in this chapter because they are so closely integrated. Strong communication skills can support collaboration, whereas excellent collaboration typically comes when individuals are able to communicate effectively. On the converse, when either communication or collaboration are ineffective, both can suffer.

The Application of Communication Skills

In schools, educators are expected to communicate daily. "When it comes to communication in schools, less is not more, and more is not necessarily better. It needs to be systematic, intentional, and transparent" (Dunbar, 2016). Teachers have to communicate lessons, directions, expectations, rules and responsibilities, excitement and disappointment, outcomes and grades, and so much more. They have to communicate with students, parents, community members, other teachers, specialists, paraprofessionals, and administrators. They have to be able to effectively communicate with busy adult professionals and distracted active kindergarteners, with those for whom English is a second or even third or fourth language, with morose teenagers and elderly grandparents who have lost their hearing, as well as with individuals who have no formal education and colleagues who may specialize in various aspects of education.

Communication comes in three forms: verbal, nonverbal, and visual (e.g., writing, video, sign language; Graham-Clay, 2005). Educators have to communicate in writing, orally, on the phone, through email, in videos, through distance learning online, and in person in front of large and small groups. They have to write lessons that others will follow, create classroom rules to teach to students, share information to increase knowledge, and even communicate nonverbally through a "teacher look" or simply by crossing their arms and using silence. Communication can be one way (e.g., notes, signs, lectures) or two way (e.g., discussions, parent–teacher conferences, phone calls; Graham-Clay, 2005). With all of these applications for communication—and typically no actual instruction on effective communication skills in teacher training (Glazier et al., 2017)—it is no wonder that strategies for effective communication are needed.

Note that whereas communication strategies (CS) have been defined by some as "verbal and nonverbal communication strategies that may be called into action to compensate for breakdowns in communication due to performance variables or to insufficient competence" (Al-Gharaibeh & Al-Jamal, 2016, p. 33), that is not the focus of the strategies provided here. These are not strategies such as those used for communicating with second language learners but rather tips for helping improve the communication of teachers as it relates to successfully including and teaching students with diverse needs.

Communication Strategies

General communication strategies. "There is a growing body of evidence that suggests student learning improves significantly when teachers collaborate. Collaboration depends on clear, consistent, and open lines of communication" (Linane, 2015). Some general strategies have been posited for effective communication no matter the content, format, audience, or situation. Table 4.1 reminds readers of these more universal techniques. Although many may seem common knowledge, we emphasize them because they are too often forgotten, and their lack of implementation results in miscommunication, misunderstandings, and misconceptions. One of the most important tips, and the one we start the table with, is to be respectful of the other person. Genuine respect for someone else will typically result in the use of many of the other strong communication techniques.

Here are additional general tips for communication:

Table 4.1

General Strategies to Support Effective Communication

BE RESPECTFUL	Use a tone that is honest and tactful. When listening, make eye contact, and focus on the speaker. Speak in turn without interrupting the speaker. Treat people equally. Recognize that you may have differing ideas but it is important to learn by listening and not always talking.
BE FOCUSED	Focus on the issue, not the person. Avoid making difficult topics personal. Try not to bring in emotions that stop you from listening and truly hearing what the other person is trying to communicate.
BE GENUINE	Be yourself rather than faking a reaction you think they are expecting. Be interested in what they are saying rather than being manipulative or calculating how to get it back to your topic.
BE CARING	Empathize with your speaker rather than remaining cold or detached. Don't overcriticize. Consider their feelings.
BE FLEXIBLE	Recognize that conversations don't always flow smoothly. Allow them to go in different directions or for speakers to communicate in a different way than you might choose.
BE POSITIVE	Use affirming responses. Avoid negativity. Be emotionally empathetic. Use facial expressions and nonverbals that indicate an interest in your speaker. Smile.
BE WELCOMING	Create a receptive atmosphere. Have a comfortable seat for you and your partner(s) if possible. Avoid places with loud noises or multiple distractions. Demonstrate that you have the time to listen.
BE ACCESSIBLE	Use simple words. Don't try to impress with a vocabulary or jargon that confuses. Use visuals, as appropriate, to make your point. Repeat your message in different ways to help the listener understand your main points. Slow the speed of your message, and ensure your voice pitch isn't too low or high for the listener to understand.
BE POLITE	Practice politeness, courtesy, and kindness. Make sure you are not speaking over the other(s) and that you aren't speaking so much that no one else can get a word in edgewise.

Table 4.1

General Strategies to Support Effective Communication (Continued)

BE ATTENTIVE	Listen graciously. Use active listening techniques. Keep eye contact as appropriate to demonstrate your attentiveness. Avoid multitasking. If you are going to take notes, make sure your partner knows that is what you are doing and is comfortable with it.
BE DIRECT	Talk to people, not *about* them. Avoid gossip. Even when speaking directly, be diplomatic; choose words that are appropriate to the situation and noninflammatory.
BE OPEN	Value others' opinions. Never assume anything. Ask questions to get more information. Open-ended questions are less misleading and get more of a response.
BE CONSISTENT	Consider your body language and tone of voice. If your arms are crossed, it may communicate a lack of openness. A sharp tone may indicate a lack of patience. Try to be consistent with your verbals and nonverbals.
BE AWARE	Check for understanding. Pay attention to the other's tone of voice, body language, and facial expressions. Consider how your communication might be misunderstood or how you might improve it in the moment.
BE QUIET	Silence may feel uncomfortable, but it allows people to think, reflect, and process. Stop talking and see if someone else has something to say or a question to ask.

- ***Always know the purpose of your communication.*** Is it to provide information, communicate disagreement, ask a question, or something else? Try to be thoughtful about why you are communicating.

- ***Avoid communicating emotional information via text, email, or notes.*** Face-to-face is almost always better to ensure the emotion is adequately transmitted, even though it may be more difficult.

- ***Avoid assumptions.*** Whether you are speaking with a parent, student, or colleague, try to obtain sufficient information with questions and through listening before you react to possibly incorrect assumptions.

- ***Try to listen more than you talk.*** It helps obtain information, and it communicates respect and interest in the other person. Do not be afraid of silence.

- **Be wary of technology.** Although texting, emailing, voice messages, and even Zoom or other online platforms can help provide options for communication, it is important to recognize that some communication issues might be caused by, or at least exacerbated by, technology. Be sure to regularly check for understanding.

- **Simplify your message.** There is no need to overcomplicate things with complex vocabulary or more verbiage.

School-wide communication strategies. While the general communication strategies presented are applicable to almost all interactions, the following are relatively quick actions that can help improve communication school-wide. Consider these strategies for increasing the interactions among members of the school community to reduce miscommunication and increase future collaboration and inclusive practices.

- **Monday Memo** (Dunbar, 2016)—Teachers can be easily inundated by daily announcements, emails, memos, and handouts. Messages can be lost. Instead, consider consolidating all of this information into one package that goes to all school staff. This Monday Memo can include information on operations, teaching strategies, calendar events, weekly goals, professional development articles, and even a cartoon or joke to add a bit of humor.

- **The Huddle** (Dunbar, 2016)—Teachers often work in their classes all day with doors shut. This results in a feeling of being cut off from other teachers and a lack of communication. Instead, school leaders can help free up 15–20 minutes once a week when teachers can all get together, preferably with snacks, to share team plans and look for opportunities to collaborate across grade levels. Ending with a unified clap (just like in American football huddles) helps raise the energy and positivity and make the session feel fun.

- **Collaborative Culture Surveys** (Dunbar, 2016; Murawski & Spencer, 2011)—What's working, and what is not? Sending out short surveys to ask for feedback on the collaborative culture of the school is a strong method of encouraging communication. All faculty and staff can share their opinions and offer recommendations for improvement. The goal can be to establish a culture that is inclusive of all adults and students through open, positive communication and collaboration.

Coffee with the Principal/Director (Dunbar, 2016)—It is important for school goals to be shared with the community and with parents. Although emails and letters home may help with this, the written word may not be accessible to all; in addition, the one-way communication doesn't encourage dialogue and questions. Instead, having an opportunity to have coffee with the principal once a month allows community members a chance to have an informal discussion with school leaders to communicate their questions and concerns in a positive, welcoming setting.

Educator-to-educator communication strategies. School-wide communication strategies, such as those mentioned here, are supportive of messaging larger groups and establishing a collaborative and communicative culture in a school. In addition to those techniques, consider these strategies for helping teachers communicate with one another as well as for teacher–leader and leader–teacher communication.

- *Communication apps* (Mccutchen, 2019)—Slack chats, Google Hangouts, Todays Meet, HipChat, WhatsApp, and Discord are all methods of quick and easy communication about a topic of interest. Email lacks the spontaneity and engagement that these apps have. Participants can invite others and have a private conversation or open it to the public. In addition, these types of communication are typically started and used by those who have interest in the topic as opposed to forcing all teachers at a school to talk about one topic.

- *Online Facebook groups*—Connecting with other educators internationally can also open communication avenues and result in increased strategies for working with diverse learners. Many Facebook groups have been created based on a need to dialogue about particular topics. For example, there is a group with more than 2,000 followers called Co-Teaching: A Collaborative Community of Co-Teachers, a group focused on twice-exceptional learners (those who have disabilities and are gifted) with more than 3,000 followers called Twice Exceptional/2E Network International, and another group that started due to the pandemic called Teaching in the Time of Corona: Resources with well greater than 11,000 members.

- **Tea with teachers** (Dunbar, 2016)—Much as coffee with the principal enables the community to dialogue with school leaders, tea with teachers can encourage open communication as well. This time might be for all teachers to get together, or it may be used for teachers to have time to talk to their administrators about their ideas and challenges, or it may even be used for teachers to be available to chat with parents. All of these are possible, and schools can use them as needed.

PROFESSIONAL DEVELOPMENT ON COMMUNICATION AND COLLABORATION

Could teachers use some practice communicating with parents, students, colleagues, or administrators? Do administrators need practice running difficult IEP meetings? Try simulation! SIMPACT offers immersive experiences where participants can interact with avatar students or adults and practice their skills in advance!

https://www.csun.edu/simpact

Teacher-to-parent communication strategies. Communicating with parents has been noted in the literature time and again as not only a critical component for student learning and engagement (Graham-Clay, 2005) but also a legal one when it comes to students with identified disabilities (Rodriguez & Murawski, 2022). McConnell and Murawski (2017) noted that families today look different than 30 years ago and that there are myriad issues that may arise when trying to communicate between home and school. They recognize that "major issues include different family dynamics and makeup, cultural differences, lack of adequate professional development for teachers, and the expected role of parent as shared educator" (p. 338). The role of shared educator is even more pronounced because some students receive their education through distance learning! Even when trying to connect with 150 students or classes that are online or hybrid, connecting with students on a personal level is one of the most powerful actions a teacher can take to help a student be successful in school (Hoover-Dempsey et al., 2005), and a major way to do that is to communicate with families.

- **Initiate first contact** (Mccutchen, 2019)—Do not wait for family members to reach out to talk about an issue. Depending on culture, some may not feel it is their right to question authority (Fallah & Murawski, 2018). In addition, the first communication between parent and teacher should not be about a question, concern, or something negative. Instead, call, text, email, or Zoom with one new parent each night in the first few weeks of school until you have connected with all families. Say something positive about the student, and do not bring up any potential negatives in the first interaction; feel free to share this role if you are co-teaching (Murawski, 2009). For some families, this may be one of the first positive communications they have had from school related to their child. This will set an excellent precedent for future contact.

- **Social media and class websites** (Mccutchen, 2019)—Technology is now an integral part of a teachers' skill sets. Class websites and social media are ways that parents can be updated on the work happening in the classroom and what major projects are impending. Settings can be on private, so only those invited can see what is posted, but these are an excellent way to keep families informed without having to do a lot of individual emails.

- **Class newsletters** (Mccutchen, 2019)—Keeping parents updated with an online (or hard copy) class newsletter is another strong strategy. Not only can students share information of interest to them, but they also can work on skills related to writing, organizing, and meeting deadlines. Invite parents to submit information to the newsletter as well; topics can include updated information on volunteer opportunities, columns from guest speakers, or parenting strategies.

- **Student work folders** (Mccutchen, 2019; Murawski, 2009)—Help students build their organizational skills by keeping a structured folder. In addition to supporting them academically, these folders can be structured in such a way that parents can see what is due, what has been graded, and what is upcoming. Some students can also have a place in the folder for communication between teacher and parent that can be checked daily to help avoid any assignments falling through the cracks or to share information on behavior, social skills, or IEP goals.

Teacher-to-student communication strategies. Finally, teachers also need to consider how they are communicating with their students. Communication with students needs to be strategic, thoughtful, and positive. Miscommunication between student and teacher can lead to negative feelings (on both sides), which can have consequential outcomes. Therefore, teachers are encouraged to embrace the concepts of Positive Behavioral Interventions and Supports, which emphasize identifying positive behaviors, words, and actions and encouraging those over providing punitive comments or repercussions (Hott et al., 2017).

- **Communicate clear expectations** (Hott et al., 2017)—Positively word the expectations for the class, and publicly post them in a place all students can see them. For example, class expectations may be to "Be Respectful, Be Responsible, and Be Ready." Then, be sure to teach students what these expectations mean by reviewing what they look like (and do not look like). Check for understanding, develop a system to reinforce students' behaviors, and regularly review the expectations and data with students.

- **Open channels for communication** (Mccutchen, 2019)—Use apps like Remind and ClassCraft to continue to send regular messages to students about upcoming assignments. Keep in mind that many students struggle with attention, memory, processing, and organization and will need regular reminders as a method of scaffolding. Using apps to send quick reminders is a universally designed option of supporting those learners, in addition to the entire class, without needing additional individualized accommodations.

- ***Celebrate those who are "On a Roll"*** (Murawski, 2010)—Many schools recognize students who succeed academically by posting and highlighting those who made the honor roll (students who have all As on their grades). However, that tradition tends to continue to emphasize the same students who are academically exceptional. Instead, teachers can communicate their appreciation of students who are improving in a variety of ways by identifying those who are "On A Roll." This can be students who have lower academic grades but are improving or students who have worked on their behavior or social skills. Having myriad ways to communicate positively with students can make a big difference in their overall success.

Collaboration

MAKING CONNECTIONS

Get additional strategies for collaboration among teachers in Chapter 5 on co-teaching and among students in Chapter 7 on collaborative learning.

True collaboration requires strong communication, which is why we have provided so many strategies, as well as a commitment to shared goals and a willingness to work together to meet those goals. Although collaborative efforts can certainly be between two individuals, such as through co-teaching, schools often require multiple individuals with different frames of reference to get together to work in collaborative teams. While schools are rampant with teams and groupwork, how common is real collaboration in schools? Unfortunately, it's not as common as one might think—or hope. According to research supported by the Gates Foundation in 2014, of almost 3,000 American teachers, only 7% of those surveyed thought their schools had strong collaboration models (Bill & Melinda Gates Foundation, 2014). "A successful team effort is not a mysterious or magical event that just 'happens' because fate brought the right group together. Real teamwork happens as a result of a deliberate and well thought-out plan, executed by a skilled team leader who has a clear vision, specific goals, and a definite strategy to get people to work well together" (Gerlach, 2015, p. 27). That skilled team leader might be an administrator who pulls together teachers to problem-solve around curricular issues, or it may be a classroom teacher who sets up cooperative learning groups of K–12 students. In either case, collaboration is not magic; it takes vision, goals, and skills.

School leaders are expected to establish the collaborative culture of their schools. They need to promote an inclusive atmosphere and encourage teachers to communicate, collaborate, and differentiate for the needs of their students. Gerlach (2015, p. 91) reviews the actions needed for strong leadership. He stated:

"An effective team leader:
- Understands and is committed to team goals.
- Is friendly, concerned, and interested in others.
- Acknowledges and confronts conflict openly.
- Listens to others with understanding.
- Includes others in the decision-making process.
- Contributes ideas and solutions.
- Values the ideas and contributions of others.
- Recognizes and rewards team efforts.
- Encourages and appreciates comments about team performance."

Collaborating with others requires an acknowledgment, acceptance, and even celebration of the fact that other individuals have different frames of reference. Frame of reference refers to the different points of view that others have, which are shaped by their past experiences, education, opinions, belief systems, and perspectives (Murawski & Spencer, 2011). These different frames of reference color and influence the exchange of ideas that can help lead to improved collaboration. Indeed, as Murawski and Spencer noted: "In many cases, understanding others' frames of reference can make or break your collaborative and communicative endeavors!" (p. 31).

Collaborative strategies. Many of the strategies provided in the sections on communication will serve to improve collaboration in a school. In addition, Table 4.2 offers strategies to help promote the institutionalization of school collaboration, keeping in mind that a collaborative culture results not only in increased inclusive practices but also improved academic and behavioral success and much happier students, parents, and teachers! Consider these strategies gleaned from *Collaborate, Communicate, and Differentiate! How to Increase Student Learning in Today's Diverse Schools* (Murawski & Spencer, 2011) to enhance the collaboration at your own site:

- ***Who's here and why?*** Start all meetings with introductions and find out what everyone hopes to get out of the meeting. This will help establish frames of reference and value.

- *Be prepared.* Have paper, pens, sticky notes, copies of materials or reports, and so on available to those who may come unprepared. This communicates an expectation that all will follow along and follow up on any tasks determined during the meeting.

- *Stop the jargon.* In meetings with families or other colleagues, be aware that educational acronyms or jargon specific to one field may isolate others in the room. Catch it and explain.

- *Mix it up.* Although some teams seem to always have the same individuals participate, consider inviting those who have not participated in the past or who may have a different perspective. This will help ensure more voices and views are represented in decision-making.

- *Crack a joke.* Humor and a positive outlook will help lighten difficult situations. Have fun!

Table 4.2

Strategies for Institutionalizing Collaboration in Schools

STRATEGY	DESCRIPTION OF STRATEGY
Create a culture of expectancy.	Create an atmosphere in which there is a bit of peer pressure to work with colleagues; expect collaboration by immersing the school in the concepts; keep the concept out in front, and create multiple opportunities to collaborate around different topics and activities.
Increase sharing of information.	Open meetings with faculty sharing successes and concerns; rotate through different departments, grade levels, or individuals; allow for personal sharing of successes and concerns as well as school-related ones; have faculty create a central clearinghouse on students with information gleaned by teachers regarding learning preferences, grading preferences, parent feedback, multiple intelligences, etc. Avoid adding confidential information.

Table 4.2

Strategies for Institutionalizing Collaboration in Schools (Continued)

STRATEGY	DESCRIPTION OF STRATEGY
Encourage sharing of expertise.	Help school members recognize and appreciate the shared expertise that exists; have an Expert in the Lounge Day each week with experts on anything from grading, foldables, skateboarding jargon, organizational tips, knitting, and working with parents; ask for newsletter articles; create an Ask the Expert website and include parents, staff, students, and community members as experts; ask teachers to conduct staff development programs so that it is not always experts from afar who are presenting.
Enable sharing of ideas.	Have a folder at every photocopier in the school, and ask teachers to make an extra copy of any good ideas or work they are doing to share with others; at the end of the year, compile a Best Ideas folder with open access; scan documents and create an internet folder with faculty access to good instructional ideas; encourage teams to share good lesson plans and avoid recreating the wheel; hold classroom walkabouts during which teachers get to visit each other's rooms and share ideas.
Allow sharing of concerns.	Create opportunities for roundtable discussions of ongoing concerns or issues; anyone who wants to can post an issue to discuss, and a small group would get together to discuss and then share results for 1 hour or less; invite community members.
Promote sharing of knowledge.	Facilitate book studies by ensuring multiple copies of books on differentiation, collaboration, and strategies are available; get funding for sending teachers and related staff to conferences; send individuals from different areas when possible; start a Critical Friends group or action research group; make a connection with a local university's College of Education, and invite ongoing communication and collaboration with faculty there.

(Continued)

Table 4.2

Strategies for Institutionalizing Collaboration in Schools (Continued)

STRATEGY	*DESCRIPTION OF STRATEGY*
Model sharing of consideration, humor, compassion, and other positive personality traits.	Regularly recognize the positive attributes of others, and model them yourself; set up opportunities for rapport building that don't have other ulterior motives—for example, a family picnic that is not also a fundraiser; allow risk taking, sharing of nontraditional ideas, and constructive criticism; laugh often and help others do so as well.

Source: Reprinted from Murawski and Spencer, 2011.

CO-TEACHING

Defining Co-Teaching

As inclusive education becomes less of a social justice buzzword and more of a reality in schools across the world, educators seek ways to meet the needs of diverse learners. One option for providing services to children in an inclusive classroom is called co-teaching. Co-teaching involves two or more professionals who "co-plan, co-instruct, and co-assess" to meet the needs of all learners (Murawski, 2010). Co-teaching takes far more than simply putting two teachers, or a teacher and paraprofessional, in the same room however.

Co-teaching involves two professionals sharing the same physical space, at least for a part of the day. During this time, both educators are expected to feel a sense of parity (i.e., equality) and to share roles and responsibilities for the entire class. They are not supposed to take ownership of only specific students (e.g., "my kids" and "your kids"), nor are they to identify their roles as purely "my job" and "your job." In a strong co-taught class, an observer wouldn't be able to tell the difference between educators as they move seamlessly, working together to meet all students' needs. Each educator would bring their own areas of expertise to the classroom and be valued for those different areas. These professionals would collaborate and share their own ideas, while valuing that of the other adult, as they work to co-plan lessons. They would then share the classroom, using a variety of instructional approaches as they co-instruct all students. Finally, they would analyze the results and outcomes as they co-assess how the students are doing and even how they feel they, as co-teachers, are doing.

Co-Teaching is when two or more educators "co-plan, co-instruct, and co-assess" a diverse group of students in the same physical classroom (Murawski, 2010).

Historical Perspective on Co-Teaching

Co-teaching is not a new phenomenon. It first became popular in the United States when Lynne Cook and Marilyn Friend wrote about the concept in the late 1980s (Friend & Cook, 1992). At that time, co-teaching was described as a way to bring a typical classroom teacher (called a "general education teacher") and a qualified special education teacher into the same room to collaborate. Cook and Friend described multiple ways that these two professional educators could interact to assist learners with and without disabilities in a classroom.

Since that time, quite a bit of research has been done on co-teaching. Researchers across the world have identified best practices regarding what works in co-taught classes as well as what components are needed for a successful co-taught class (e.g., Cook et al., 2017; King-Sears et al., 2014; Murawski, 2006). Because co-teaching requires the interaction of two or more adults, much of the literature also cautions that the personalities of both educators can have a significant impact on the outcomes of the relationship with and without the other factors in place (Karten & Murawski, 2020; King-Sears et al., 2014; Murawski, 2006).

Benefits and Barriers to Co-Teaching

Benefits. The most obvious benefit of co-teaching is the inclusion of all students into the same general education classroom. Teachers who previously felt ill-prepared to teach students with special needs, second-language learners, slower learners, or even gifted learners, now have an educational partner in the same room who can help. Indeed, that second individual is often an expert in those things! While the general education teacher takes lead on knowing the content, curriculum, and typical development of grade-level learners, the other teacher or specialist takes lead on identifying strategies for improved pedagogy, adapting curriculum or experiences, and ensuring all students are getting their individual needs met.

There are many additional benefits to educators, above and beyond having an additional adult with whom to share ideas and frustrations, to plan curriculum and lessons, and to identify the needs of varying students. Some of these benefits include having multiple frames of reference; learning skills, content, and strategies from one another; and being able to connect with different students. In addition, educators collaborate more, have another adult in the room to get their jokes, and even get to take brief brain and bathroom breaks when needed (Karten & Murawski, 2020).

Benefits to students are even more profound. Because all learners are in the same general education class, rather than being pulled out to a segregated setting, students who previously may have received watered-down instruction are now receiving access to the same educational content as their grade-level peers. This access, in conjunction with a belief that we should maintain high expectations for all students, leads to increased academic outcomes for students with and without special needs (Lochner et al., 2019).

Academic benefits are only the start. Students with behavioral challenges actually do better in inclusive classes with co-teachers there to help manage their behaviors. They are with nondisabled, grade-level peers who can model appropriate behaviors and social skills. Students' self-concept is increased because they are no longer pulled out to a separate setting to receive different, and often diluted, instruction.

Barriers. Despite a plethora of benefits, there are certainly numerous barriers to effective co-teaching as well. Unfortunately, one of the most often cited barriers relates to the lack of adult collaboration. Many educators are resistant to the idea of sharing their classroom and giving up the complete control they are used to having. Although teachers emphasize the need to collaborate, communicate, and "play nicely" to their students, they do not always jump at the chance to do the same themselves!

MAKING CONNECTIONS

Chapter 4 is all about how to effectively communicate and collaborate, not only with students but with colleagues and administrators. Chapter 10 will give you tips on making time to plan with your co-teacher.

Scheduling is another oft-cited barrier to co-teaching. Educators need to have the time to plan together, not only show up in the room at the same time. In addition, specialists (such as special education teachers, speech teachers, occupational or physical therapists, sensory-motor integration specialists, counselors) require schedules that allow them to truly co-plan, co-instruct, and co-assess with a partner. Having too many partners results in a specialist who is spread too thin to be effective or someone who doesn't have the time to truly co-plan. The result is someone walking in to the room unprepared and saying, "What are we doing today?" This is not true co-teaching.

When educators are unable to co-plan, due to scheduling or a lack of willingness, the result is a class with two adults but no real collaboration. When one teacher continually takes the lead, the other can get relegated to the role of "glorified aide" (Zigmond et al., 2013). This is frustrating for the educator but also doesn't result in any real learning support for the students. Co-planning is absolutely critical for the successful co-taught class.

Best Practices for Effective Co-Teaching

Although the literature on co-teaching has been termed "confusing, contradictory, and yet cautiously optimistic" (Murawski & Goodwin, 2014), specific best practices have been identified consistently as playing a key role in its effective application.

Educators need to consider one another as equals, without losing their unique roles, administrators need to provide support to the co-teaching teams, and planning time needs to be provided. In addition, professional development should be provided so that educators are prepared for their roles, they should use a variety of instructional approaches when working together, and Universal Design for Learning (UDL) should be an integral part of their planning.

Parity in roles. Murawski's (2009, 2010) analogy of co-teaching is that of a marriage. She has stated that co-teachers are "two adults who are raising children together" and that their actions will affect the children academically, behaviorally, socially, and even—down the road—financially. Consider the role of parents: both are considered equals in the relationship, although they often have different roles that help the team function. One parent may always do the dishes, whereas the other takes out the trash. In co-teaching, educators should also discuss how to feel that they are equal and have parity but that they also are able to use their own distinct skills and areas of expertise.

For example, if a specialist and a classroom teacher are co-teaching, it is unreasonable to expect that the specialist would or should take lead on all the instructional planning (Gulløv, 2017). Instead, as the classroom teacher brings in information on the content that needs to be taught in upcoming weeks, the specialist should bring in information on possible ways to enhance the students' social, collaboration, and communication skills. If a special education teacher and a classroom teacher are co-teaching, and the special education teacher has to do quite a bit of testing on students with disabilities in the class, that would be considered part of the assessment tasks; thus, the classroom teacher may take on more of the grading that week to balance the duties.

Administrative support. School leaders play important roles in the success of co-teaching (Murawski & Dieker, 2013). They are the ones who determine which teachers get selected to co-teach, whether co-teaching will occur solely between teachers or if other specialists will be involved as well, how the schedule will be arranged, and how to ensure common planning time between co-teachers. Administrators help set a collaborative and inclusive culture of the school, which makes co-teaching so much easier. School leaders also help share the vision of co-teaching with the school community to include parents. They help communicate that co-teaching is designed to help all children in the inclusive classroom, not only those with disabilities.

One of the best practices identified frequently in the early literature on co-teaching was the importance of volunteerism—or rather, having teams select their own partners (Friend et al.,

2010; Murawski, 2010). Although this is still considered best practice, many researchers now recognize that administrators often select teams and simply tell them they will be co-teaching in what is jokingly referred to as an "arranged marriage" (Karten & Murawski, 2020). Because the personalities and relationships of teachers do have such a profound impact on the outcome of the co-taught class, administrators are cautioned to provide educators with as much say in who their partner will be as possible. When that is not possible, leaders should try to provide those educators some time to get to know one another before they start to co-teach.

School Leader Spotlight

Are you a school administrator or leader who wants to start co-teaching? Consider having a "speed dating" activity during a faculty meeting. Get all faculty to line up in two rows facing one another, and call out something to talk about for 4 minutes (e.g., "Your funniest moment." "Your worst date." "Your ideal day."). After each person talks for two minutes, the leader rings a bell, and everyone moves over one seat to get a new partner. This activity leads to a more collaborative school environment, educators who get to know one another better, the start of some great new relationships, and a bucketful of laughs! Don't forget to include your paraprofessionals, therapists, coaches, and other educators.

Planning time. We cannot emphasize enough the importance of shared planning time. If co-teachers do not co-plan, they do not meet the definition of true co-teaching. Remember, they need to "co-plan, co-instruct, and co-assess" (Murawski, 2010)! It is during co-planning that both educators proactively infuse their areas of expertise (Keefe & Moore, 2004). As a math teacher states that students need to learn a particular math skill, the special education teacher might encourage them to create a step-by-step checklist, use manipulatives, write the formula on the board with different color markers, or create a graphic organizer. As a Social Studies teacher describes what students need to learn about the causes of World War II, the specialist might suggest this is a perfect time to practice positive debating skills, work in small groups, and brainstorm ways world leaders might have used negotiation techniques over going to war.

Although time that is built into an educator's schedule is always preferable, not all school leaders are able to create common planning times for co-teachers. Some teams meet before or after school, at lunch, or in the evenings via Teams or Zoom. Many others use Google Docs and other shared platforms to allow them both to contribute to a lesson plan. Some educators like to co-plan entire units with macro-planning, choosing to work out the details later for their micro-planning (Murawski, 2012).

In an article on using co-planning time more efficiently, Murawski (2012) recommended that teachers divide and conquer and avoid getting bogged down in details as they collaborate. She also recommended that teams create an agenda to help focus their planning times, meet in an area free of distractions, and even bring snacks. Murawski also shares a strategy for co-planning called the What/How/Who approach, wherein co-teachers first identify what needs to be taught soon (the content), how it might be delivered together (the co-instructional approaches and universal design), and who may still need additional support or enrichment (the differentiation).

PROFESSIONAL DEVELOPMENT ON CO-TEACHING

PD comes in a variety of ways. Check out this Padlet with articles, templates, checklists, lesson plans, and other resources related to co-teaching:

https://bit.ly/3tDNkqt

Professional development. Many educators appear to be dropped into a co-taught class without professional development (PD) or training. The result is often a specialist who doesn't want to interfere or interrupt the general education teacher and so waits patiently before they can work with individual students and a general education teacher who is frustrated by the lack of initiative being taken by the specialist! This situation arises from simple miscommunication and misunderstanding due to a lack of knowledge.

Educational consulting companies that focus on promoting inclusive practices, like 2Teach® Global (www.2TeachGlobal.com), provide training for new teams by identifying what co-teaching should—and should not—look like as well as by offering concrete practical strategies for the co-taught class. Presenters model the co-teaching environment during their professional development sessions so that educators experience for themselves what Parallel, Station, and Alternative Teaching approaches feel like. Time is provided for potential co-teachers to discuss possible areas of contention, like how they will address in-class behavioral issues or how they may grade students with different abilities. Taking time to proactively discuss how educators may deal with differences in philosophy, opinion, or instruction is truly helpful and results in teams who are more eager to collaborate and feel more optimistic about their upcoming relationship.

Regrouping approaches. Cook and Friend (1995) identified five co-instructional approaches, sometimes called models. These five approaches are ways in which co-teachers can interact with the students and one another in a meaningful, systematic, proactive manner. When teachers use a variety of approaches during their instruction, they not only avoid the possibility that one educator is seen as merely an assistant but they also more actively engage their students. Students do not all learn in the same way, and using a variety of instructional approaches validates that knowledge.

Table 5.1, which follows, provides a visual of each of the five co-instructional approaches as well as a brief description of each (Murawski & Spencer, 2011). Consider how two of these approaches (One Teach, One Support and Team Teaching) allow for students to remain in the typical large group setting as the teachers interact in different ways, while the other three remaining approaches (Station, Parallel, and Alternative teaching) have students regrouped into configurations. This too allows educators to interact with the students in smaller student–teacher ratios and for different purposes. If co-teachers keep students in the same large-group setting all of the time and continue to lecture at them in the way they have for years, even if they sometimes vary which teacher is talking at the students, how can we possibly expect that change will occur?

Table 5.1

Commonly Used Co-Teaching Approaches to Instruction

CO-TEACHING APPROACH	CLASS SETUP	QUICK DEFINITION
One teach, one support (OT/OS)	A, B — Whole class	One teacher is in front of the class leading instruction. The other is providing substantive support (e.g., collection or dissemination of papers, setting up labs, classroom management). Both are actively engaged.
Team teaching	A, B — Whole class	Both teachers are in front of the class, working together to provide instruction. This may take the form of debates, modeling information or note-taking, compare/contrast, or role-playing.
Parallel teaching	A, B — Regrouping	Both teachers take half of the class in order to reduce student—teacher ratio. Instruction can occur in the same or a different setting. Groups may be doing the same content in the same way, same content in a different way, or different content (Murawski, 2009).

(Continued)

Table 5.1

Commonly Used Co-Teaching Approaches to Instruction (Continued)

CO-TEACHING APPROACH	CLASS SETUP	QUICK DEFINITION
Station teaching	A, B — Regrouping	Students are divided into three or more small, heterogeneous groups to go to stations or centers. Students rotate through multiple centers, though teachers may rotate also. Teachers can facilitate individual stations or circulate among all stations.
Alternative teaching	A, B — Regrouping	One teacher works with a large group of students, while the other works with a smaller group providing re-teaching, pre-teaching, or enrichment as needed. The large group is not receiving new instruction during this time so that the small group can rejoin when finished.

Source: Reprinted from Murawski and Spencer, 2011.

Universal Design for Learning (UDL) is when educators proactively plan to provide multiple means of representation, engagement, action and expression. It values student voice and student choice.

UDL. UDL became popular through the work of the Center for Applied Special Technology (CAST, www.cast.org; Murawski & Scott, 2019). CAST started the concept of UDL by applying knowledge obtained by universally designing buildings proactively to be more accessible rather than retrofitting them with ramps and elevators after the fact (which was time, labor, and cost intensive). David Rose and other CAST founders recognized that education also used the concept of retrofitting by differentiating lessons to meet the needs of diverse learners after the lesson for the typical learners was created (Murawski & Scott, 2019). UDL became the concept that, by proactively considering the needs of all learners and planning lessons to teach to the margins, teachers wouldn't have to recreate, differentiate, or retrofit as much after the fact (Dieker et al., 2013).

UDL fits within the philosophy of inclusive education in that teachers now think less about individual students with special needs and instead consider all learners as diverse. Students are encouraged to have a voice in the lessons and are provided with choice in anything from the content, to the environment, to the instructional design. Planning lessons and units that offer multiple options and methods for representing content to students, to engaging and motivating them within that content, and to allowing them to demonstrate their learning through various actions and expressions is key to UDL. When co-teachers plan their lessons collaboratively through a UDL lens, far less after-the-fact differentiation needs to occur. Lessons are universally designed, accessible, and inclusive. This enables the specialist (e.g., special education teacher, therapist, coach) to focus more on integrating their own areas of specially designed instruction.

MAKING CONNECTIONS

Chapter 6 is devoted to Universal Design for Learning, where you can learn more about what UDL entails and how it is relevant to almost every aspect of teaching.

Strategies for Effective Co-Teaching (More Tools!)

Data collection with One Teach One Support. All educators need data. Without it, they can't engage in data-based decision-making! Data doesn't need to be complicated, however. When one educator is leading a whole-class lesson, the other educator can be circulating the room. During this time, in addition to providing proximity control and answering individual questions, the circulating teacher can also be collecting data.

Take a simple clipboard and print out a picture of the class seating chart. Put small sticky notes on each area indicating where a student sits (Murawski, 2009). As the second educator walks around the room, they can take data on areas of interest that both co-teachers identified at an earlier time. For example, a checkmark might go on all the sticky notes of children who did their homework. A "T" might go on any student who is talking out of turn and asked to be quiet; a second "T" might indicate a second talking infraction. If a student with a disability has been working on raising their hand before yelling out, a star might be written on their sticky note every time they manage to do so. After class is over, the teachers can file these sticky notes in documentation folders. In the case of the student who was earning stars, you might even share that information with their parents that evening.

Musical chairs with Station Teaching. Stations involve students getting up at preordained times and moving to another location. It can be loud and unruly, but it doesn't have to be!

Providing students with the opportunity for a brain break and some kinesthetic movement between groups is helpful for their learning, but it doesn't mean that teachers have to endure chaos. Instead, consider asking students about the types of music they like, and even having them bring in some songs. Use that music to create mini-clips (i.e., 30 seconds to 2 minutes).

Now, use those music clips as cues to let students know it is time to change groups. They are allowed to talk quietly as the music plays in the background. Much like the game Musical Chairs, however, as soon as the music stops and turns off, they are expected to sit down and turn off their socialization. This positive environment validates students' choice of music, allows them to socialize (on the teachers' terms), and provides a structure for classroom management.

Heterogeneous grouping with Parallel Teaching. Getting students in small groups is important in a co-taught, inclusive setting. Large lecture groups tend not to work for many children and not only those who have identified disabilities. Having two educators in the room means that they can maximize the options for a smaller student-to-teacher ratio. One frequent misstep by many co-teachers is that they tend to have the same students go with the same teacher, resulting in a feeling of "my kids"/"your kids."

Co-teachers can avoid this conundrum by using systematic ways of getting students in heterogeneous groups. You can do this by numbering them off (e.g., 1, 2, 3, 4, 1, 2, 3, 4), handing out colored cards (e.g., if you have blue, go to this group; red, go to that group), or other systems (e.g., if your birthday is in January, February, or March, you are in group 1). Another strategy is to proactively create heterogenous groups that you can use throughout the year.

Provide each student with a card. Ask them to put their name in the center. On the upper right-hand corner, ask one-half of the class to write an "A," and ask the other half to write a "B." On the upper left-hand corner, ask one-quarter of the room to write a "1," followed by the other three-quarters writing a "2," "3," and "4," respectively. Collect the cards. Together with your co-teacher, identify the upper, middle, and lower third of your class academically. Assign a square to one group, a triangle to another, and a circle to the third, and write these on the bottom left-hand corner of the card. Finally, on the bottom right-hand corner of the card, assign students with one of six colors (e.g., red, blue, green, yellow, purple, orange). You will do most of these randomly, but do consider any behavioral or social needs some students may have and if they should be separated from any other student. Plan in advance for two of your colors to never get together; for example, co-teachers will never put the red and blue groups together. Then, if Flora and Eva are best friends and tend to talk too much, teachers can put Flora in the red group and Eva in the blue group.

Now, any time teachers want to get students in groups, they are ready! Want two groups? Students can be told to get into their A/B groups, or even numbers and odd numbers, or Red/Green/Orange and Blue/Yellow/Purple. Want three groups? Consider if it is important that the groups are homogeneously grouped by ability or skill; in which case, shape groups would be appropriate. If not and heterogeneity is important, you can use color groups again (e.g., Red/Orange; Green/Blue; Yellow/Purple).

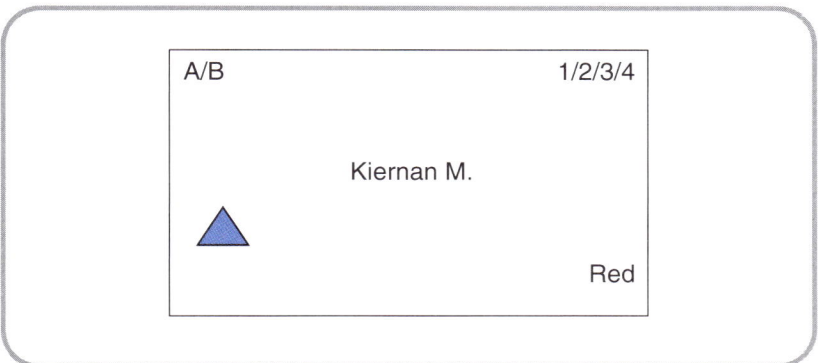

Interactive white boards with Alternative Teaching. Alternative teaching is the approach in which one educator is with the large group, while the other is with a small group. The tendency here can be to use the small group as a default intervention or pull-out group. It is important that co-teachers recognize that both educators should take time with the large group and with the small group. Also, the small group—though a good opportunity for reteaching or pre-teaching material—is also an excellent way to offer enrichment for those who need additional challenge.

Whenever two educators are talking concurrently and in the same room, noise can be an issue. Using quieter voices that project only to the group with whom they are working is a skill that co-teachers need to build. When one teacher is at a table with a small group of students, they should consider using more interactive ways to communicate. This can involve technology, like smart phones and iPads or interactive white boards. Interactive white boards allow students to write their answers using dry erase markers so the noise level is much quieter. They also allow teachers to pose questions in writing. These interactive boards do not have to be expensive. They can be created by putting white paper inside a sheet protector or pages from a photo album. You can use some plastic plates to write on with dry erase marker and then wipe them off with a paper towel and reused. The key here is to interact with the students, not to do yet another lecture in a different smaller venue.

Nonverbal signals with Team Teaching. Communication between co-teachers is essential. As with married couples who have kids, co-teachers will sometimes want to communicate in ways that their "children" don't understand. Creating visual, verbal, and nonverbal codes is a great way to interact and communicate with your partner without sharing too much in front of the students. For example, imagine Ms. Becker wants to ask her co-teacher if they might want to consider taking one of the groups outside for an upcoming activity. If she asks that aloud in front of the students, she knows they will begin to yell and beg to be part of the group to go outside. She also knows there might be a reason her co-teaching partner, Mr. Anderson, may not think this is a good idea. After catching Mr. Anderson's eye, Ms. Becker is able to give him a signal that she has a question for him, adults only.

Other signals can be shared with students. For example, co-teachers can instruct all students in some sign language signs for "May I go to the bathroom?" or "I need a brain break" or "May I sit somewhere else?" By teaching these to all learners, the communication is more inclusive and can be done without interrupting instruction. Both co-teachers are empowered to respond.

There can also be visual cues, such as noise meters that show all students how loud they are able to be (e.g., no talking during testing, open talking during Socratic seminar). Visual schedules are helpful for students with special needs or those who struggle with time management or transition (Flores, 2019). Co-teachers can create these as they co-plan, supporting their students but also helping them remember what activities are coming up as well.

Getting Started With Co-Teaching

Schools that have never experienced co-teaching are encouraged to investigate the idea with their educational community. Consider reading articles about co-teaching or even doing a book club with a book on co-teaching. Ask a co-teaching expert to do a Zoom call to answer questions or to do a mini-webinar explaining how it works. Provide a survey to teachers and specialists asking if they are interested in learning more and if they have other individuals with whom they might like to collaborate in more depth. Conduct a diagnostic to determine how inclusive the school site already is and how ready it is to embrace co-teaching (Lochner & Withrow, 2019).

Familiarize yourself with the co-teaching competencies (Murawski & Lochner, 2011) and what to look, listen, and ask for related to the co-taught classroom. The competencies (known as the Co-Teaching Solutions System [CTSS] Co-Teaching Competencies) can be found on www.2TeachGlobal.com, on the Padlet noted on page 142, in the Murawski and Lochner (2011) article, or in the book *Beyond Co-Teaching Basics: A Data-Driven, No-Fail Model for Continuous Improvement* (Murawski & Lochner, 2018). Use these competencies as the standards by which co-teachers should operate. Have different groups (e.g., general education teachers, special education teachers, counselors, administrators, specialists) look over the competencies and create additional adaptations that meet their unique needs. Invite experts in to help plan a coordinated sequence of events to move from less inclusive to more inclusive using co-teaching as one of the tools in the inclusive tool box. One such sequence is offered by the Protégé system of Co-Teaching Coaching (www.2TeachGlobal.com). No matter how you choose to start, any baby step is a step in the right direction for more inclusive practices with co-teaching!

UNIVERSAL DESIGN FOR LEARNING

Defining Universal Design for Learning

Universal Design for Learning (referred to simply as UDL) is not a curriculum. It is not a pedagogical strategy. It is not even all that new. UDL, however, is a way of embracing teaching and learning that respects the diversity of our students and even ourselves as teachers. UDL takes into account that we do not all learn in the same way despite the fact that most of our classrooms across the world expect students to sit and learn in a large-group setting.

When educators of all sorts (e.g., general education teachers, special education teachers, specialists, coaches, therapists, counselors, administrators) understand, and more importantly truly believe, that all students can learn when provided different options, the concept of UDL helps determine how to make that happen. A class that is universally designed is one that might have some students sitting on the floor, others working at a computer at a desk, and others sitting in a small group at the back of the room. It may have some students who prefer to learn through direct instruction with the teacher, whereas others prefer to read a book or learn from a video. When demonstrating their learning, some students may prefer to write a paper alone, while others choose to do a group project or design a graphic novel. Getting nervous? Relax. In this chapter, we will share the premise behind UDL as well as the strategies that will make it work for you.

Historical Perspective on UDL

In the foreword of the book *What Really Works With Universal Design for Learning* (Murawski & Scott, 2019), Novak shared a story about how the concept of UDL came about when colleagues shared a pizza one evening. These researchers were lamenting the lack of accessibility for students with learning needs. As individuals strong in technology, they recognized how technology could help with that accessibility if it were only used more proactively as opposed to reactively (after the fact). They made a connection between proactively building a lesson or curriculum and proactively adding accessibility features in a new building construction.

In the United States, the Americans with Disabilities Act was passed in 1990 and affected construction of buildings. No longer could buildings be constructed with only stairs and no ramps, or with multiple floors and no elevator, or without large bathrooms or wide hallways. Retrofitting, wherein ramps or other accessibility features are added after the fact, is far more expensive and time-consuming than adding those features during new construction. Taking this premise to education, David Rose and colleagues began to disseminate the idea of UDL (Bacon, 2014): Proactively plan for diverse students rather than be surprised by them after the fact!

Any educator who has been in schools for more than one year—or more than one day—knows that there is always at least one student who struggles with paying attention. There will be at least one student who struggles with following directions, and one who struggles with reading, and one who struggles with writing, and one who struggles with behavior. The list goes on! Rather than trying to address these needs after the fact, UDL asks educators to create lessons and environments that consider these needs before the students even walk in the room. It seems like such an obvious pedagogical choice, and yet it is one with which educators have difficulty.

Policymakers, politicians, and educational decision-makers have fully embraced the concept of UDL. In fact, UDL has been embraced worldwide as an educational practice and goal (Rao et al., 2016). In the United States, UDL has been represented in federal-level policy since 1998 in major laws such as the Assistive Technology Act, the Individuals with Disabilities Education Act (IDEA), the Higher Education Opportunity Act, and the Every Student Succeeds Act (ESSA; Gordon et al., 2009; Rodriguez, 2019). In the United Kingdom, researchers report the need to continue to embed UDL principles into higher education to do a better job with inclusive teaching and learning (Martin et al., 2019). In Sweden, Pia Häøggblom, a lecturer at the University of Kristianstad, conducted a project on implementing UDL with other lecturers working in higher education. The response from the university teachers was positive, and now many primary schools in Sweden are also trying to learn more about UDL to widen the participation of all students (Häøggblom, 2016).

Benefits and Barriers to UDL

Benefits. The benefits to UDL are not only multifaceted but also research based. Research has found that application of UDL principles can increase achievement in reading and writing across grade levels and abilities (Coyne et al., 2017). Australian researchers found that engaging students with math topics helped increase their strategy development, problem-solving, reasoning, and understanding of solutions (Buchheister et al., 2017). There also is an established connection between UDL and science, technology, engineering, and math (STEM), demonstrating that such a link helps support the development of deeper learning and opportunities to engage in higher-level cognitive tasks (Basham & Marino, 2013). There also is evidence of the benefits of using UDL with the performing arts and how that connection can improve student outcomes in academic areas (Ashton & Ashton, 2019).

At the postsecondary level, Seok and colleagues (2018) conducted a systematic review of empirically based studies on UDL for students with and without disabilities and determined that overall, the findings, as supported by the existing literature regarding the effectiveness and practicality of UDL, were quite promising. In yet another review of peer-reviewed and empirical research, Al-Azawei and peers (2016) found 12 studies over a 3-year period and determined positive results from 11 of the 12 studies. Like most researchers, they suggested further research "to confirm the positive impacts of UDL in different educational settings and cultural backgrounds" (Al-Azawei et al., 2016). In a nutshell, the concept of UDL is a positive one and continues to be applied and researched in a variety of content areas, grades, and educational arenas. What then are the drawbacks?

Barriers. Nothing in education is easy, especially for busy teachers! There is no quick fix to teaching students, especially those who struggle due to disabilities, language issues, or social needs. Although many aspects of UDL are things teachers already do, and simply need now to do more systematically, intentionally, and thoughtfully, there are still aspects that may be daunting.

Teachers who want a classroom where students are sitting in rows quietly, ready to listen and learn, will find UDL a difficult transition. The fact that choice is a major aspect of UDL will be daunting to many. Teachers often feel their students are not ready for this and are unable to make choices. We encourage you to think differently! It is entirely possible that the behaviors that make you think your students are not ready for this autonomy are actually caused by the lack of autonomy they currently have.

MAKING CONNECTIONS

Learn more about options for setting up the physical environment for UDL by reading Chapter 1 on sensory-motor development.

When students are given choices that appeal to them, it frequently changes their behavior and academic outputs for the better (Spencer, 2015). Teaching to the middle, as so many teachers do, actually ends up missing the majority of students.

Check out the excellent TEDx Talk by Todd Rose about this particular phenomenon.

https://bit.ly/3yYTmnH

The barriers to UDL then are primarily adult-related. Educators are the ones who need to be willing to create open, accessible physical environments where students might stand or even sit on different types of chairs (or even balls!). The adults are the ones who have to be ready to bring in real-world examples and be open to students learning in ways that were not available when teachers were students themselves. Teachers, administrators, and even policy makers need to build evaluation systems that are open to multiple means of action and expression, meaning that students have different ways that they can demonstrate their learning above and beyond a standardized assessment.

Best Practice Components of Effective UDL

UDL does not result in students running the classroom. Certain components, or best practices, have been identified that make UDL a concrete, effective, and positive pedagogical practice. The following practices are the foundation of UDL and are critical to ensuring that its implementation is evidence based and not a free fall into chaos.

Accessibility. Think about physical accessibility into a building. If you have use of both of your legs, and you see a ramp and some steps, you have options for accessing the building. You can choose which to use, and neither will slow you down or limit your access. If you have broken your leg and are in a wheelchair, you would look at steps as a barrier and a ramp as an accommodation for the time you need it. If you have a disability and are always in that wheelchair, the ramp is not merely an accommodation, it is the only way you will enter that building. It is your sole method of access.

Now apply this same analogy to the classroom. In the past (and honestly, for many classrooms, in the present), teachers often create lessons that should be appropriate for a particular grade level or group of students; let's say it is a whole-group reading lesson. In the analogy, the reading lesson is the building. When a student presents with a disability or special need, the teacher needs to create an accommodation for that student. Let's say that student is allowed to listen to the book, so now the teacher has to obtain a digital or taped version. That is like having to build a ramp to the lesson—only for that student. The next student gets their own ramp (e.g., a graphic organizer for following along with the story), and so on and so forth. What a lot of work!

Instead, what if the teacher had considered accessibility in advance and planned for it? We'll address proactive planning in the next section, but for now consider the concept of accessibility. It is not only that the students had access to the physical book or even to the instruction or lecture of the teacher. They need to have access to the learning! Without adaptations such as hearing the book, having a graphic organizer or checklist, stopping to check comprehension, using assistive technology to assist with annotation, and other options, these students would not have had *access* to the actual *learning*. Remember, being in the room does not equate to access to learning!

Proactive planning. As previously mentioned, a key component of UDL is being proactive rather than reactive. In the building analogy, retrofitting involves adding items like ramps, elevators, and handrails after the building is built; compare that to how educators often add accommodations or other adaptations to their lessons *after* the lessons have been created. By recognizing that there will always be students who struggle—with reading, writing, math, transitions, directions, attention, motor tasks, behavior—teachers can be more prepared in their lesson design and perhaps ultimately less stressed by the increasing diversity of the inclusive classroom.

Murawski and Novak (2019) have suggested that teachers take baby steps to their lesson planning for UDL. It can be intimidating to think that each lesson is supposed to meet the needs of every learner. Instead, they recommend that teachers start in these ways:

1. **Rewrite objectives** for the lesson to ensure they acknowledge learner variability. Instead of "write an argument about why lunch should be longer," students can be told they need to "compose an argument" and that they can choose the topic.

2. **Reexamine procedures** (to include routines, rules, approaches to instruction) to see which can be more flexible. Do students have to write with a pencil or sit in the same desk?

3. **Mix up your materials so you are not always using the same format** (e.g., worksheets, packets, presentations, lectures) for instruction. What are some options that might change things up a bit?

4. ***Ask for evidence of learning***. If a student can show you that they met the objective, what is the rationale for making every student use the exact same format?

Multiple means of representation. The National Center on UDL (https://medium.com/udl-center) reminds educators that learners vary greatly in the way they perceive and comprehend information that is presented to them. The Center for Applied Special Technology (CAST), the lead in UDL internationally (www.cast.org), has defined having multiple means of representation as identifying the "what" of the learning and presenting it to learners in a variety of ways. The CAST website shares:

> For example, those with sensory disabilities (e.g., blindness or deafness); learning disabilities (e.g., dyslexia); language or cultural differences, and so forth may all require different ways of approaching content. Others may simply grasp information quicker or more efficiently through visual or auditory means rather than printed text. Also learning, and transfer of learning, occurs when multiple representations are used, because they allow students to make connections within, as well as between, concepts. In short, **there is not one means of representation that will be optimal for all learners**; providing options for representation is essential. (UDL Guidelines, n.d., emphasis added)

Multiple means of engagement. School leaders enter a classroom and want to see engaged students. What does engagement look like, and how do teachers engage diverse learners in the same room? UDL identifies the need for engagement as an essential role in learning but emphasizes that one-size does not fit all. In a classroom that is truly universally designed, educators have deliberately designed the environment to maximize engagement. Defining engagement as the "how" of learning, CAST emphasizes the need for options for self-regulation, options for sustaining effort and persistence, and options for recruiting interest. CAST also provides 10 tips for designing an engaging learning environment (CAST, n.d.):

1. Create clear, specific goals.

2. Minimize distractions.

3. Present flexible assessment options.

4. Present frequent, formative feedback.

5. Incorporate authentic, relevant examples.

6. Ensure resources and supports meet the demands of the tasks.

7. Increase opportunities for collaboration.

8. Share examples and nonexamples.

9. Offer time for active reflection on learning and engagement.

10. Support risk taking.

Multiple means of action and expression. Consider a topic you know well. Perhaps it is the content you teach, or maybe it is a hobby of yours (knitting, fishing, crafting). You might be an expert in this particular field, but how would you feel if we told you we were going to test you on it? You might feel fine, confident that you know your topic well. Now how would you feel if we told you that the test would be given to you in Braille, or in Chinese, or that you would have to sing your answers in opera, and you would be evaluated in that format. You might not feel as confident; would you?

UDL asks educators to consider the diverse skills and strengths of learners not only in how they obtain information (representation) or interact with the information (engagement) but also with how they demonstrate their learning (action and expression). By assessing individuals in one particular way, which often is in the form of tests, quizzes, or writing assignments, we may be putting students at a disadvantage and not actually identifying what they have learned about the topic. Spencer (2015) emphasized this conundrum, stating, "The truth is that many exams and assignments are not testing what our students with disabilities know; they are testing their disabilities. Let me say that again: *we aren't always assessing what they know; we may be assessing their disabilities*" (p. 115). Thus, it is critical that educators provide students with different options to demonstrate their comprehension of the content; this might include reports, posters, group projects, poems, app designs, tests, papers, social media posts, debates, and more.

Figure 6.1 depicts a UDL VennBrella designed by Sally Spencer to demonstrate how multiple means of representation and expression fit with a culture of engagement (Spencer, 2015). Key components help to create that culture of engagement. They include active learning, mastery-oriented feedback, empowered informed learners, options for collaboration, relevant high-value learning, diversity that is accepted and valued, balance of routine and novelty, and self-regulated learners.

Figure 6.1

UDL VennBrella

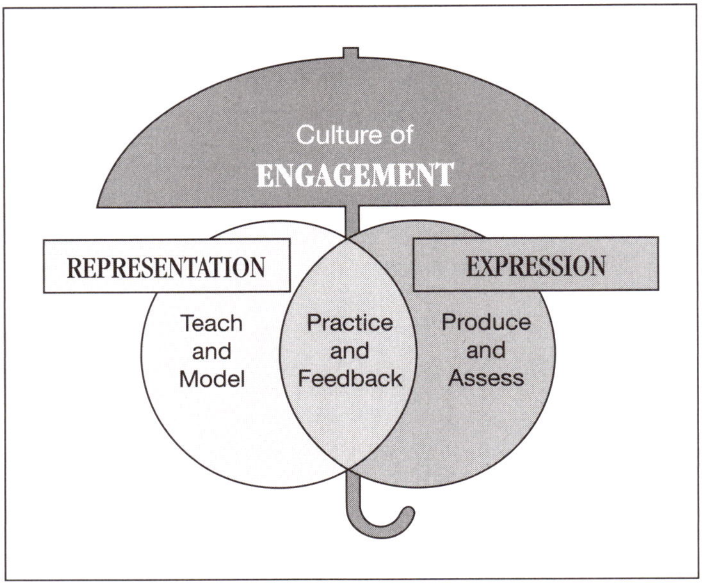

Culture of
ENGAGEMENT

REPRESENTATION

EXPRESSION

Teach
and
Model

Practice
and
Feedback

Produce
and
Assess

Source: Reprinted from Spencer, 2015.

Providing choice. Students are bored. Don't believe it? Research found that 66% of students surveyed were bored *every day* in school (Yazzie-Mintz, 2010); that's 2/3 of the students! If teachers keep telling students what they need to learn, and more importantly how they need to learn it, we will never get out of this loop. In the UDL classroom, teachers consider the goals of the learning and unlink them from the means by which they need to be achieved (Rose et al., 2014). In UDL, choice is one of the most important components.

There are myriad ways for providing choice in the inclusive classroom. In fact, research has demonstrated that providing choice to students helps reduce escape behaviors (Romaniuk et al., 2002; Trussell et al., 2018). Certainly teachers can let students choose where to sit or what to sit on (see Chapter 1). They can also allow students options for working independently, in pairs, or in small groups. They can let children select their partners, their topics, their medium, and their final products. As long as students are meeting the standards and objectives of the class, which can be assessed on a rubric to ensure all students are meeting the same criteria, the more options students have, the more empowered and engaged they are to learn!

Providing student voice. Student voice is equally important in a truly universally designed classroom or school. It is a bit different from student choice. In choice, teachers can provide students with options from which to select. That might look like "Would you write your persuasive essay on skateboarding, fashion, or animals?" When educators are truly open to student voice, that same question might instead become "How would you like to show me you understand how to create a persuasive essay?" Although many students might eagerly choose a topic on which to write, one student might suggest they find a published persuasive essay and label the parts that make it persuasive, whereas another may ask to create a PowerPoint outlining the steps in writing a persuasive essay. Truly respecting and valuing the voice of the students, from the youngest to the oldest, can be difficult to do, but it is the hallmark of a truly inclusive and universally designed classroom.

PROFESSIONAL DEVELOPMENT ON UDL

PD comes in a variety of ways. Check out this Padlet with articles, templates, checklists, lesson plans, and other resources related to UDL:

https://bit.ly/41QQmnV

Professional development. Teachers are bombarded with new information daily. Rather than feeling like UDL is "just one more initiative," we recommend helping teachers identify the elements of UDL they already have in place. Many teachers already provide forms of representation of information, and now they merely need to do that more thoughtfully and consistently. Many are already seeking ways to engage their students more actively and may quickly embrace the ideas of student choice and voice. The menu of UDL teaching options created by Murawski and Novak (2019) offered as a UDL Lesson Planning Checklist in Table 6.1 provides an example of how a diverse group of students can have their academic needs met without teachers going stir-crazy.

Table 6.1

Menu of UDL Teaching Options

A UNIVERSALLY DESIGNED UDL LESSON PLANNING CHECKLIST				
UDL doesn't have to be overwhelming. Take baby steps to ensure you have multiple means of representation, engagement, action, and expression. Start small and keep adding options!				
Clear lesson objective:				
Multiple Means of Representation:				
Mini-lecture	PowerPoint	Visuals	Realia	Kinesthetic movement
Humor	Art	Music	Video	Technology

(Continued)

Table 6.1

Menu of UDL Teaching Options (Continued)

A UNIVERSALLY DESIGNED UDL LESSON PLANNING CHECKLIST				
Reading	Writing	Numbers	Partners	Individual work
Web-Quest	Social media	Hands-on	Real world	Cultural examples
Multiple Means of Engagement:				
Parallel teaching	Station teaching	Alternative teaching		Team teaching
Partner work	Individual work	Small group work		Online work
Choose your seat	Choose your topic	Choose your partner(s)		Choose your medium
Read about it	Write about it	Talk about it		Draw about it
Blog about it	Tweet about it	Think about it		Act about it
App about it	Game about it	Problem-solve about it		Sing about it
Connect personally	Connect culturally	Connect academically		Connect emotionally
Multiple Means of Action/Expression:				
Oral presentation	PowerPoint/Prezi	Visual presentation		Artistic presentation
Quiz/Test	Ticket in the door	Ticket out the door		Homework
Design something	Discuss something	Present something		Analyze something
Compare something	Solve something	Write something		Show something
Reflection on this lesson:				
Goal for making the next lesson even more UDL:				

Source: Reprinted from Murawski, 2019.

Strategies for Effective UDL (More Tools!)

Data collection with UDL. Not sure what choices to offer that will engage students? In addition to asking the students themselves, teachers can collect data to see which choices get the most students interested. Keep a simple table with frequency counts documenting how many students created a poster, wrote a paper, did an online activity, and so on. After providing multiple means of representation (e.g., a lecture, reading, video, discussion), ask students to fill out a short survey on which of these options seemed to work best for them. Another option is to have students collect data themselves. Ask them to do a few different types of assessments (e.g., a test or quiz, writing assignment, group project) and then reflect on which resulted in the higher grade and if they think that grade is reflective of how they learn best.

Using technology. Technology is a friend to UDL. Certainly, using PowerPoint or Prezi or YouTube in creating a visual to align with a verbal presentation is part of almost every teacher's repertoire. Teachers know that many students prefer to work on a computer than to write longhand or to go online rather than go to the reference section of a library. However, have you also thought of using social media? Consider the increase in interest if students can chat a response in real time, use Instagram to demonstrate comprehension of a concept, or send you a picture on Snapchat. Because UDL is about student voice and choice, in addition to the multiple means, there may be many apps, online forums or blogs, digital games, and so on that students may bring to your attention. Even students with more significant special needs can use assistive technology to engage, connect, and demonstrate learning.

Ask the kids! You won't know what is out there or, more importantly, what interests your students unless you ask them. Teachers tend to make assumptions about what their students will like. Starting the class by saying "Hey, class. You are going to like today's lesson. It's super fun!" tends to make many students skeptical and even resistant. What a teacher thinks is fun and engaging isn't always the students' idea of fun. Instead, consider telling students what the overall objective is and then ask how they might want to go about accomplishing it (e.g., "We have 2 weeks to read this novel and demonstrate comprehension of what happened as well as identify the major themes in the book. How do you all think we might meet that objective?"). Worried that students might not agree on how to meet the objective or that they may want to go about it in a variety of ways? Don't be! In fact, expect that will be the case and plan for it. Remember, part of UDL is student voice, and by asking them, you'll better be able to identify what works for them.

Be prepared to be flexible. If you are asking students their opinions and for them to have input into how they learn or are assessed, then you also have to be prepared to go along with their choices—as long as they are reasonable. Having a rubric that clearly identifies the objective and any subgoals is critical to help students know how to meet those goals and objectives.

Getting Started With UDL

In the book, *What Really Works With Universal Design for Learning*, Wendy Murawski and Katie Novak (2019) share strategies for taking baby steps to engaging in UDL. Teachers do not have to be overwhelmed by the concept of choice and student voice. One suggestion is to take a particular lesson and simply provide choice in the representation, engagement, action, *or* expression—not in each area. For example, teachers may choose to provide many different ways to introduce a concept to their learners (a lecture paired with PowerPoint and a video followed by the choice of a hands-on activity or an article to read or listening to a guest speaker) but then choose to have the students engage in one particular way (a group project) and demonstrate their understanding in one way (a test).

Conversely, a teacher may choose to present the material to the students in one way (everyone gets the same lecture and PowerPoint), but then students can choose how to make the information meaningful (working online, small-group activity, reading material, working with the teacher) followed by the same assessment (a final paper). The last example has the teacher providing the choice in only the action and expression phase of the learning. After students are presented the information and engage in the same way dictated by the teacher, they are allowed to choose how they want to display their competencies. Teachers may present multiple options or even have students identify how they would prefer to have their competencies assessed. By selecting one aspect of the learning process (representation, engagement, action, expression), educators might not be as overwhelmed with providing choice.

UDL PROGRESSION MATRIX

Their UDL progression matrix is available online.

https://bit.ly/3ySjRvh

Novak and Rodriguez (2018) have provided guidance for moving through a progression of UDL proficiency from emerging, to proficient, to progressing toward expert practice. This type of rubric not only helps schools identify promising practices, but it also enables them to self-assess their current practices to determine how universally designed they are.

Finally, building off of Murawski's (2012) work on co-planning for co-teaching, Murawski and Novak (2019) have also recommended asking four specific questions as schools and teachers begin to embrace the UDL model. Using a What/Why/How/Who approach to lesson planning, the authors recommended that these questions be applied to all of the principles of UDL.

1. **What** is the overall goal or objective? What are you trying to accomplish with students?

2. **Why** is it critical to be done in a particular way? Or is it?

3. **How** can you let students have choice in what is done and choice in how to meet the goal?

4. **Who** may still require specially designed instruction to bridge some remaining gaps?

UDL needs to be a whole-school initiative. While individual teachers can universally design their environments or their specific lessons, without school leadership backing, this can be difficult to sustain. When a school leader establishes to all educators that accessibility and participation of all students is important—and goes beyond simply being present in the classroom—teachers will recognize the importance of providing various ways for students to learn, engage, and demonstrate understanding. School leaders also need to model this belief in UDL in the way they run the school, how they interact with families and stakeholders, how they organize the environment, and how they support students and faculty. We recommend administrators read *What Really Works With Universal Design for Learning* (Murawski & Scott, 2019) and pay special attention to the chapters on "UDL and Administrators," "UDL and Home School Collaboration," and "UDL and Policy."

COOPERATIVE LEARNING

Defining Cooperative Learning

In a nutshell, cooperative learning involves "the instructional use of small groups so that students work together to maximize their own and each other's learning" (Johnson & Johnson, n.d.). Merely putting students in small groups and asking them to work together is not sufficient. To achieve results, true cooperative learning involves positive interdependence, wherein the group members need to work together to achieve their group learning goal, as well as individual accountability, wherein a student's grade is based on their individual performance (Rappaport et al., 2017). Too frequently, teachers randomly cluster students to answer a question, work on a project, or solve a problem with little thought to who is in the group or what the purpose of such a group might be. Research has found that when students are thrown into a group with little thought to its makeup, purpose, or interaction, students merely share their answers with one another without explaining the process behind those answers (Webb, 2008); when that occurs, learning is actually inhibited, not supported.

It is important that groups be provided a learning goal. Depending on how that learning goal is structured, groups may find themselves engaging in cooperative, competitive, or individualistic efforts (Johnson & Johnson, n.d.). In *cooperative* groups, students work collaboratively toward the learning goal, sharing knowledge and achievements. In the *competitive* structure, students may work as one team against another or as individuals trying to achieve the highest score in the class. In the *individualistic* structure, students work solely to improve their own skills and outcomes. "In the ideal classroom, all students

Cooperative learning groups work together collaboratively to solve a joint problem. They are created purposefully, and each member has an interrelated role.

would learn how to work cooperatively with others, compete for fun and enjoyment, and work autonomously on their own" (Johnson & Johnson, n.d.).

Features of Cooperative Learning

Johnson and Johnson (2009), American researchers well-known for their focus on cooperative learning strategies, identified the core features that work to ensure the success of cooperative learning. First, they emphasized the need for positive interaction among group members, wherein team members are supportive and encouraging of one another. Next, they promoted the need for group members to have and employ skills for small-group interaction. These skills might include communication, decision-making, problem-solving, negotiation, and conflict management. Third, the authors recommended that group members take the time to reflect upon their processes, skills, relationships, and outcomes and that they discuss these with one another during the cooperative learning process.

It is no secret that students like to work with their peers. Cooperative learning is a strategy that builds on this innate desire of children but provides a structure to help adults manage the interaction in a more positive, outcomes-driven manner. Once students are taught the process and the rules for interaction, children at all ages can actively participate. Unfortunately, too many educators try to merely put students in small groups and expect them to figure out those rules and processes themselves. This can result in chaos, leading the educator to feel it is not worth the time and effort and going back to the "tried and true" (albeit boring and ineffective) method of lecture as students sit in rows facing forward. In fact, chaos and groups without ground rules are not fun for students either. They can be stressful for many; high-achieving students may feel they will be stuck with all the work, whereas students with special needs may feel increased anxiety due to a lack of structure and a need to work with peers in a way that might highlight their disabilities.

Historical Perspective on Cooperative Learning

The concept of social interdependence, in which groups are created by individuals whose members affect one another, began in the early 1900s. In the 1920s and 1930s, psychologist

Kurt Lewin defined, clarified and made popular the term "interdependence" and began to promote the concept that group interdependence creates a "dynamic whole" so that changing a member of the group actually changes the outcome of the group and that the way group members work together affects the accomplishment of a desired goal. In the late 1940s, and into the 1960s, Morton Deutsch, one of Lewin's graduate students, took this concept further by coining the term *positive inter-dependence* and promoting the social interdependence theory. Positive interdependence can be achieved when a goal structure is set up in such a way that the group achieves its goal, while each individual team member also reaches their own personal goals (Van Ryzin et al., 2020).

Although cooperative learning as a specific interaction was introduced in 1954 by Herbert Thelen in his book *Dynamics of Groups at Work*, its use did not become popular until the 1970s and later (Mandel, 2003). Since the 1970s, schools have become more interested in developing students' collaborative skills as opposed to merely individualistic or competitive skills. A meta-analysis of 122 studies comparing cooperative, competitive, and individualistic goal structures on students' achievement and productivity was published in 1981 and increased interest in how educators could structure lessons to increase collaboration among students (Johnson et al., 1981). A great deal of research on cooperative learning and teaching in schools has occurred in the past decades. Two more large meta-analyses were conducted more recently (Kyndt et al., 2013; Roseth et al., 2008) and, validating the earlier work by Johnson and colleagues, both found that cooperative learning structures increased student achievement. Researchers such as Johnson and Johnson and Robert Slavin are renowned for their work in this area over the past four decades. These individuals, among others, have helped identify the key characteristics to successfully cooperative learning.

Currently cooperative learning is one of the "few empirically supported instructional approaches that specifies the establishment of positive interdependence in small group learning activities" (Van Ryzin et al., 2020). There are many different terms used in the literature to describe cooperative learning. These include small-group work, peer learning, active learning, collaborative learning, and teams. In addition, there are numerous uses of cooperative learning in action for a particular type of task; these include reciprocal teaching, jigsaw, peer tutoring, and other group activities (Van Ryzin et al., 2020). For the purposes of this chapter, we will use cooperative learning as an umbrella term, describing the aspects that teachers can use to successfully engage their students and reap the many benefits frequently identified in the literature.

Benefits and Barriers to Cooperative Learning

MAKING CONNECTIONS

Cooperative learning can be an excellent building block for developing students' social-emotional skills. You can read more about the importance of these skills in Chapter 9.

Benefits. A great deal of research has identified myriad benefits to cooperative learning. These benefits have found robust effects on student motivation, academic achievement, and positive peer relationships. In a meta-analysis of almost 150 studies, cooperative learning was associated with more positive peer relationships and greater academic achievement than competitive or individualistic goal structures (Ginsburg-Block et al., 2006). In a 2020 study using close to 2,000 students, Van Ryzin and colleagues found that cooperative learning significantly increased prosocial behaviors. Prosocial behaviors include behaviors that benefit others and may include helping, sharing, cooperating, and even volunteering. Through engaging in cooperative learning groups, students learn more about the potentially hidden strengths of their peers as well as how to use their own strengths to mitigate any potential weaknesses (Altun, 2015). In addition, results suggested that cooperative learning is one of the strongest methods of eliminating the prejudices among students and increasing student success, when compared to traditional classroom teaching, because students learn more about the strengths and talents of their classmates than they would have by simply by sitting and listening to a teacher lecture (Altun, 2015).

Other research has found that cooperative learning was more effective than numerous other instructional practices, including the use of technology and curriculum textbooks (Gillies, 2016). Cooperative learning has been linked with increased motivation, cooperation, relatedness, enjoyment, and novelty (Fernandez-Rio et al., 2017). In addition, researchers have even found a reduction in alcohol and tobacco use as well as a reduction in bullying behaviors linked to the peer reinforcement for positive behaviors that occurs through the use of cooperative learning (Van Ryzin & Roseth, 2018a, 2018b).

The importance of developing collaborative skills as students move into college, career, and the workforce cannot be overemphasized. Universities often require students to work collaboratively on group projects and culminating activities (Premo et al., 2018). Businesses frequently espouse the need to have employees who can collaborate, communicate, problem-solve with others, and deal with interpersonal conflict appropriately (Mandel, 2003). Problems in the science, technology, engineering, and math (STEM) fields are typically too complex for one person to solve independently, requiring individuals to have the skills to work collaboratively and cooperatively (Premo et al., 2018). Not all students have the innate ability or social skills necessary for interacting with their classmates in a prosocial manner (Dean, 2015). This skill needs to be taught and then reinforced. Teaching students how to collaborate with peers is not a luxury that teachers can choose to include or not include in their curriculum; it is a necessity for today's students.

Barriers. As previously mentioned, simply putting students into work groups together is insufficient for cooperative learning to occur. In fact, some research has found that unstructured groups can actually have negative effects on students and outcomes. It can lead to social loafing (Meyer et al., 2016), negative relationships, and interpersonal conflict (de Jong et al., 2014). Without the specific structures in place for true cooperative learning, students are merely thrown together and told to "collaborate." This may lead to class chaos, disengaged students, students who do the work for their group, and unsatisfied teachers. Naturally, these outcomes may increase the resistance of teachers to use cooperative learning strategies despite the fact that what they were doing previously would not, in fact, have met the criteria for true collaborative learning.

In addition, cooperative learning may also be stressful for some students. There is a group pressure involved to work collaboratively and to do one's part successfully (Altun, 2015). Because the group tasks are interdependent, students are no longer able to drop the ball, not show up, or not do their part because it affects the whole group and not only themselves individually. Although this can be a positive motivator, it can also be a stressor for some. Also, students who are typically high achievers or academically successful on their own now may have the additional stressor of wondering how their peers' actions will affect their own achievement. These students may not be comfortable having an aspect of their grade or score dependent on another person's work (Altun, 2015).

Unfortunately, despite the plethora of evidence showing how beneficial cooperative learning is across a multitude of factors for students, including academic achievement, many teachers still believe that learning can only be achieved through teacher-directed instruction (Buchs et al., 2017). Even teachers who say they recognize the power of cooperative learning may use it only occasionally. They want quicker delivery of content, and certainly lecturing or having students read something is more efficient (although not necessarily more effective) (Jacobs & Ivone, 2020). In addition to needing a mindset that values cooperative learning and its benefits over the need to be at the front of the room or to zip through content, educators need to put the appropriate structures in place for true cooperative learning; for many, this seems to be too much work. In fact, research shows that the more difficult teachers believe

MAKING CONNECTIONS

Many teachers worry about the time it might take to design cooperative learning strategies and whether students might become disruptive during cooperative activities. Chapter 10 on time management provides advice on how to make more time in your day, and Chapter 3 provides some tips on managing classroom behavior.

embedding cooperative learning into the curriculum will be, and the more time they worry it will take, the less they implement it (Buchs et al., 2017; Jacobs & Ivone, 2020). This chapter will provide the key elements to effective collaborative learning and easy-to-use strategies for educators so that implementation is not as daunting.

Key Components of Effective Cooperative Learning

In their research on collaborative learning, Johnson and Johnson (2009) offered five key components that need to be in place for effective cooperative learning to occur. These five components include structuring positive interdependence, facilitating promotive interaction, encouraging individual accountability, teaching interpersonal and social skills, and embedding group processing and reflection (Gillies, 2016). We will briefly describe each of these.

KEY CONCEPTS

Cooperative learning requires:

- Positive interdependence
- Promotive interaction
- Individual accountability
- Interpersonal and social skills
- Group processing and reflection

Structuring positive interdependence. A key element of strong cooperative learning is that each group knows the goals of the task and that the task is structured so that each person's actions are important. One way to do this is to have students take specific roles for the task (e.g., Recorder, Reporter, Facilitator, Timer, Technology Enabler; Jacobs & Ivone, 2020). If students recognize that each group member's actions will lead to the accomplishment of the task, or could derail the whole group, they will see that their success leads to the success of the entire group.

Facilitating promotive interaction. In addition to supporting one another academically and with individual parts of a group task, cooperative learning also requires that students share resources and provide one another with personal supports as well. Students are urged to help, encourage, and praise one another throughout the shared task. To address this aspect of cooperative learning, teachers can explain to students why they are working together and what the goals of this interaction are (above simply completing the task). Providing examples of how collaboration was instrumental in a personal goal or demonstrating how adults in the real world promote and encourage one another would help students recognize these skills as valuable (Jacobs & Ivone, 2020).

Encouraging individual accountability. A downfall of many groups is when one or more members allow the others in the group to essentially do all the work. In essence, they ride the coattails of their peers. In true cooperative learning, each group member is also assessed individually so that is less likely to occur. Each student is held accountable for an aspect of the task, so it is clear when one person has not done their work and it may hold up the rest of the group. Techniques to increase individual accountability include keeping groups small, allowing time for students to reflect on answers before being put into groups to discuss them, encouraging turn taking, having students document their individual efforts on a group roster, using apps like Padlet and Trello for collaboration, regularly reflecting on and discussing group dynamics and individual accountability, and so on (Jacobs & Ivone, 2020).

Teaching interpersonal skills. Teachers should not assume that all students already possess interpersonal skills. Instead, students should be taught how to engage in groups proactively (Jacobs & Ivone, 2020). Mini-lessons on taking turns, conflict resolution, problem-solving, communicating, and even building trust, should be offered. Teachers might differentiate and offer different mini-lessons for different students based on need. For example, whereas one small group of students may need some instruction in how to complete tasks or give compliments to group members, another small group that already has those skills might benefit from a workshop on effective leadership skills and demonstrating patience with peers.

Embedding group processing. In addition to merely completing a task together, strong cooperative groups also engage in communication about the task and how they are approaching it. They need to have the skills to share frustrations or concerns as well as provide one another feedback and give praise when it is due. Teachers can encourage students to regularly take a processing break to discuss how it is going and to identify behaviors that are both helpful and unhelpful to their group interaction.

Logistics for Effective Cooperative Teaching

Group composition. Mandel (2015) explained that the optimum size for a group is between four and seven members. His rationale is that having more than seven students in a group is unwieldy, whereas three-person groups are the most challenging because they often result in a two-versus-one dynamic. In addition, he recommended that teachers consider even-sized groups over uneven. Although an uneven group may make voting on an issue easier, "when group votes have to be decided by a significant consensus rather than a one-vote margin, it leads to stronger decision-making process" (Mandel, 2003, p. 9).

In terms of heterogeneous versus homogeneous group makeup, teachers should consider the goal of the task. Most literature on the inclusive classroom recommends heterogeneous groups, wherein students of mixed ability are put together so they learn from one another (Karten & Murawski, 2020). However, there are times when having students of similar ability or challenge may be appropriate. For example, Hughes wrote "grouping has to be flexible. Heterogeneous groups are great for some things, but gifted learners need to have like-minded peers around to challenge them" (2015, p. 237). Consider what the goal of the group is. If it is to learn new content for all, heterogeneous groups are appropriate. If it is to engage in problem-solving around different problems of interest, it might behoove teachers to let students choose their team members, and if a group of students with like ability get together, that would be acceptable.

Teachers do need to consider students with special needs and how they will best fit in each group configuration (Mandel, 2003). One area to be especially cognizant of is reading ability. If a reading component is part of the group task, there needs to be at least one strong reader in each group, and the teacher needs to encourage groups to have one member read the required information to the entire group. This removes the stigma of only one student needing information read aloud to them. The need for literacy support, in both reading and writing, will arise for students with identified disabilities as well as for second-language learners, so these supports are helpful for many students in the classroom. As long as teachers have considered the components of the task and ensured there are multiple ways for students to participate, heterogeneous groups tend to work better (Mandel, 2015). Ultimately, "the teacher must also assure that the groups are required to perform certain tasks in which these students can inevitably succeed (e.g., nonreading special education students should not be in a group activity where all investigation, tasks, and reporting are dependent on higher level reading abilities. That situation is sure to lead to failure, social stigma, or at the very least, a critical drop in the students' self-esteem as they become 'useless' to the group)" (Mandel, 2003, p. 12).

Finally, there are times when either students can choose their peers themselves or a learning management system might do it for them. For example, if instructing online, Zoom can break students into groups randomly. There are also apps that can do the same thing. Ultimately, teachers should use a variety of strategies when engaging students in cooperative learning groups to continue to mix it up.

Determining and managing leaders. In addition to considering those students who may struggle, teachers need to also consider how to distribute the natural leaders in the class. There are various leader types they should consider (Mandel, 2003). A student who is concerned with the actions of the group and what they must do to follow directions and complete the goal of the project is typically one who would be considered a *task leader*. This is a student who says things like "What's next on the list?" and "Who will bring in those materials?" A student who offers new ideas to the group and is constantly challenging themself or others cognitively is considered an *intellectual leader*. This student may bring in new content or say things like "Last night, I was wondering about … so I researched it and found out…" A third type of student leader is one who continues to offer peers support and encouragement throughout the process, motivating them to continue and try. This leader is considered a *social-emotional leader* and may say things like "Oh, that's really helpful" and "I love how you drew that." Finally, a fourth leader that may be considered when distributing natural leaders is one who takes attention and control in a more negative way. This person is considered a *coercive leader* and may use negative comments or humor to get attention and derail the group. Comments by this person may include phrases like "Shut up" and "That's stupid" and jokes (Mandel, 2003).

Teachers should consider who these natural leaders are and place them carefully in the groups. Recognize that natural leaders will almost always take a leadership role, whether the teacher has given it to them or not (Mandel, 2003), so it makes sense to let students select their own roles. However, Wilson (2004) has also encouraged teachers not to neglect those who are not leaders. Having other students identified as *observers* gives them an important role as well. She wrote, "Whereas the leader's purpose is to be goal oriented and achieve whatever task the teacher devises, the observers are to pay attention to the individuals on the team. Their job is to promote or solicit participation from any student who doesn't immediately feel comfortable in adding to the discussions" (Wilson, 2004, p. 32). She stressed that these types of cooperative learning activities build community in the classroom and also offer students a sense of team unity.

Materials. "Nothing will sabotage a cooperative work group experience faster than having the students run out of materials to use in their investigation" (Mandel, 2003, p. 25). With the increased use of technology, most students can access information on their laptops, tablets, or even phones. Ultimately then, teachers need to determine the goal of the project. Is it to:

- Have the students work with the information contained within the material?

  or

- Have the students learn how to conduct research?

If the goal is the former, teachers are encouraged to provide as much material as possible (e.g., bookmark websites, bring in books and articles), so groups do not waste valuable time trying to find articles or other information. In contrast, if the goal is the latter, then the finding of appropriate materials is part of the group task. Thus, one of the major considerations for teachers in determining how to proceed with cooperative learning is to what extent materials should be provided to students or gathered by them.

Teacher role. Much literature on cooperative learning stresses the teacher as merely a facilitator, requiring students to take the lead roles (Gillies, 2016). However, many teachers argue that students are ill prepared to immediately take on the independent roles cooperative groups may require. Instead, without these skills, groups may devolve into chaos, and teachers find themselves spoon-feeding groups and individuals with the information that was supposed to be gleaned through the group interaction (Buchs et al., 2017). This doesn't mean that teachers should abandon cooperative learning in favor of more traditional (and less impactful) lecture techniques; instead they should consider themselves facilitators who are also directly responsible for the critical thinking levels of the groups (Mandel, 2015). What this means is that teachers need to be purposeful about the directions they give groups, the questions they ask students, and the feedback they offer throughout the interactions. If teachers ask low-level, closed questions, they are likely to get low-level work at the knowledge and comprehension levels of Bloom's taxonomy (Mandel, 2003). If they want higher-level work at the analysis and evaluation levels, they need to be sure to pose open-ended questions that challenge students to problem-solve and interact collaboratively around the topic as opposed to merely regurgitating findings from a book. Based on the makeup of the group, teachers can differentiate their types of questioning and the level of support they provide the group.

Strategies for Effective Cooperative Learning (More Tools!)

1. **Try the jigsaw technique.** The jigsaw technique was developed by Aronson in the early 1970s (Aronson, 2000). In this approach to cooperative learning, students are divided into groups, and each student is provided one aspect of the task. It might be one page of a reading or one problem on a math worksheet or one part of a lab activity. Students from different groups working on the same subject can gather and create expert groups. For example, all of the students who are working on math problem four would get together to share how they approached the problem, and if they all answered it in the same way, or perhaps if they answered it in different ways but got the same answer. After students feel confident in their responses and their subject, after working with their subject matter expert groups, they return to their own group to share their responses with that group. Ultimately, all students learn all of the material, even though they had to become experts in only one aspect of the task. This requires cooperation because all students will be responsible for learning all of the material for subsequent activities or assessments (Altun, 2015).

2. **Play games!** The Teams–Games–Tournament (TGT) technique is another application of cooperative learning. Developed by Slavin in the early 1980s, TGT embeds a bit of competition into the cooperative learning process (Slavin & Madden, 2021). After students receive direct instruction on a topic by the teacher (or other students), they are divided into small groups to review the material and teach one another to mastery. After a set amount of time, student

groups then compete with other groups at the same level at a tournament table. As students accrue individual points with correct answers, those points are added to their small group's score. Team points are calculated by summing the points of the individual students in that group, and the small group with the highest amount of points is considered the winner (Altun, 2015).

3. **Involve everyone.** Another flexible application of cooperative learning is the Everyone Can Explain technique (Jacobs & Renandya, 2019). In this approach, groups do tasks or respond to questions but then check to ensure every one of the group members is able to explain what they have done and why. Teachers then choose a group member at random to present the group's work and explain what they accomplished. This technique encourages students to engage in peer support and ensure no one is left confused.

4. **Collect data.** Not sure what choices to offer that will engage students? In addition to asking the students themselves, teachers can also collect data to see which choices get the most students interested. Students can choose who they work with, the topics they research, the projects in which they want to engage, and the tasks they take once in a small group. Universal Design for Learning (UDL) principles (see Chapter 6) encourage student choice and student voice, and cooperative learning can allow for both if teachers are open and use data to inform their decisions (Murawski & Scott, 2019).

5. **Use rubrics.** Even the most independent of students may struggle with project-based learning, student-led groups, and open directions. Having a rubric that clearly identifies the objective and any subgoals is critical to help students know how to meet those goals and objectives. Rubrics can also lay out the steps that students need to take, which will help with those groups who may lack in direction or organization. Finally, rubrics can also allow for a lot of creativity in how students demonstrate mastery without losing the original goals of the teacher or overall standards the activity is meant to address (Bernhardt, 2019).

6. **Teach digital citizenship.** Many teachers are, rightfully, concerned about students working independently, especially when they may be using technology. Issues, such as the inappropriate use of social media, the increase of cyberbullying, the misuse of the internet to engage in gaming or shopping, or even a lack of understanding regarding how to identify appropriate content or know-how to trust online information, are rampant. Thus, teachers who want to have their students engage in cooperative

learning groups who use technology should also teach those students about digital citizenship. (To be fair, we think all teachers should teach all students about digital citizenship regardless of whether or not they engage in cooperative learning!) Digital citizenship includes "respectful, informed communication, tolerance of various voices and opinions, equity of all individuals, and responsibility for one's actions" in the digital environment (Porter & Bernhardt, 2018).

7. **Manage conflict.** Although proactive grouping, clear directions, and tasks that invite multiple ways to be successful are all ways to minimize conflict, interpersonal collaboration is always rife with the possibility of conflict. Conflicts may occur within and between groups, requiring teachers to be agile in both preventing and solving intragroup conflict (Altun, 2015). If the issue seems to stem from one individual, consider having a quiet conversation with that student to determine the function of their behavior and what needs to be done to help the student work collaboratively with the group. Try using techniques to differentially reinforce that student's behaviors (Hott & Limberg, 2015; see Chapter 3 on applied behavior analysis). Despite best efforts, some students will have substantial social skills deficits that make it difficult or aversive to work in groups. In those situations, teachers can create an alternative assignment (Mandel, 2015).

8. **Assess both the group and individual.** A key aspect of cooperative learning is to assess students both as a whole group and also as individuals. This is not to be done in a punitive way or even in a competitive one, pitting teams against one another. It should be done in a collaborative and supportive manner as a way to provide feedback (Jacobs & Ivone, 2020). Criterion-based assessments require all students to be assessed against a standard, reducing competition and allowing all students to get an A if they meet the standard. Ipsative assessments assess students based on their own individual past performance as opposed to compared to a standard or their peers (Jacobs & Ivone, 2020).

9. **Design learner-centered spaces** (Sheninger & Murray, 2017). Classrooms in which all the chairs are in rows facing forward, spaced out equidistant from one another, are not conducive to cooperative learning groups. Students need to work in pods of chairs and desks moved together. They need to move their seats to work with their expert groups and then move back to their home group. As mentioned in Chapter 1, having a variety of types of seating arrangements and the ability to move is critical. Allow students to stand, lie on the carpet, sit on the floor, or move around as long as it is not

disturbing. Being able to move between groups as needed is a hallmark of strong collaboration and cooperative learning groups.

10. **Be flexible.** Despite the intrinsic motivation that is built into the use of cooperative learning groups, some students may still struggle. Those who have high absences in class or who are self-conscious of their own skills may not feel the same culture of collaboration and teamwork as their peers do. They may struggle to engage at the same level and may need additional motivation to participate. Teachers may need to differentiate for some learners, offering additional motivation for engagement such as having one-on-one conversations, building in a point system, identifying clear procedures for specific infractions, maintaining high expectations, and focusing on preventative measures as a first line of defense against problematic behaviors (Porter & Bernhardt, 2018).

11. **Encourage asking for help.** In years past, working with others might have been seen as an indicator of dependency, an inability to work alone. Nowadays, however, "learning together and asking for help is considered among the best strategies for learning how to learn" (Altun, 2015, p. 451). This concept needs to be reinforced, especially for students who come from an individualistic culture as opposed to a collectivistic one. Rothstein-Fisch and Trumbull (2008) have encouraged teachers to build on students' cultural strengths by acknowledging differences and bringing them to the forefront.

12. **Flip the classroom.** Flipping the classroom requires teachers to provide students with direct instruction via videos, readings, and other methods of providing information to students prior to their entry in the classroom. Essentially the opposite of the traditional method of teaching (i.e., hear direct instruction from the teacher in class and go home to do an application of that new knowledge via homework), flipping the class means that students get new content knowledge at home and then come into the classroom to engage in an application (Bergmann, 2017). Being able to engage in cooperative learning groups during the school day allows teachers to check for comprehension of the material and provides for additional peer tutoring and scaffolding. Teachers can also use flipping the class as an method for developing a more inclusive classroom with increased differentiation (Embury & Clarke, 2023).

13. **Get in breakout rooms.** When most of the world turned to virtual and online education for the COVID-19 pandemic, teachers across the globe were thrust into having to figure

out how to move instruction from a brick-and-mortar environment into a digital one. Quickly, the use of breakout rooms became popular as a way to get students into smaller groups for instruction, group work, discussions, and checking for understanding. Murawski and Gaines (2021) have offered a variety of ways for educators to meet the needs of students with exceptionalities (such as those with disabilities, those who are gifted, and those who are working in a second or foreign language) when working in online or hybrid model. They strongly recommend breakout rooms for smaller student-to-teacher ratios, especially when classes can be co-taught.

Distance learning can be a major adjustment for both students and teachers, and including peer interaction in that distance learning presents yet another adventure for students and teachers. Fortunately, it can be a rewarding adventure, as cooperative learning provides students with more communication opportunities, more opportunities to give and receive assistance, and more opportunities to add a social element to their learning.

(Jacobs & Ivone, 2020, p.12)

LITERACY STRATEGIES

What Is Literacy?

The word *literacy* is bandied about quite a bit. Educators today hear about *digital literacy, media literacy, linguistic literacy, visual literacy, emotional literacy*, and other similar terms. In the past, literacy seemed to merely be comprised of its constituent parts, reading and writing (Paran & Wallace, 2016). The National Reading Panel identifies reading, writing, listening, and speaking as the four primary components of literacy instruction (Toews & Kurth, 2019). Most educators now promote the teaching of literacy, wherein all of these skills are taught concurrently and in context, as opposed to the discrete teaching of reading (e.g., decoding, fluency, comprehension) or writing (e.g., spelling, grammar) without an eye to how these skills will be used in regard to communication (Paran & Wallace, 2016; Spencer, 2015). "While 'reading' and 'writing' are conceptualized as individual, cognitive skills, 'literacy' is indexed to particular societies at a particular time in history: literacy is seen in terms of what it allows you to do, that is, what social roles you are able to play in your community and the wider society" (Paran & Wallace, 2016, p. 441). As inclusive classes welcome students from varying cultures and backgrounds, those students may have diverse experiences around what it means to be literate. Even the most research- or evidence-based practices may not have been normed on the same type of student group in one's class, especially because current inclusive classes have students with a variety of needs and abilities. This is why we do not advocate only one approach or philosophy to instruction; we embrace a myriad of high-leverage practices that have been identified as impactful

Evidence-based practices are those teaching practices that have substantive research to support their use.

High-leverage practices are not specific to a particular curriculum or activity and can be generalized; the four main aspects of practice include collaboration, assessment, social/emotional/behavioral, and instruction (Jenkins & Murawski, 2023).

with all learners, regardless of differences (Jenkins & Murawski, 2023). High-leverage practices are "a critical set of practices that are essential to improving student learning and behavior and can be learned in coursework, deliberately practiced in field experiences carefully structured by faculty, and generalized to more loosely structured field experiences" (McCray et al., 2017).

Teaching and learning is always relational and situational; there is no one way to teach literacy (Smagorinsky, 2018). Strong teachers of literacy consider their teaching to be focused on literacy events as opposed to strictly reading or writing lessons. A literacy event is simply any occasion wherein one interacts with written text or in which a piece of writing is integral to an interaction. Therefore, teachers might engage students by discussing a billboard, a tweet, a menu, a sign, a social media post, or each other's writings as a way to teach literacy rather than providing worksheets on grammar, spelling, or sentence structure.

Early literacy. Readers, from a young age, "learn to read" by decoding. They begin with learning the alphabet, then they learn the names of the letters, the sounds of the letters, words, and finally sentences. However, by focusing primarily on the code, meaning is sometimes lost. They might develop into "master decoders" but have no idea what they are reading about. They are simply saying words, not reading. As schools progressively include students of all abilities and cultures, "early childhood development and literacy learning and teaching in inclusive classrooms are at the forefront of education systems worldwide" (Nel et al., 2016, p. 47). In a study of early literacy practices in South Africa, researchers found that the teaching of reading needs to be adapted to local conditions; include the developing of decoding, comprehension, and meaning making even at a young age; and consider multilingual practices in different contexts (Nel et al., 2016). Early literacy activities need to be embedded in all academic tasks, but researchers stress that educators need to avoid relying on traditional teacher-driven lecture, memorization, and recitation teaching styles (Paran & Wallace, 2016; Spencer, 2015; Toews & Kurth, 2019). Instead, they concur with other researchers (e.g., Nel et al., 2016; Nie et al., 2013) who recommend instructional methodologies that facilitate students' thinking, understanding, and communication as it relates to literacy attainment, even for young learners.

Related to the need to consider context and teaching methodology when it comes to literacy, so too must teachers think about the types of reading and writing skills they are emphasizing with their young learners. Fundamental literacy skills can be conceptualized as falling into two categories: constrained and unconstrained skills (Snow & Matthews, 2016). Constrained skills include things like identifying the letters of the alphabet and the basic spelling rules; they are skills that are easily teachable and finite. Unconstrained skills, in contrast, include information primarily acquired by experience, including vocabulary, discourse, and background knowledge; these skills may be largely influenced by students' socioeconomic status, home backgrounds, and parents' level of education. Research shows that focusing too much on constrained skills, such as teaching phonemes and graphemes to decode, can actually decrease literacy scores (Snow & Matthews, 2016). Experts in literacy instruction emphasize the need for teachers to also address the unconstrained skills, even in early childhood and primary classrooms (Snow & Matthews, 2016).

What strategies can teachers employ to build those unconstrained skills? Talk to students! The quality of teachers' talk increases their ability to learn unconstrained language and literacy skills. Research has suggested that, even in preschool, students who had teachers or family members who used more sophisticated language, who talked to them actively about books, and who utilized complex sentence structure and syntax began to use improved grammar, had larger vocabularies, and had better reading skills (Dickinson & Porche, 2011). Patterns of such research strongly encourage teachers to use more sophisticated talk with their students to promote unconstrained skills related to literacy.

In an inclusive class, students' needs with respect to literacy activities vary. Although modeling think-alouds (whereby teachers work out a problem in front of children while expressing their thinking aloud, so students can hear their thought processes) and using a varied vocabulary are strong pedagogical choices, not every student will benefit in the same way. Differentiation is key to literacy instruction. However, differentiated literacy instruction means identifying students' literacy needs and addressing them strategically, not merely offering a variety of choices or simply doing many different things with students. In fact, there is substantive research demonstrating that

> differentiated literacy instruction is an effective evidence-based practice at the elementary level. When teachers are supported to differentiate instruction, students have significantly higher literacy achievement scores, particularly for letter-word and writing outcomes. The most successful programs took very different approaches to differentiation, including individualization, choice, and an alternate curriculum.
>
> (Puzio et al., 2020, p. 459)

Clearly, there is no one size fits all. One of the ways teachers can individualize and differentiate their literacy instruction is through co-teaching (Lyon et al., 2021). More information on co-teaching is provided in Chapter 5.

MAKING CONNECTIONS

Whether you are teaching early readers or advanced readers, assessing what learners know and can do as they are learning is imperative. Chapter 2 provides helpful advice on incorporating formative assessment in your teaching.

Secondary literacy. Most teachers are aware that elementary education is where students learn to read, whereas secondary students are expected to read to learn. Thus, there is an expectation that all foundational literacy skills have been addressed prior to secondary school. Naturally, for students with disabilities and those learning to read and write in a second or even third language, those skills may not yet be fully formed. In addition, at the secondary level, students are expected to "use complex literacy skills to construct meaning from many types of text to communicate understanding in a variety of ways" (Smith & Waegerle, 2016, p. 678). Yet, most secondary teachers report that they do not directly teach reading or writing, nor have they been taught evidence-based literacy strategies to use with their students (Smith & Waegerle, 2016). Teachers need professional development on how to incorporate such strategies (including information on constrained and unconstrained skills such as those mentioned in early literacy approaches) into their varied content areas in such a way as to support those students for whom reading and/or writing are difficult or nonpreferred tasks.

As mentioned in the box "Changing the Way We Think About Learning," teachers need to embrace the notion that presenting content is no longer their key role as an educator. Content is available online and at the touch of a button (or even via a voice prompt). Even the concrete acts of reading and writing are no longer required for literacy; assistive technology can allow one to use speech to text or text to speech. Other assistive technology, such as mobile devices, graphic organizers, and apps can help with reading and writing, and even artificial intelligence (AI) can support learners who struggle. In one study, students with and without special needs in an inclusive classroom who were provided with a mobile-based graphic organizer, instruction on self-regulated learning strategies, and content instruction significantly outperformed students with and without disabilities in the control group (i.e., students who did not receive those supports) on persuasive writing tasks (Regan et al., 2018). Results such as these emphasize the need for teachers to focus more on meaning making, critical thinking, analysis, inquiry, and skills-based instruction. By incorporating specific literacy skills into content instruction, teachers can help students continue to build their unconstrained skills to address the increased and more complex vocabulary and the less generalizable content introduced in the more advanced classes.

Changing the Way We Think About Learning

BY ADRIENNE GEAR

I went to school at a time where the teacher at the front of the room was the keeper of knowledge, the provider of facts. My job as a student was to listen to the teacher, study the information, and always be ready with "the right answer." A literal understanding of information was all I was ever asked to provide: read–memorize–regurgitate–repeat. No teacher ever asked me what I thought, only what I knew, and so I learned to study by cramming facts into my brain, memorizing them, and spewing them out on cue. Looking back, I realized now how much I learned but how little I understood. When I became a teacher, I asked of my students what had been asked of me—give me the "right answer." My way of assessing a student's level of competence was based solely on how many correct answers they were able to provide. And, like many teachers of my generation, I thought that this was the goal. Give them the information, and see how much they can give back to you. Teach them what to think.

In 1991, the worldwide web became public, and in one fell swoop, the internet rained on our educational parade and changed the role of teachers forever. No longer were we needed to be the keepers of the facts, the givers of the lectures, because with one quick tap, swipe, or click, every bit of information our students could ever need to know was at their fingertips. And so curriculums, districts, and teachers needed to quickly figure out a way to adapt to this fast-paced information overload; they had to figure out a way to teach students not *what* to think, but *how* to think. Because in this fast-paced and ever-changing world, it is no longer enough for students to tell you what they know but what they think about what they know. This dramatic shift became a challenge for educators, particularly those who have been engrained in the "old-school" way of teaching knowledge and facts. And let's face it—"right and wrong" lessons are much easier to teach and much easier to mark.

Educators are now searching for ways to integrate deep learning and deep thinking into their curriculum. Fact-finding and memorizing have become a way of the past, and the need now is to focus on inquiry-based, student centered, process-based learning rather than product-based, teacher-directed, knowledge-based learning. Teach them to uncover the facts rather than covering them; teach them *how* to think rather than *what* to think. For students to be successful in their adult lives, they need to learn how to become independent thinkers, to articulate their

(Continued)

(Continued)

perspectives, to question, to adapt, to succeed through failure, to con-
front ethical issues, and to problem-solve. These essential soft skills are
not found within the pages of a textbook but rather through experiences
in classrooms where thinking is at the center, where critical and creative
thinking are encouraged, and where students experience learning
through the lens of a constructivist pedagogy.

Literacy and Learners
With Exceptionalities

Second-language learners. Although most researchers and
educators agree that a strong basis of literacy in one language
(L1) can help facilitate a stronger basis in a second language
(L2), "current global migration patterns have led to a situation
where many migrants need to achieve some sort of L2 literacy
without being literate in their L1" (Paran & Wallace, 2016, p.
442). For those students who do have a measure of literacy in
their own native languages, researchers suggest that they be
allowed to identify the strategies they use in that L1 and work to
apply them in the L2. This requires encouraging students to
work between their respective languages while reading, writing,
listening, and speaking as opposed to requiring them to keep
them distinct. Experts remind teachers that context is critical,
and culture is often a driving force in the classroom and should
not be ignored or assumed (Smagorinsky, 2018).

In their article on preparing teachers for equitable inclusive
classes, authors Coady et al. (2015) recommended that teachers
who are working with second-language learners obtain skills in
three primary areas. They need to understand how language is
learned and the role of language and culture in a classroom. To
do so, first, they should learn how languages work and the
influence of a first language on the acquisition of future languages. Second, they should understand that language is both
the content and medium for learning. Third, they need to employ
effective instructional practices that recognize the need for differentiation, accessibility, and opportunities for group learning.
Currently, it appears that most teachers resort to typical
instructional practices instead of planning proactively for the
second-language learners' linguistic development through differentiated instruction or assessment (Coady et al., 2015).
Instead, teachers should engage in activities (such as surveys,
games, and discussion groups) that allow them to obtain information about their students' cultures, backgrounds, home
languages, parents' educational level and involvement, and

learning preferences (Alasim, 2019). This will help them develop appropriate literacy and learning activities for their students.

Students with disabilities. Intentional planning of instruction around literacy goals is critical for students with exceptionalities (disabilities, sensory differences, giftedness, second-language learners). Teachers cannot simply implement general "best practices" and expect them to work for all students (Coady et al., 2015). Spencer offered a poignant metaphor for why literacy skills, and in her example specifically writing, are so important for students with disabilities. She wrote,

> *Writing is, indeed, a very big deal for many kids, especially for those with learning challenges and disabilities. In some ways, writing an essay is like constructing a building: you need exceedingly strong foundational materials, all of which need to be functioning exceedingly well in order for the building to stand. If a single beam or girder is faulty, the whole thing can tumble. Just like a building, writing involves a slew of foundational skills (spelling, vocabulary, fine motor skills, and sequencing, to name a few), all of which need to be functioning efficiently for a student's writing to succeed. Additionally, for a student to be a competent writer, all of these foundational systems need to work simultaneously. That's the challenge of writing—it involves an enormous amount of cognitive and physical resources, all of which need to function at one time. If we return to our building metaphor, it's as though we are asking our kids to mix the mortar, lay the bricks, operate the steam shovel to dig the foundation, and bury the rebar, all at the same time. For those of us who write well, all of our foundational systems interact seamlessly to allow us to imagine, plan, sequence, recall, spell, and operate a pencil simultaneously as we get our thoughts on paper. For kids with disabilities, these coinciding demands are frequently overwhelming. (2015, pp. 6–7)*

Clearly, teachers in inclusive settings need to be prepared to break down skills, provide additional scaffolding (such as explicit instruction, graphic organizers, additional time, clear directions, and peer supports), and offer accommodations and modifications as appropriate (Alasim, 2019). The positive aspects of inclusive education increase when teachers are able to provide the appropriate supports and services to students (Toews & Kurth, 2019), but this may require teachers to obtain additional instruction on what those supports and services may entail. Because disabilities and students' needs vary so much, experts like Spencer and others strongly recommend using a

MAKING CONNECTIONS

Chapter 6 provides information and strategies about UDL and its application to the inclusive classroom.

Universal Design for Learning (UDL) approach to providing supports so they are accessible to all students, regardless of special need. You can read more about UDL in Chapter 6.

While some disabilities, such as learning disabilities (LDs), attention deficit/ hyperactivity disorder (ADD/ADHD), and emotional or behavior disorders (EBDs) are more common in classrooms and can often be addressed with simple accommodations, other disabilities may require more specific or specialized modifications or adaptations. Proponents of inclusive education emphasize that these specialized supports can still be provided in the general education environment. Two examples of disabilities that may require more intensive intervention when it comes to literacy are students who have more extensive support needs (e.g., those with intellectual disabilities and those who communicate nonverbally or through augmentative or assistive technology) and those students who are Deaf or Hard of Hearing (D/HH).

Toews and Kurth (2019) have reminded readers that literacy includes listening, speaking, and interacting, as well as reading and writing, and highlighted the need for literacy skills not only for academics but also for employment and for interacting in typical school, home, and community activities. Although additional research is needed on literacy instruction for students with extensive support needs in inclusive settings, current research-based literacy strategies for this population include time delay and systemic prompting, shared story reading, repeated reading, graphic organizers, and age-appropriate texts (Toews & Kurth, 2019). Research has found that students with significant disabilities are 10 times more likely to be exposed to academic literacy instruction when in inclusive general education settings than those students who are in self-contained or pull-out special education settings (Ruppar et al., 2018). Because it is clear that reading, writing, and speaking are significantly influenced by a learner's surroundings, all students—including those with significant disabilities—need the opportunity to be in environments rich in text, language, and writing and in which literacy is clearly valued for *all* students.

Students who are D/HH, who are increasingly included in general education classes, often struggle with literacy (Alasim, 2019). These students "have a variety of language histories, learning needs, and communication preferences" (Dostal et al., 2017, p. 1). Some D/HH students may have learned language through visual means (such as a signed language), whereas others have been taught to sight or lipread, and still others may have been exposed to language through the filter of a hearing aid or cochlear implant. For those D/HH students who are in an inclusive setting, educators must remember that their needs and communication preferences are as varied as a class is diverse. Simply providing an interpreter is insufficient for many and doesn't truly provide access to language. Dostal and colleagues (2017) identified two primary principles that apply both to D/HH students and to many students with special needs: optimize access and make content and thinking visible. The first (optimize access) links nicely to the concept of UDL, which is described in Chapter 6, whereas the second (make content and thinking visible) aligns with support for a constructivist philosophy. Both of these principles are supportive of the majority of learners in an inclusive class, and strategies related to their implementation are offered in Table 8.1. There is no surprise these go hand in hand as "UDL supports constructivist learning principles" (Dalton, 2017, p. 17).

Table 8.1

Strategies for Supporting Literacy Through Two Principles

Principle One: Optimize Access
Inquire about students' language history and communication preferences.
Set a classroom expectation for having only one speaker at a time with a brief pause between speakers. This is helpful as a strategy both in person and when teaching online or in a hybrid situation.
Repeat questions and comments verbatim when there is naturally overlapping or rapidly occurring classroom talk. This is supportive of students with language, hearing, learning, and attentional deficits.
Create a nonverbal cue that allows students to ask for clarification without calling attention to themselves. This avoids stigma and embarrassment.
Make sure you understand the purpose and function of accommodations or assistive technology students may use. Support other students as they learn them also because they may be able to provide the most natural of peer supports.
Remember that the common accommodation of "preferential seating," often provided to students who are D/HH or who struggle with behavior or attention, is not only for whole-group instruction, but it also applies to small-group and independent work. Consider what preferential seating might look like when applied to an online format.

(Continued)

Table 8.1

Strategies for Supporting Literacy Through Two Principles (Continued)

Principle Two: Make Content and Thinking Visible
Support visual cues for word learning. This provides multiple means of representation.
Create visual representations for oral explanations. For example, instead of using a brief oral aside, you might keep a whiteboard or chart paper nearby during read-alouds so that you can briefly pause, write the word on the board or paper, and discuss its definition in context out loud.
Construct written records of think-alouds. When teachers make their thinking visible by creating model written responses, the quality of written responses among all students will rise.
Invest in extended conversation to enhance word knowledge. Extended explanations only take an additional moment, but they ensure repeated exposure to new vocabulary (before, during, and after reading), which supports more efficient acquisition for all students.
Use semantic mapping. This allows teachers to visually capture multiple, meaningful connections to new words and word meanings. Semantic mapping exposes students to various forms of a word and helps them build meaning with a visual graphic that assists them in identifying, understanding, and recalling words in text.

Source: Adapted from Dostal et al, 2017.

Using Technology to Support the Development of Literacy

Technology has provided a wider array of readers in addition to a wider array of writing possibilities. Students can write blogs, post threads on social media websites, email, respond in tweets, create cartoons and memes, or even self-publish entire books. Pen pals can be self-created or identified by partnering schools across the world, and responses can be instantaneous. Generative AI (e.g., ChatGPT, Bing) offers myriad writing opportunities when presented with strong prompts. In addition, the use of assistive technology such as speech to text, text to speech, spellcheck, graphic organizers, and so on have significantly and positively provided access to writing for those who may have heretofore struggled (Spencer, 2015). Students with significant and complex communication needs include those who are nonverbal or who communicate primarily through augmentative or alternative communication means, such as with high-tech, low-tech, or no-tech communication devices. Too often, these students are denied education with their grade-level peers due to these communication needs despite clear evidence that context and environment play such significant roles in literacy attainment (Toews & Kurth, 2019).

As demands to increase writing across the curriculum continue to grow, and as classes continue to become more diverse, technology is simply no longer an option; it is a necessity. Teachers need to familiarize themselves with the hardware, software, and internet applications that can support students with everything from letter formation to idea generation to written expression. This is often easier said than done. In addition to identifying the different technological tools necessary for different students' needs, teachers need to have the ability to then use those tools appropriately. Regan and colleagues also emphasized that "planning for classwide mobile technology implementation in the classroom should not be underestimated. Implementation requires first learning the technology and learning how to evaluate its use" (2018, p. 12). Even then, educators need to identify who would benefit from what, when, and how it will be used. As with all aspects of literacy instruction, there is no one-size-fits-all solution, and technology is not a quick fix. It is, however, a critical tool when determining how to support the development of students' reading and writing.

The Role of Meta-Cognition in Literacy Development

Thinking is the foundation of any classroom (Gear, 2018), and thinking is obviously critical when it comes to literacy. Integrating thinking into all aspects of your classroom and teaching is essential. Talking about thinking, making thinking visible, and providing students with a language to articulate their thinking in reading, writing, and the content areas are important first steps in building this foundation. By transforming this abstract concept of thinking into something concrete, we can begin to help our students construct meaning in all areas of their learning.

METACOGNITION INVOLVES:
- Awareness of thinking
- Thinking about your thinking
- Articulating thinking

Strategies to Support Thinking and Meta-Cognition in Literacy

BY ADRIENNE GEAR

WHAT DOES THINKING ABOUT LITERACY LOOK LIKE?

With older students, introduce metacognition by inviting them first to draw a picture of an apple on a piece of paper. After a few minutes of drawing, invite the students to share and compare their apple picture with a partner. Once they share, discuss the fact that drawing an apple was a relatively easy task: most drew a round shape with a stem, a leaf, and possibly some shading or a shiny spot. Ask them why it is easy to draw an apple. Discuss the fact that it is something we have all seen before; therefore, it is easy to draw.

Source: Photo by Adrienne Gear.

Next, invite them to draw a picture of thinking. Most will draw a thinking bubble, but after explaining that this is more of a symbol and that thinking does not actually happen in a bubble in the air, invite them to draw what they think thinking looks like inside someone's head. After sharing and comparing, discuss the fact that it was more challenging than drawing an apple because we can't see thinking. From there, explain thinking as an important part of literacy (reading, writing, speaking, listening), but because we can't see it, it becomes rather challenging. "What does thinking look like?" Tell them you are going to show them inside someone's brain!

Create a visual of a person's head (a real person or an imaginary one), and introduce the five reading strategies, or "reading powers": connect, question, visualize, infer, and transform (McLeod, 2019). Explain that when someone is reading, these five strategies help them think about the story and that is what helps make the story more meaningful. Ask the students if they have ever read a book but realized that they were not actually thinking about the story but about something else. They were still "reading" but not understanding. These five reading strategies can help readers stay focused and pay attention to their thinking so that they aren't only reading the words but making meaning. Next, ask students how they might apply those reading powers to also help them with their writing as well as with their own listening and speaking skills!

WHAT DOES THINKING ABOUT LITERACY SOUND LIKE?

The visual or poster described can certainly help answer the question, "What does thinking look like?" You can take that a step further by exploring the question, "What does thinking sound like?" Developing a language for thinking in your classroom and modeling that language as often as you can is one of the most effective ways to promote meta-cognition you can use. Create an anchor chart (see the example) with thinking prompts or cues as a reminder to your students and yourself what thinking sounds like. Use this language as often as you can, while you teach and encourage your students to do the same.

WHAT DOES THINKING SOUND LIKE?

Anchor Chart

That reminds me of...

I'm thinking...

I'm wondering...

I'm noticing...

Maybe...

I'm picturing...

I learned that...

I'm figuring out...

I'm feeling...

I used to think... but now I'm thinking....

Constructing Meaning in the Content Areas

For many teachers, if a child can read a book and then describe what it was about in their own words, there is an assumption that child understood the story. If they got 50/50 on their multiple-choice Social Studies test, teachers assume they understood the content. More veteran teachers recognize that there are different levels of understanding. A literal under-standing, or the ability to retell or summarize information is what Gear (2018) has referred to as a basic "Level One" understanding. Although retelling and summarizing require intellect and skill, there is more to understanding than the simply retelling the content. This would equate to the first levels of the cognitive process dimension of Bloom's Revised Taxonomy, which essentially require students only to "remember" (e.g., list, recognize, recall, identify) or to "under-stand" (summarize, classify, clarify, predict; Anderson et al., 2001).

Of more interest to teachers should be whether the student has constructed meaning, interacted with the text or the informa-tion, and added their thinking, made connections, wondered, inferred, or visualized. A "Level Two" understanding, therefore, is if a student could make a connection, ask a question, or draw some inference from the text (Gear, 2018). This aligns with the next levels of Bloom's Revised Taxonomy as well, requiring students to "apply, analyze, and evaluate." Action words associated with each are apply (respond, provide, carry out, use), analyze (select, differentiate, integrate, deconstruct), and evaluate (select, determine, judge, reflect; Anderson et al., 2001).

"Level Three" understanding, the final "nudge of thinking," is when a child is able to transform their thinking into new understanding (Gear, 2018). This is the highest level of thinking and one that requires a learner to reflect on how their thinking has shifted or changed. In Bloom's Revised Taxonomy, this would be the "create" dimension (generate, assemble, design, create). Although this may be challenging, providing concrete activities that scaffold thinking and encouraging students to move beyond a literal interpretation can be the starting point to achieving this level of understanding (Hyland, 2011). Using these strategies, and recognizing not only how critical literacy is—but more importantly, how diverse it and our students are—will help educators find success in their own literacy endeavors.

LIFE SKILLS AND SOCIAL-EMOTIONAL LEARNING

Defining Social-Emotional Learning

Social-emotional learning (SEL) is not a new concept, nor is it foreign to most American educators. In fact, in an evidence brief created by the RAND Organization, authors noted, "Although ESSA (Elementary and Secondary Schools Act) does not explicitly reference SEL, its policy language includes calls for improving school conditions for student learning; enhancing peer interactions; providing a well-rounded education; and incorporating programs and activities that promote volunteerism, community involvement, or instructional practices for developing relationship-building skills. These are all related to SEL" (Grant et al., 2017, p. 2). In 2019, the National Practitioner Advisory Group reported that in more than half of the United States, "SEL standards link student behaviors to research-based outcomes intending to increase attendance, reduce bullying incidents, shrink suspensions, and generate fewer office referrals" (as cited in Gimbert et al., 2023, p. 3). Clearly then, SEL is a major component of a solid education for American students.

Naturally, SEL is not the only—or even primary—focus of schools. All teachers should be familiar with their curricular standards. Forty-one states, the District of Columbia, four territories, and the Department of Defense Education Activity have adopted the Common Core Standards (www.thecorestandards.org), whereas other states use their own standards (e.g., Virginia has the Standards of Learning; Texas has the Texas Essential Knowledge and Skills) that emphasize necessary curriculum. Naturally, schools most typically keep their primary focus on the academic performance of their students. Educators constantly seek strategies on how to improve academic outcomes, and student performance is constantly measured and assessed. Yet educational researchers, policymakers, and practitioners are increasingly recognizing the impact SEL has on students' academic and behavioral outcomes in schools as well as their future as engaged and involved citizens. These concerns are slowly making their way into policy; for example, "in 2019 Washington State enacted a Social Emotional Learning bill, that included the establishment of a social emotional learning committee, in addition to a Children's Mental Health bill. Though few in number, these resolutions demonstrate a trend in recognizing the importance of addressing students' social-emotional health and well-being and its direct impact on students' academic and behavioral successes in school" (Rodriguez & Murawski, 2022, p. 501). It is becoming abundantly clear—especially after the COVID-19 pandemic and the increase of school violence and trauma—SEL simply cannot be pushed to the side; it needs to be incorporated into our daily schoolwork.

In this chapter, we define SEL and the benefits of prioritizing and making room for evidence-based strategies on social development and well-being. Note that Chapter 3 on applied behavior analysis (ABA) and Chapter 7 on cooperative learning also contain strategies that support the development of pro-social skills and can work complementary to SEL. In addition, schools that are already implementing Positive Behavior Intervention and Supports (PBIS; Chapter 3) and/or the Multi-Tiered System of Supports will find that aligning SEL strategies into the school's culture is much easier to do and sustain (CASEL, 2018).

Social-emotional learning (SEL) is the process through which we understand and manage emotions, set and achieve goals, feel and show empathy, establish and maintain relationships, and make decisions.

The most well-known, research-based organization focused on SEL is called Collaborative for Academic, Social and Emotional Learning (CASEL). CASEL was established in 1994, almost at the same time as SEL initiated its development as a key element needed in schools. We use the CASEL definition for SEL: "SEL is the process through which children and adults understand and manage emotions, set and achieve positive goals, feel and show empathy for others, establish and maintain positive relationships, and make responsible decisions" (CASEL, 2020b).

Historical Perspective on SEL

SEL has its historical base in the research on emotional intelligence (EI). The term EQ was first coined by Reuven Bar-on in 1985 from *emotional quotient*, a way to assess based on a standardized score like IQ. A paper by Salovey and Mayer in 1990 is often considered the origin of the construct of EI. In that paper and subsequent scientific articles, the authors present and propose a framework for EI. They define emotional intelligence as "the subset of social intelligence that involves the ability to monitor one's own and others' feelings and emotions, to discriminate among them and to use this information to guide one's thinking and actions" (Salovey & Mayer, 1990). Daniel Goleman (1995), however, is credited with bringing the concepts of EI and EQ (which have been frequently interchanged) to the mainstream through his 1995 book *Emotional Intelligence: Why It Can Matter More Than IQ*. There is an obvious link then between those individuals with strong EI and those who possess excellent SEL skills.

In 1997, CASEL introduced SEL as a field for educators through the book *Promoting Social and Emotional Learning: Guidelines for Educators* (Elias et al., 1997). This text provided additional information on the importance of SEL and its need to be included in every K–12 classroom. Whole-school evidence-based SEL programs have been integrated in and adapted to the regular and complex school environments in some districts (e.g., Chu & DeArmond, 2021; Oberle et al., 2019; Porche et al., 2014); however, they are not yet common practice and, recently, controversy has surrounded the inclusion of SEL into the school day.

The most current issues and controversy around SEL—leading to bills in eight states at the writing of this book to limit or ban SEL—include that the programs are part of a "woke agenda" to teach progressive ideas in school (e.g., critical race theory and gender diversity) and that they distract from academics (American Psychological Association, 2023). Much of the controversy stems from a lack of real understanding regarding what SEL entails and the politicizing of the term.

> Yet data show that families, lawmakers, and communities do value the principles underlying SEL. ... In a nationally representative survey commissioned by the Thomas B. Fordham Institute, an education policy think tank, parents overwhelmingly wanted schools to teach the skills that SEL emphasizes, including managing emotions and communicating with peers (Fordham Institute, 2021).
>
> (as cited in American Psychological Association, 2023)

Overwhelmingly, the preferred term for parents, regardless of political party, has been *life skills*. So, now you know why that term is added to the title of this chapter! We promise we are not making any kind of political statement. Our focus, and the focus we espouse for all educators, is to help students with setting and achieving goals, improving their understanding of emotions, building empathy and tolerance, navigating social situations, improving their problem-solving skills, and increasing their own self-efficacy and self-worth. We believe all educators and families concur these are worthwhile skills—no matter what they are called.

Benefits and Barriers to SEL

Benefits of SEL. A meta-analysis of 213 SEL programs found that school-based universal social and emotional learning programs improve social and emotional skills, attitudes, behavior, and academic performance (Durlak et al., 2011). Some of the programs included in the meta-analysis were conducted by schoolteachers, whereas others were delivered by nonschool personnel (e.g., consultants, researchers). Interesting from a school perspective is that the programs run by teachers from the schools were effective in all of the categories that were measured. Academic performance is clearly important in schools, and SEL programs significantly improved academic performance but primarily when the programs were conducted by the school staff themselves (Durlak et al., 2011). This is important to readers because it emphasizes the need for buy-in and utilization of SEL programs and strategies by teachers themselves.

Research shows long-term positive effects for school-based SEL programs. In fact, the best and most impactful effects were on academic performance, which demonstrates the link between SEL and academics. The programs demonstrated positive effects for all subgroups (Taylor et al., 2017). That indicates that SEL programs can be helpful for supporting a diverse classroom with students of varying needs, abilities, and exceptionalities.

Social-emotional competence is an important factor for reducing problem and disruptive behavior among students in schools. In a review that covered more than 300 studies and 300,000 students, the level of students' social-emotional competence was the strongest predictor for positive effects on behavior (Domitrovich et al., 2017). The takeaway here is that, by proactively addressing students' social-emotional competence, educators can positively influence the behaviors in their classes and ultimately the students' learning and success. Students' social-emotional skills are not merely "fluffy," "soft skills," or kind things to do; they are inherently linked to students' behavior and academic outcomes.

Six school SEL programs from different countries were reviewed from an economical perspective. Is it even worth spending the money to implement these programs? The short answer was yes. The most important finding was that the measurable benefits exceeded the costs. On average, for every invested Swedish crown (krona), the programs gave a return of 11 crowns (Belfield et al., 2015); that's like going from 10 cents to $1.05 in American dollars. That is not a bad return on investment!

Barriers. Although teachers can implement SEL strategies individually, successful SEL programs normally require a whole-school approach. The school also needs a program implementation of high quality. This means support from school leaders to allocate resources that are needed and to secure professional development for all the educators who will conduct the program selected (Chu & DeArmond, 2021; Oberle et al., 2019; Rimm-Kaufman & Hulleman, 2015). Not surprisingly, even the most well-meaning of teachers might get disgruntled if there is no administrative or school support in place.

A school environment is complex, and all schools have to make priorities. Even when a school has made SEL a priority, the program might need to be adapted to fit in with the current school culture, organization, and resources. This can be successfully accomplished, but the school might require some external SEL expertise support to maintain the active ingredients of the program when adapting it. To achieve all the possible positive outcomes of an SEL program, this cannot be viewed as a quick fix. Both as an educator and as a school leader, one must be patient and focus on sustainability and quality (Durlak, 2015). In general, the most often heard barriers to the implementation of SEL programs are cost, the time requirement, a lack of professional development, and the need for consistent buy-in.

Best Practice Components of Effective SEL Programs

Educators in every school have to make tough priority decisions each day. They have many tasks to fulfill, and it can feel overwhelming to add one more to the list. Although the demonstrated SEL benefits exceed its costs, it is not easy to implement new initiatives and activities. While SEL activities can serve as a natural part of the school curriculum, most school days are already busy with instruction on academic subjects. Therefore, an SEL program that can be included in the regular teaching of subjects will likely be preferred by both educators and school

MAKING CONNECTIONS

Chapter 3 on applied behavior analysis describes a framework for implementing whole-school intervention approaches that are responsive to individual needs. The strategies for creating cooperative learning opportunities in Chapter 7 can be helpful in promoting social-emotional learning.

leaders than an add-on or supplement. Strategies whose implementation save time and reduce stress, while still meeting the SEL criteria, are optimal.

A good example of an evidence based SEL-program that meets those criteria is called the RULER. Developed at the Yale Center for Emotional Intelligence, the name RULER uses a mnemonic (a memory trick) that stands for *Recognizing* emotions, *Understanding* emotions—including identifying their source and their influence on our behavior, *Labeling* emotions with a nuanced vocabulary, *Expressing* emotions adapted to the context, and *Regulating* emotions instead of being regulated by them (Brackett, 2019). These five actions are the core skills in developing emotional competence (Brackett & Kremenitzer, 2011).

RULER MNEMONIC

Recognizing emotions
Understanding emotions
Labeling emotions
Expressing emotions
Regulating emotions

(Brackett, 2019)

Once students have been taught how to recognize and understand their emotions, they need the academic vocabulary to label them. Labeling emotions has a key role, like a midfielder in soccer, because of how it links *Recognizing* and *Understanding* to *Expressing* and *Regulating*. Once labeled, students can use that vocabulary to express their emotions in the situation and then use that knowledge to regulate them as needed. In the book *Permission to Feel*, Brackett (2019) highlighted the importance of learning to label emotions and how that ability also can serve as a way of regulating those emotions.

In the RULER approach, the process begins with teachers. The first step is to give the educators the tools they need, which means personal and professional development. When a school wants to start using the RULER approach, it begins with a year of personal and professional learning for the school staff. The next step is to start working with the students through direct instruction in emotion vocabulary (Hoffman et al., 2020). The work with students focuses on emotional literacy that will be integrated in the academic classroom. Three main tools or anchors used are the classroom charter, the mood meter, and the emotional literacy blueprint.

The classroom charter. For a positive and functional classroom climate, both students and staff need to be in agreement on what defines their best classroom. Everyone needs to identify mutual values and goals for their classroom. When a class is about to create their charter within the RULER approach, students are asked how they would like to feel during interactions with their teachers and classmates and what emotions they think are important for success in school. A classroom charter is created to demonstrate a shared classroom vision. Within the program, it is also common to expand from the classroom charter to a school-wide charter.

In Chapter 3 on ABA, we introduced the concept of PBIS. Under a PBIS framework, school values are defined in every context of the school. These values can be set up exactly as the classroom charter. Chapter 3 also introduced the Good Behavior Game as positive ways to reinforce desirable behavior. These approaches help teachers create a vision for their classroom, the same way as the classroom charter establishes a vision. The classroom charter is based on feelings and emotions; how does this class and actions within it make the students and teachers feel? All of these strategies can easily be combined. If you are already working with some sort of positive behavior support philosophy, the SEL approach of RULER will fit nicely.

Consider this application: A school that has embraced PBIS on a school-wide level selects "Show kindness" and "Be responsible" as its two key school values. Next, the school staff, along with the students, create a classroom vision. If this school also was aiming at implementing the RULER approach, they would start making a classroom charter based on the two school values that are already agreed upon in a process together with students and staff. They would then follow the RULER process for the vision based on how the students and teachers should feel as well as what that vision would allow you to hear, see, and do. In this way the classroom charter and overall vision would be based on what showing kindness and taking responsibility would feel like, look like, sound like, and what students will be doing to demonstrate those values. Both the SEL strategy of RULER and the aforementioned ABA-based strategies are student centered. All aim at improving self-regulation and result in sustainable outcomes.

The mood meter. In their book about the RULER strategy, Brackett and Kremenitzer (2011) introduced the mood meter by arguing that *identifying and discussing how everyone in the classroom community—students and teachers—are feeling is the core of developing emotional literacy.* The mood meter is a tool that teachers can use in the classroom with students for the development of emotional awareness and self-regulation of emotions.

The Mood Meter From *Permission to Feel*

Enraged	Panicked	Stressed	Jittery	Shocked	Surprised	Upbeat	Festive	Exhilarated	Ecstatic
Livid	Furious	Frustrated	Tense	Stunned	Hyper	Cheerful	Motivated	Inspired	Elated
Fuming	Frightened	Angry	Nervous	Restless	Energized	Lively	Excited	Optimistic	Enthusiastic
Anxious	Apprenhensive	Worried	Irratated	Annoyed	Pleased	Focused	Happy	Proud	Thrilled
Repulsed	Troubled	Concerned	Uneasy	Peeved	Pleasant	Joyful	Hopeful	Playful	Blissful
Disgusted	Glum	Disappointed	Down	Apathetic	At Ease	Easygoing	Content	Loving	Fulfilled
Pessimistic	Morose	Discouraged	Sad	Bored	Calm	Secure	Satisfied	Grateful	Touched
Alienated	Misrable	Lonely	Disheartened	Tired	Relaxed	Chill	Restful	Blessed	Balanced
Despondent	Depressed	Sullen	Exhausted	Fatiguied	Mellow	Thoughtful	Peaceful	Comfortable	Carefree
Despair	Hopeless	Desolate	Spent	Drained	Sleepy	Complacent	Tranquil	Cozy	Serene

HIGH ENERGY — LOW ENERGY

LOW PLEASANTNESS — HIGH PLEASANTNESS

Source: Marc Brackett, 2019. Reprinted with permission.

You can use the mood meter as a tool with a whole group. You can try to work with your class to shift their current mood on the mood meter into a more desired mood (= the desired quadrant of the mood meter). Consider this: your class arrives back from lunch with many students stressed, restless, and anxious, although you are about to start a lesson where you'd prefer that they be calm and relaxed. Based on the mood meter, you might choose to start the lesson with a mindfulness or a breathing exercise. You need to know your students to choose the most adequate activity. The main message is that educators can use the mood meter for feedback to make adaptations and take the actions needed to give students the best conditions for a successful lesson.

From a mood and emotional perspective, you might notice that your students have such different needs and moods that a whole-group activity simply will not work. Then it is nice that you have more strategies in your toolkit, isn't it? You can organize your classroom so that it can meet a number of different sensory motor needs at the same time (see Chapter 1 on sensory motor development), or use cooperative learning strategies (see Chapter 7) and UDL strategies (see Chapter 6) to give your students opportunities based on those differing needs. You might even break the class into small groups with your co-teacher (see Chapter 5). Note that "based on their needs" does not mean you have to create individual solutions for each student. It means to work on a group level using a perspective (UDL and cooperative learning) that can be helpful in managing a diverse classroom; making use of the mood meter concurrently can assist you in training students on their own self-regulation and emotional awareness.

The emotional literacy blueprint. The emotional literacy blueprint is a tool for problem-solving when in emotionally challenging situations. The blueprint also has a function for training the development of SEL skills. At the beginner's level in the RULER approach, the blueprint contains five questions with student response as a base for the process. The questions are: *(1) What happened? (2) How did I feel? (3) What caused me to feel this way? (4) How did I express and regulate my feelings? (5) What could I have done better?* (Brackett & Kremenitzer, 2011). Ultimately, the blueprint approach is a way to prompt student self-reflection and help with conflict management. The questions help students gain a new perspective and prompt empathy. Restorative practices have a similar purpose and are increasing in use in schools. These practices may include restorative conversations, circles, and conferences and may be both informal or formal in nature. They include both proactive practices and responsive practices that respond to conflict with the goal of repairing harm and rebuilding relationships (CASEL, 2020a).

RESTORATIVE PRACTICES

An emerging social science that studies how to strengthen relationships between individuals as well as develop social connections within communities. In schools, restorative practices help to create a trusting environment by giving both students and adults an opportunity to make positive choices and interact respectfully in the classroom and throughout the school.

(CASEL, 2020a)

The feeling words curriculum. When students don't have words to express how and what they feel, it can often lead to miscommunication and conflict. Feelings can also be suppressed. Students need words to express their feelings and the feelings they observe in others in addition to being able to express their thoughts. Within the RULER approach, students develop a feeling-words curriculum from kindergarten to eighth grade. This curriculum is developed to enhance emotional literacy being integrated into the school's regular curriculum. The feeling-words curriculum was developed for the United States, but it can serve as a model for other international school contexts.

To implement the feeling-words curriculum in the classroom, Hoffman et al. (2020) described a process that follows four steps where the aim is for the students to learn 12 emotion words per year in grades K–5:

1. "Teachers and students share stories about times they have experienced the feeling;

2. Teachers infuse the feeling word into the standard curriculum (e.g., character analysis);

3. Students teach the feeling word to family members; and

4. Students participate in "strategy sessions" to brainstorm helpful emotion regulation strategies in small groups or creative activities."

(Hoffman et al., 2020)

Implementing this type of curriculum into an academic one needs to be intentional, but it needn't be time-consuming or overwhelming. The need to use academic language when working with students is well-known by teachers. This merely asks you to be thoughtful about integrating emotions-related terms into your typical repertoire. For some, it may also support teachers themselves in helping identify their own emotions!

Professional development. Teachers have always been faced with the social-emotional needs of their students. Even educators who have never seen research on SEL or have never been able to attend professional development on the topic have had a student who is crying or angry or excited. Teachers recognize that it is simply impossible to teach only academics in today's inclusive classrooms. In a typical day, most teachers need to take the role of nurses, therapists, police, and parents. Clearly then, the need for SEL strategies is strong.

We don't want readers to feel like addressing students' SEL needs are "one more weight on my shoulders." As you are likely already are doing some work in your classroom that addresses students' social-emotional needs, a good first step is merely the awareness of SEL. Once you are more aware of what SEL entails, you can identify the SEL elements you already have in place. We promise they are there! Why not create a vision for your classroom together with your students? Don't have a feeling-words curriculum? No problem. You can still get started using the process described here. An excellent resource to learn more about SEL is through CASEL (https://casel.org/).

Getting Started With SEL

Ready to get serious about addressing your students' SEL needs? Check out the book *Creating Emotionally Literate Classrooms* by Brackett and Kremenitzer (2011). This text offers an introduction to the RULER approach mentioned previously. In addition, the authors give four recommendations regarding how teachers can prepare to implement an SEL program. Their recommendations include: (1) enhance your own emotional literacy, (2) strengthen your relationships with students, (3) hold regular class meetings, and (4) lead open class discussions. The authors also point out that there is not one "right" way to include emotional literacy for students. Teachers need to take into consideration that every student, educator, and school is unique. Feel free to adapt how you include emotional literacy, but at the same time strive to follow the key principles of the program.

A few years later, Brackett (2019) suggested that including an additional step prior to number one ("enhance your own emotional literacy"). He recommended that at the start of the whole development process, educators simply need to give themselves "the permission to feel" (Brackett, 2019). Although this may not seem challenging, it actually may be a difficult task for some educators. Worried about bringing feelings into the classroom? They are already there! Now is the time to acknowledge those feelings—those of teachers and of students.

Class meetings and open class discussions about feelings and social issues are helpful with SEL but can also be challenging. Educators can benefit from implementing other strategies in this book to help ensure discussions are inclusive and well managed. Two chapters that offer related strategies are Chapter 4 on communication and Chapter 7 on cooperative learning. In addition, when you want to work on strengthening relationships with your students, Chapter 2 on formative assessment offers ways to use different kinds of feedback that can be beneficial. As you can see, the different strategies in this book are complementary to each other and can often have positive synergistic effects. Remember, you are building your own teacher's toolkit; we encourage you to reach in frequently and pull out anything you need!

School Leader Spotlight

SEL is best as a whole-school initiative. For a sustainable result, support from school leadership is crucial. Teachers need opportunities for professional development and mutual time for reflection. As a school leader, you have the challenging task of identifying the top priorities for your school. *Managing* a school is about ensuring the effectiveness in what is being done, but *leading* a school is about ensuring the prioritization of what needs to be done; ultimately, this is about prioritizing the right things (Covey, 2013). Each school has its own unique organization, conditions, resources, and challenges, and a leader's job is adapting programs and curricula to match those unique elements. Select an evidence-based SEL program that you believe in, and work with your school colleagues to help fit it into your school culture.

Recommended readings for school leaders include the two books mentioned previously: *Permission to Feel* (Brackett, 2019) and *Creating Emotionally Literate Classrooms: An Introduction to The RULER Approach to Social and Emotional Learning* (Brackett & Kremenitzer, 2011). For those who would like a more in-depth overview of SEL, the *Handbook of Social and Emotional Learning* (Durlak et al., 2015) is a strong choice.

TIME MANAGEMENT

Defining Time Management

Time management refers to how we use available time. It can be viewed and experienced in several ways depending on different perspectives and disciplines. It might focus on how to structure personal time, but it can also involve how we prioritize activities or arrange them within our day, given our personal strengths and preferences. Good time management requires the ability to estimate the time to accomplish different tasks and how to use that knowledge to effectively organize one's activities most efficiently.

Although there are a number of ways to define time management, we have selected one that is complex enough to cover different perspectives. Thus, for the purpose of this chapter, time management is defined as "a form of decision making used by individuals to structure, protect, and adapt their time to changing conditions" (Aeon & Aguinis, 2017).

Time management is "a form of decision-making used by individuals to structure, protect, and adapt their time to changing conditions" (Aeon & Aguinis, 2017).

Historical Perspective on Time Management

How to manage time—especially at work—is not a new concept. Although it hasn't always been referred to as *time management*, the concept has been reflected upon and discussed for centuries. As early as the first century, renowned Roman philosopher Seneca wrote about how to best use time and avoid wasting it (Gribetz, 2018). In the beginning of the 20th century, Frederick Winslow Taylor developed a form of time management with focus on productivity and workflow at work places—initially in the steel industry. It was called *scientific management* and, in 1911, he published a book about that strategy that has since been bundled with his other works and republished (Taylor, 2003).

In modern times, Stephen Covey is probably one of the most well-known figures in discussions of time management. He has described the development of time management over the last decades as four "generations" of time management, which mimic development in society (Covey, 2013). Taylor's scientific management had its focus on checklists and detailed work procedures and was considered the first generation. The next generation was more proactive, focusing primarily on planning and scheduling using different types of calendars. The third generation, which is widely used today, focuses on setting the right priorities and valuing different activities based on those priorities. It includes setting goals and making daily plans toward reaching those goals. The fourth generation of time management focuses on managing ourselves rather time. It involves prioritizing what we value rather than merely focusing on setting a schedule and meeting goals (Covey, 2013). This fourth generation will be what we share and describe in this chapter, providing some new ideas and examples.

Benefits and Barriers to Time Management in Education

Benefits. In the past, efficient time management has been emphasized as a way to enhance job performance and make workers more efficient. However, a recent meta-analysis, which included outcomes from nearly 54,000 participants, found that time management skills had a greater effect on general well-being than it did on job performance (Aeon et al., 2021). In other words, time management seems to benefit our general life satisfaction to a greater extent than it improves our work productivity. The study further found that time management can relieve the stressful effects of high workloads even when workers have low autonomy (Aeon et al., 2021).

Even the best time managers have to deal with unexpected interruptions in their work and of their priorities. For example, a teacher might be in the middle of explaining a complex topic to their students, and someone interrupts class to ask a student to come to the front office. A principal might be trying to explain a new school policy to a group of parents, and one parent keeps interrupting with questions. Or perhaps a teacher is at home trying to plan lessons for the week, and their toddler keeps coming up to show their toys. Each of these interruptions stops workflow and increases time pressure to get tasks finished on time. The more they occur, the more pressure they exert. Fortunately, time management skills have been found to work as a protective measure to mitigate the negative impacts of such interruptions (Ma et al., 2020). In fact, research has found that time management skills may also be useful for other types of stress relief (Aeon & Aguinis, 2017).

Barriers. It is clear that good time management has a number of benefits, so what makes it so difficult to accomplish? Put simply, teachers need more time! A survey of more than 400 primary and lower secondary schoolteachers in Sweden found that almost 80% felt they lacked sufficient time to talk with colleagues about scheduling, teaching and learning issues, and school development. About 60% of the participants reported lacking sufficient time to talk about student issues (Schad, 2019). Without time for problem-solving and collaboration, teachers may feel they are on their own when it comes to solving complex problems, which may lead to feelings of isolation and burnout.

Research shows that there are at least four predictors of teacher burnout: discipline problems, time pressure, low student motivation, and value dissonance (Skaalvik & Skaalvik, 2017). Perhaps unsurprisingly, time pressure was the strongest predictor, with researchers reporting a high correlation between time pressure and emotional exhaustion (Skaalvik & Skaalvik, 2017). In another study, researchers examined the factors that affected teachers' perceptions of their work–life balance (Nilsson et al., 2016). Teachers' experiences with time at work—and whether they felt they had time to accomplish everything expected of them—was the most important factor in determining whether they had a good work–life balance. Taken together, these studies emphasize the impact that time, including the way it is used and managed, has on teachers' emotional well-being.

Another barrier to time management is that there is only so much time in the day, which may increase pressure to multitask, whereby we attempt to get multiple tasks done in the same space of time. However, despite feeling that we are accomplishing more, some researchers suggest that persistent multitasking can be self-defeating (Koch et al., 2018). In one study related to technology-related tasks, the impact on performance related significantly to the tasks' difficulty. For difficult tasks, multitasking resulted in lower performance, whereas for tasks considered easy, those who multitasked had higher performance (Adler et al., 2020). In other words, depending on the task, trying to do too much at one time might actually decrease the quality with which more difficult tasks are completed.

Caposey (2018) identified eight possible working styles that could exacerbate time management issues (Table 10.1) as well as some simple strategies to help mitigate the negative effects of those styles. For example, do you tend to start multiple tasks at one time but have a difficult time completing them? You might be a *Prisoner of the Moment.* Do you spend more time making checklists of little tasks that you need to do rather than focusing on the bigger picture of what needs to be accomplished? You could be on your way to being *checklist dependent*. Most of us have struggled with time management at some point in our working lives; finding out your typical patterns of responding could be helpful in identifying the best solutions, thereby reducing time pressure and improving your overall well-being.

Table 10.1

Working Styles Related to Time Management

WORKING STYLE	DESCRIPTION	STRATEGY
Work avoidant	Wants to avoid complex tasks; procrastinates & blames it on time	Build in small rewards to get started & to persist
People pleaser	Struggle to say no; tries to help everyone	Identify the purpose of each task; try to prioritize your own
Prisoner of the moment	Constantly starting new tasks & having ideas; doesn't finish one	Slow your brain; try yoga or meditation; check it off
Checklist dependent	Focused on mini-tasks over big-picture items	Create if/then lists to help prioritize most important
Disorganized	Loses time because can't find items; inefficient	Create systems to help with efficiency (e.g., piles)
Technology avoidant	Scared of technology so doesn't benefit from apps, lists, etc.	Get someone to teach you; use YouTube tutorials
Self-serving	Focus on what you want to do instead of need to do	Practice empathy; think of your actions' impact on others
Perpetually imbalanced	Flit from one priority to exclusion of others & back again	Find a combination schedule that works & stick to it

Source: Adapted from Caposey, P.J. (2018).

Best Practice Components of Effective Time Management

Although there are many time management strategies based on matrixes, this chapter will focus on a matrix based on Covey's Time Management, which appears in his book titled *The 7*

Table 10.2

Teachers' Priority Matrix

	NOT URGENT	URGENT
IMPORTANT	**A** **ACTIVITIES** Building and maintaining relations Physical activity Recreation Long-term planning Co-planning with colleagues Lesson tuning Reflection Development (professional, school)	**B** **ACTIVITIES** Crises or serious incidents Setting grades School requirements and projects with deadlines
NOT IMPORTANT	**D** **ACTIVITIES** Workflow interruptions such as emails, messages via your digital school platform, social media notices and messages, and phone calls Venting sessions Gossip Some school meetings	**C** **ACTIVITIES** Workflow interruptions such as text messages, emails, and phone calls Interruptions from colleagues Some school meetings

Source: Adapted from Covey, 1989.

Habits of Highly Effective People (2013). The goal of the matrix offered in Table 10.2 is to help teachers prioritize activities and use their time more wisely by categorizing tasks according to their urgency and their importance. Former U.S. President Dwight D. Eisenhower was famous for many things, and among these were his thoughts about time management. Eisenhower is cited as saying, "What is important is seldom urgent, and what is urgent is seldom important." Clearly, Eisenhower was an early proponent of fourth generation time management.

Teaching should be about educating, motivating, and engaging students. It is not likely that most educators joined the field eager to complete a lot of paperwork or do a bunch of grading. However, teachers can often be heard complaining that they spend more time on paperwork than they do on actual teaching. Look back at Eisenhower's quote. Although the paperwork may have a due date that makes it more "urgent," would anyone argue that it is more important that the actual time invested in

MAKING CONNECTIONS

Effective time management is difficult for most of us. You might try some of the self-assessment strategies described in Chapter 2 to track improvements in your time management skills.

front of pupils? Hopefully not. The rest of this chapter is aimed at helping educators identify ways to spend more time with students—and with family and friends—and less time worrying about how to manage other items that seem to suck one's time away.

Doing What Is Important, Not Only What Is Urgent

In Covey's time management matrix, like in the adapted matrix in this chapter, there are two key factors that define all activities: is an activity *urgent* (or not) and is it *important* (or not)? In every school, there are daily matters that demand an educator's attention, and they are frequently considered "urgent." These urgent matters also often have a tendency of being workplace interruptions—interrupting what was planned and what was occurring (e.g., teaching). Urgent activities are often considered important by default. Thus, based on this assumption, educators are regularly interrupted with demands that are both urgent and important. We would like to take a moment to point out the term *assumption*. Past school culture often has set a precedent that urgent matters such as calling a parent back, completing a form, answering an email, and so on are important and warrant immediate attention.

We suggest taking a moment to analyze the task. Ask yourself if perhaps many of the urgent activities are important for other people but maybe not for you. Or maybe they are not as urgent or important as they appear. Or perhaps someone else has called them urgent, but they may be able to wait a bit. Naturally, teachers have activities they are obligated to do on a specific schedule, but except for class lessons and mandatory staff meetings, there is still autonomy regarding when tasks are completed and how much time is allocated per task. In some cases, you can also choose if you should do it at all. The key factors of *urgent* and *important* form the matrix that can help educators with decision-making that leads to the creation of a life balance above and beyond trying to schedule a week's worth of activities.

Quadrant A—*not urgent but important.* This quadrant is proactive. Here you have the activities that best help you reach your goals. As a teacher this could include long-term planning, co-planning with a colleague, and lesson tuning. Because you are not only a teacher, but a human being, you also need balance in your life, which includes recovery and good health. Therefore, in this quadrant you also have activities like building and maintaining relationships and exercising. During a school day, you might accomplish this by engaging in a walk and talk with a colleague during lunch; this not only provides you a break from the school environment, but you are concurrently able to exercise and work on a relationship.

You will benefit from expanding this quadrant to allocate time for your important but not urgent activities. Think about what is important to you. Is it connecting with your students? Keeping Sundays for family time? Creating lesson plans that embed engaging activities and physical movement? We know that time is limited. Starting to identify those tasks in your life that hold the most meaning for you will help you to prioritize them while simultaneously recognizing the need to minimize time spent on activities that simply do not hold as much weight in your overall quality of life.

Quadrant B—urgent and important. Activities that are both urgent and important are matters at your school with a deadline you are required to meet. For example, this might include inputting grades or running reports that your school requires. It can also be dealing with some sort of crisis or serious incident that needs your attention, like a student who has gotten injured. Activities in this quadrant are by nature *reactive*. If you have your focus here, you will often feel like you are constantly running around putting out fires. It is also possible that because so much is urgent and immediately requiring your attention, you will start to feel like everything that is urgent is important. Try to put the brakes on and analyze what you are doing or being asked to do.

If something is both urgent and important, you obviously can't ignore it. However, see if you can identify some items that are definitely important but maybe not as urgent as they seemed at first. This will allow you to move them to Quadrant A. By doing so, you can go from being reactive to being more proactive. That normally gives better results and creates less stress. By its nature, Quadrant B tends to be a reactive quadrant (urgent and important), resulting in many workflow interruptions, which hamper performance and cause stress (Aeon & Aguinis, 2017; Ma et al., 2020).

Quadrant C—urgent but not important. In this quadrant, you have different interruptions like text messages, emails, and phone calls. Consider putting aside specific times to respond to these, so they are not constantly bombarding you throughout the day and interrupting your flow. This quadrant also includes interruptions from colleagues at your school who may want to talk to you about something *they* find urgent. Consider the issue; perhaps it is neither urgent nor important for you personally. Could you politely defer from talking about the issue right then without offending your colleague as a way to find time for more important issues? Consider asking your colleague if you can walk and talk about the issue at lunch, thereby achieving a few of your own goals while still being there for a friend.

Some meetings may also fall in this Quadrant C. Naturally, some meetings are indeed important, but that does not mean all of them are critical for you. Rather than agreeing to be on every committee, try to be selective. See if you can join some meetings via an online platform to reduce time at school. Remember, if much of your time is in this quadrant, you won't have much time for your own priorities and what you value as important.

Repeatedly getting interrupted and having to constantly react to things that appear to be urgent is stressful and results in a feeling of being out of control and lacking sufficient time to deal with everything. (Pretty much every teacher everywhere has had that feeling!) Interruptions hamper the work task and can result in emotional reactions. While in a complex workplace like a school, you may not be able to eliminate all interruptions, but being aware of which are important and urgent and which are not may help you reduce the negative effects of those you can't eliminate altogether (Puranik et al., 2020).

Quadrant D—not urgent and not important. A number of emails, messages via your digital school platform, social media notices and messages, and phone calls fit in to this category. They are not urgent, and they are not important for your work tasks and goals, yet they take time and result in interruptions from your planned activity. Try to avoid getting sucked into Candy Crush on your phone or looking at Facebook, unless you are doing it during a scheduled brain break or life balance time. Avoid getting involved in gossiping or venting sessions with colleagues that can take precious time and don't serve a positive purpose. Building relationships are important, but those can be done in more positive ways. Investing time on those belongs to Quadrant A.

Using the Teachers' Priority Matrix to Create a Life Balance

The way to get time for what is important for you is to do less of what is not important. That means reducing time spent in Quadrants C and D. It may seem easier said than done. Spending more time and focusing on what is important but not urgent (Quadrant A) will help reduce the time needed to spend in Quadrant B (important and urgent). Because you can't avoid doing what is important and urgent, instead try to eliminate activities that are not important, or at least minimize time spent on them. Although some cannot be eliminated, you can still to some extent choose when to do them and how much time to allocate for them.

When you start to use the time management matrix, we recommend that you take into account your whole life. It is not only at work you need balance. Think about all your activities in work and your private life. Based on your own priorities of importance, consider what will be in each quadrant. Create a table for yourself, print it out, and keep copies where they will be visible at home and work. Refer to it often to keep yourself on track.

Reducing Multitasking to Improve Performance

Time management is about the best possible use of one's time, but that does not necessarily mean trying to do as much as possible by squeezing more into a daily schedule. Let's compare time management with the process an athlete might use to optimize their performance. Training is an essential part of performance, but research clearly shows us that *over*training can lead to poor performance and even impair health (Cadegiani & Kater, 2018). It might be helpful for teachers to look at their work as a sport that requires a training regime to optimize performance. However, as in sports training, they also need recovery time. Naturally, teachers have both work time at school and some work tasks to complete at home—much as athletes spend time training and preparing prior to a performance or match. It can be challenging to find a balance. Educators, like athletes, need to find balance between training and recovery to perform well and stay in good health (Kellmann & Heidari, 2020).

As noted, good time management is about prioritizing the right things and allocating enough time for what is most important. Elite athletes do different types of training on specific times of the day based on what works best for their bodies, needs, and desired outcomes. They also have allocated time for rest and recovery. In the same way, educators might find it helpful to identify specific days or times of a day when they find it most effective to do specific tasks. Allocating the best times during the day and/or the week to the tasks that are most important or when it would be most efficient becomes part of a time management system. This will require identifying priorities and including activities that are *recovery activities* (e.g., time with family, exercising). For example, one teacher may tell parents that she responds to emails in the mornings between 7:30 and 8:30 a.m., whereas another may tell parents that they get back to emails on Tuesday and Thursday evenings. Even holding Sunday mornings as family time, and letting family, friends, colleagues, and students know that you are unavailable during that time, can help with time management and stress reduction.

Be Proactive Rather Than Reactive

When we are overwhelmed by tasks and deadlines, it is quite common to plan from day to day. Unfortunately, this strategy often prevents us from seeing the bigger picture. It is a little like trying to understand a whole puzzle based on only one piece. This approach makes it difficult to prioritize tasks effectively and puts us at risk of becoming reactive rather than proactive. Instead, try looking at a week as a micro-cycle for planning how to best use your time, thinking ahead to what you need to accomplish over the longer term. This is called *backwards planning* (Wiggins & McTighe, 2005), and it can be hugely helpful for time management. In the same way that we might sort puzzle pieces according the color or edge, this approach helps you see the scope of the work ahead without feeling overwhelmed. For example, let's say you have to prepare for a parent–teacher event where there are many factors that come into play. Instead of waiting until the night before to cut, paste, type, or print, and ultimately stay up all night trying to pull the different items together, you could instead put "Prepare for Parent Event" on your calendar each day from 4:00 to 4:30 p.m., and break up the tasks into manageable, bite-sized, 30-minute chunks.

TIME MANAGEMENT TIPS

- Do what is important rather than what is urgent.
- Be proactive rather than reactive.
- Select the activities you choose to do at different times of the day.
- Schedule your own priorities, and allocate time based on that (amount of time and when).

Being proactive rather than reactive is not only about planning; it also has much to do with identifying which activities will get the most time and focus. As Covey has said, "The key is not to prioritize what's on your schedule, but to schedule your priorities" (2013, p. 170). This is where those four quadrants come in on the matrix provided. A proactive plan for managing your time not only helps ensure that the most meaningful tasks are accomplished but also helps relieve the stress of having to react to forgotten deadlines or critical activities.

The Importance of Colleagues in Time Management

Most educators are part of some sort of working group or team. As such, we recommend completing the teachers' priority matrix exercise together with your colleagues. This exercise can have many benefits. You will learn more about your colleagues' priorities as they learn about yours. Upon learning you have different priorities from your peers, another potential benefit can be taking over some activities from each other. As you reflect and discuss activities together, trying to determine which activities go in Quadrants A–D, you may further improve your own personal time management matrix. You can identify mutual priorities, and through this mutual understanding, colleagues can help one another in the process of allocating time and focusing on the most important outcomes. They can help one another say no when appropriate and warranted. In addition, groups can support each other with regular matrix follow-ups, feedback, and reflections.

The Impact of Trust on Time Management

In several other chapters of this book, we describe the importance of relationships and communication; see for instance Chapter 2 on formative assessment, Chapter 4 on communication and collaboration strategies, and Chapter 5 on co-teaching. Trust is important in every organization, and the level of team trust is linked to job performance (Feitosa et al., 2020). There are many ways to build trust within a working group of teachers or other school staff or within the entire school organization.

How does trust relate to time management? It is not a common topic in time management literature, but a high level of trust makes things go faster and smoother. Working as an educator means that quite a lot of your work relates to collaborating with others. This may include colleagues, staff, administrators, and even parents and students. In their book *The Speed of Trust*, Covey and Merril (2018) described how trust makes things go quicker and how a lack of trust slows down decisions, communication, and relationships. They also write about how to build trust and restore trust; one of those tools to restore trust is to make and keep commitments (Covey & Merril, 2018). Thus, although working on trust is perhaps not traditional time management in itself, it can definitely serve as an important catalyzer. Knowing that one can divide and conquer when working with a colleague saves time in the long run (Karten & Murawski, 2020) if you can trust your partner to follow through and they can equally trust you.

Professional Development on Time Management

As an educator, you have a busy work life. You can't do everything, and it is important to make priorities and a good use of your time. Therefore, it is beneficial that you find a strategy for your own time management that is simple and easy to apply. There are many books with different approaches and models for time management. We recommend that you choose a strategy that is principle driven such as the matrix we used as an example adapted to an educator's context. Once you identify the strategy that fits your personality and style best, also consider getting an app to help support that strategy. We like Todoist and Outlook, but there are plenty out there. In addition to creating a time schedule, using an app, working with the priority matrix, and maybe even creating an interruptions log so you can systematically reduce your most common interruptions, you may also want to check out the Pomodoro Technique for helping break up tasks into manageable chunks. Ultimately, finding the style, strategy, or app that works for you is a personal decision, but putting the time in to figure that style out will be time well spent!

School Leader Spotlight

As a school leader, you can help your teachers make priorities from a school perspective. Help them reduce stress and make a better use of their time by not making everything a high priority in their schedule. Make time for teachers to talk and reflect together—not only at faculty meetings, professional learning communities, or other predetermined meetings. Allow some time to be unstructured but focused on communication and co-planning. You can also enhance time management at your school by engaging in a whole-school approach related to time management (e.g., using the matrix approach). Furthermore, you can proactively work on building trust within your organization by emphasizing its impact on time. If you or your teachers are not familiar with Covey's text, consider creating a book club to read and discuss its merits. We recommend *The 7 Habits of Highly Effective People: Revised and Updated* (Covey & Covey, 2020) version.

Additional Strategies for Regular Time Management: More Tools!

While the time management matrix is a strong organizational tool, teachers frequently seek additional strategies for managing their time within those quadrants. Table 10.3 offers some additional techniques that support organization and can save time. These activities can be done outside of class time but will support teachers' time management. You can complete Table 10.4's strategies during the day, as they relate more to managing time when working directly with students.

Table 10.3

Out-of-Class Time Management Strategies for Teachers

SMART goals (Chong, 2018)	Strategic, measurable, applied, realistic, time-sensitive goals can help teachers create priorities that are doable and have a deadline.
Mega-, macro-, micro-planning (Karten & Murawski, 2020)	Mega-planning is done at the beginning of a school year and gets an overview of the whole year of standards and curriculum. Macro-planning is done for major units, chapters, or projects. Micro-planning is for weekly or daily instruction, materials management, and activities.
Bullet journals (Carroll, 2018)	Bullet journals can contain checklists, goals, exercise and food notes, parent communication, and more. Keeping it all in one journal helps teachers stay organized.
Weekly consistent schedule	Create a schedule with all regular activities noted to include time allocated for things like meeting with paraprofessionals, creating lesson plans, calling parents, eating, exercising, spending time with family, and even TV.
Email management (Murawski & Hughes, 2021)	Keep emails to minimum in your in-box. Have one set time daily to respond, and let others, especially parents and administrators, know when that is, so they don't expect immediate responses. "Touch" each email once, and deal with it rather than reading it and putting it aside for later.
Self-advocate for personal time (Murawski & Hughes, 2021)	Let parents know when you are available and that you too need personal time to recharge; self-advocate for time to relax, exercise, and reflect with your family, administrator, and others.

Table 10.4

In-Class Time Management Strategies for Teachers

....

Co-teach (Karten & Murawski, 2020)	Being able to divide roles and responsibilities can significantly help with time (after the initial time required to develop routines); trust one another to follow through.
Manage time during class (Bridgers, 2018)	Work on transitions, procedures, and student ownership of specific activities; use peer mentors; try flipping your class, so class time is focused on application, not lecture (Embury & Clarke, 2023).
Develop routines in class (Handley, 2018)	Reflect on how time is being used; find the root problem; respond to the issue; refine your routine.
Find more time for your content (Lott et al., 2018)	Use different digital technologies strategically; flip the classroom; have students track their own progress; create recorded mini-lessons; build in small-group instruction and one-on-one conferencing to check understanding.
Be strategic about homework, grading, and instruction (Chong, 2018; Handley, 2018)	Identify what is losing time and annoying you the most; fix broken classroom routines; strategically plan homework assignments; grade small batches of work daily rather than letting it pile up; develop lesson plan and presentation templates; be mindful in how time is used for yourself and your students.

REFERENCES

Abel, M. H., & Sewell, J. (1999). Stress and burnout in rural and urban secondary school teachers. *The Journal of Educational Research, 92*(5), 287–293.

Adler, R. F., & Benbunan-Fich, R. (2015). The effects of task difficulty and multitasking on performance. *Interacting with Computers, 27*(4), 430–439.

Adler, R. B., Rosenfeld, L. B., & Proctor, R. F. (2020). *Interplay: The process of interpersonal communication* (15th ed.). Oxford University Press.

Aeon, B., & Aguinis, H. (2017). It's about time: New perspectives and insights on time management. *Academy of Management Perspectives, 31*(4), 309–330.

Aeon, B., Faber, A., & Panaccio, A. (2021). Does time management work? A meta-analysis. *PLoS One, 16*(1), e0245066. https://doi.org/10.1371/journal.pone.0245066

Alasim, K. N. (2019). Reading development of students who are Deaf and Hard of Hearing in inclusive education classes. *Education Sciences, 9*(201), 1–15.

Al-Azawei, A., Serenelli, F., & Lundqvist, K. (2016). Universal Design for Learning (UDL): A content analysis of peer-reviewed journal papers from 2012 to 2015. *The Journal of Scholarship of Teaching and Learning, 16*(3), 39–56.

Al-Gharaibeh, S. F., & Al-Jamal, D. A. (2016). Communication strategies for teachers and their students in an EFL setting. *International Journal of Bilingual and Multilingual Teachers of English, 4*(1), 33–44.

Alter, P., & Haydon, T. (2017). Characteristics of effective classroom rules: A review of the literature. *Teacher Education and Special Education, 40*(2), 114–127.

Altun, S. (2015). The effect of cooperative learning on students' achievement and views on the science and technology course. *International Electronic Journal of Environmental Education, 7*(3), 451–468.

American Psychological Association. (2023, September 1). Teaching social-emotional learning is under attack. *Monitor on Psychology, 54*(6). https://www.apa.org/monitor/2023/09/social-emotional-learning-under-fire

Anderson, L. W., Krathwohl, D. R., & Bloom, B. S. (2001). *A taxonomy for learning, teaching, and assessing: A revision of Bloom's taxonomy of educational objectives.* Longman.

Aronson, E. (2000). Nobody left to hate. *The Humanist, 60*(3), 17–21.

Ashton, R. M., & Ashton, T. A. (2019). UDL and the performing arts: Inspiring creativity. In W. W. Murawski & K. L. Scott (Eds.), *What really works with Universal Design for Learning* (pp. 81–94). Corwin Press.

Austin, J. L., & Soeda, J. M. (2008). Fixed-time teacher attention to decrease off-task behaviors of typically developing third graders. *Journal of Applied Behavior Analysis, 41*(2), 279–283.

Ayres, J. (1972). *Sensory integration and the child.* Western Psychological Services.

Bacon, K. (2014). All along. *Harvard Ed Magazine.* https://www.gse.harvard.edu/news/ed/14/01/all-along

Barbetta, P. M., Heron, T. E., & Heward, W. L. (1993). Effects of active student response during error correction on the acquisition, maintenance, and generalization of sight words by students with developmental disabilities. *Journal of Applied Behavior Analysis, 26*(1), 111–119.

Barrish, H. H., Saunders, M., & Wolf, M. M. (1969). Good Behavior Game: Effects of individual contingencies for group consequences on disruptive behavior in a classroom. *Journal of Applied Behavior Analysis, 2*(2), 119–124.

Bartholomew, J. B., Golaszewski, N. M., Jowers, E., Korinek, E., Roberts, G., Fall, A., & Vaughn, S. (2018). Active learning improves on-task behaviors in 4th grade children. *Preventive Medicine, 111*(6), 49–54.

Basham, J. D., & Marino, M. T. (2013). Understanding STEM education and supporting students through Universal Design for Learning. *Teaching Exceptional Children, 45*(4), 8–15

Belfield, C., Bowden, B., Klapp, A., Levin, H., Shand, R., & Zander, S. (2015). The economic value of social and emotional learning. *Journal of Benefit-Cost Analysis, 6*(3), 508–544.

Bellocchi, S., Muneaux, M., Huau, A., Lévêque, Y., Jover, M., & Ducrot, S. (2017). Exploring the link between visual perception, visual-motor integration, and reading in normal developing and impaired children using DTVP-2. *Dyslexia, 23*(3), 296–315.

Belsky, J., Vandell, D. L., Burchinal, M., Clarke-Stewart, K. A., McCartney, K., & Owen, M. T., & NICHD Early Child Care Research Network. (2007). Are there long-term effects of early child care? *Child Development, 78*(2), 681–701.

Beltman, S., Mansfield, C., & Price, A. (2011). Thriving not just surviving: A review of research on teacher resilience. *Educational Research Review, 6*(3), 185–207.

Bembenutty, H. (2011). Meaningful and maladaptive homework practices: The role of self-efficacy and self-regulation. *Journal of Advanced Academics, 22*(3), 448–473.

Benzing, V., Chang, Y.-K., & Schmidt, M. (2018). Acute physical activity enhances executive functions in children with ADHD. *Scientific Reports, 8*(1), 1–10.

Bergmann, J. (2017). *Solving the homework problem by flipping the learning.* ASCD.

Bernhardt, P. E. (2019). UDL and social studies: Applying project-based learning. In W. W. Murawski & K. L. Scott (Eds.), *What really works with Universal Design for Learning* (pp. 49–64). Corwin.

Berrong, A. K., Schuster, J. W., Morse, T. E., & Collins, B. C. (2007). The effects of response cards on active participation and social behavior of students with moderate and severe disabilities. *Journal of Developmental and Physical Disabilities, 19*(3), 187–199.

Berry, A. (2020). Disrupting to driving: Exploring upper primary teachers' perspectives on student engagement. *Teachers and Teaching, 26*(2), 1–21.

Bill and Melinda Gates Foundation. (2014). *Teachers know best: Teachers' views on* professional development. https://s3. amazonaws.com/edtech-production/re ports/Gates-PDMarketResearch-Dec5. pdf

Bjork, R. A., & Bjork, E. L. (2019). Forgetting as the friend of learning: Implications for teaching and self-regulated learning. *Advances in Physiology Education*, *43*(2), 164–167.

Black, P., & Wiliam, D. (1998). Inside the black box: Raising standards through classroom assessment. *Phi Delta Kappa International*, *80*(2), 81–90.

Black, P., & Wiliam, D. (2009). Developing the theory of formative assessment. *Educational Assessment, Evaluation and Accountability*, *21*(1), 5–31.

Bloom, B. S. (1968). *Learning for mastery. Instruction and curriculum.* Topical Papers and Reprints, Number 1. Regional Education Laboratory for the Carolinas and Virginia.

Bohan, C., Smyth, S., & McDowell, C. (2020). An evaluation of the caught being good game with an adolescent student population. *Journal of Positive Behavior Interventions*, *23*(1), 42–52.

Bowman-Perrott, L., Burke, M. D., Zaini, S., Zhang, N., & Vannest, K. (2016). Promoting positive behavior using the good behavior game: A meta-analysis of single-case research. *Journal of Positive Behavior Interventions*, *18*(3), 180–190.

Bowman-Perrott, L., Burke, M. D., Zhang, N., & Zaini, S. (2014). Direct and collateral effects of peer tutoring on social and behavioral outcomes: A meta-analysis of single-case research. *School Psychology Review*, *43*(3), 260–285.

Brackett, M. A. (2019). *Permission to feel.* Celadon Books.

Brackett, M. A., & Kremenitzer, J. P. (Eds.). (2011). *Creating emotionally literate classrooms: An introduction to the RULER approach to social and emotional learning.* Dude Publishing.

Bradberry, T., & Greaves, J. (2009). *Emotional intelligence 2.0.* TalentSmart.

Braswell, J., & Rine, R. M. (2006). Evidence that vestibular hypofunction affects reading acuity in children. *International Journal of Pediatric Otorhinolaryngology*, *70*(11), 1957–1965.

Bridgers, G. (2018). Five tips to reclaim instructional time. *ASCD Express*, *13*(21). https://www.ascd.org/el/articles/five-ti ps-to-reclaim-instructional-time

Bryan, T., Burstein, K., & Bryan, J. (2001). Students with learning disabilities: Homework problems and promising practices. *Educational Psychologist*, *36*(3), 167–180.

Buchele Harris, H., Cortina, K. S., Templin, T., Colabianchi, N., & Chen, W. (2018, May 28). Impact of coordinated-bilateral physical activities on attention and concentration in school-aged children. *BioMed Research International*, 2539748. https://doi.org/10.1155/2018/2539748

Buchheister, K., Jackson, C., & Taylor, C. E. (2017). Maths games: A universal design approach to mathematical reasoning. *Australian Primary Mathematics Classroom*, *22*(4), 7–12.

Buchs, C., Filippou, D., Pulfrey, C., & Volpé, Y. (2017). Challenges for cooperative learning implementation: Reports from elementary school teachers. *Journal of Education for Teaching*, *43*(3), 296–306.

Bulotsky-Shearer, R. J., Fernandez, V., Dominguez, X., & Rouse, H. L. (2011). Behavior problems in learning activities and social interactions in Head Start classrooms and early reading, mathematics, and approaches to learning. *School Psychology Review*, *40*(1), 39–56.

Cadegiani, F. A., & Kater, C. E. (2018). Body composition, metabolism, sleep, psychological and eating patterns of overtraining syndrome: Results of the EROS study (EROS- PROFILE). *Journal of Sports Sciences*, *36*(16), 1902–1910.

Cameron, J., Banko, K. M., & Pierce, W. D. (2001). Pervasive negative effects of rewards on intrinsic motivation: The myth continues. *The Behavior Analyst*, *24*(1), 1–44.

Caposey, P. J. (2018). Time management problems? Check your working style. *ASCD Express*, *13*(21). https://www. ascd.org/el/articles/time-management -problems-check-your-working-style

Carr, N. S. (2013). Increasing the effectiveness of homework for all learners in the inclusive classroom. *School Community Journal, 23*(1), 169–182.

Carroll, R. (2018). *The bullet journal method: Track the past, order the present, design the future.* Portfolio Press.

CAST. (n.d.). *Top 10 UDL tips for designing an engaging learning environment.* http://castprofessionallearning.org/project/top-10-udl-tips-for-engagement/

Cerasoli, C. P., Nicklin, J. M., & Ford, M. T. (2014). Intrinsic motivation and extrinsic incentives jointly predict performance: A 40-year meta-analysis. *Psychological Bulletin, 140*(4), 980–1008.

Chavez, J., & Lahav, O. (2023, Fall). *Collaborating with educational professionals: The TAG framework.* TCARE, 15, 5. California State University Northridge Center for Teaching and Learning.

Chong, S. C. (2018). Top ten time management tips for teachers. *Modern English Teacher.* https://www.modernenglishteacher.com/top-ten-time-management-tips-for-teachers

Chu, L., & DeArmond, M. (2021). *Approaching SEL as a whole-school effort, not an add-on: Lessons from two charter networks* [ED615152]. Center on Reinventing Public Education.

Clarke, L. S., Haydon, T., Bauer, A., & Epperly, A. C. (2016). Inclusion of students with an intellectual disability in the general education classroom with the use of response cards. *Preventing School Failure, 60*(1), 35–42.

Clifton, C., Jr., Ferreira, F., Henderson, J. M., Inhoff, A. W., Liversedge, S. P., Reichle, E. D., & Schotter, E. R. (2016). Eye movements in reading and information processing: Keith Rayner's 40 year legacy. *Journal of Memory and Language, 86*, 1–19.

Coady, M., Harper, C., & de Jong, E. (2015). Aiming for equity: Preparing mainstream teachers for inclusion or inclusive classrooms? *Tesol Quarterly, 50*(2), 340–368.

Codding, R. S., & Smyth, C. A. (2008). Using performance feedback to decrease classroom transition time and examine collateral effects on academic engagement. *Journal of Educational and Psychological Consultation, 18*(4), 325–345.

Collaborative for Academic, Social and Emotional Learning (CASEL). (2018). *Connecting schoolwide SEL with other school-based frameworks.* https://schoolguide.casel.org/uploads/2019/01/SEL_MTSS-and-PBIS.pdf

Collaborative for Academic, Social and Emotional Learning (CASEL). (2020a). *Restorative practices and SEL alignment.* https://schoolguide.casel.org/uploads/sites/2/2020/12/2020.12.11_Aligning-SEL-and-RP_Final.pdf

Collaborative for Academic, Social and Emotional Learning (CASEL) (2020b). *What is SEL?* https://casel.org/what-is-sel/

Cook, L., & Friend, M. (1995). Co-teaching: Guidelines for creating effective practices. *Focus on Exceptional Children, 28*(3), 1–16.

Cook, S. C., McDuffie-Landrum, K. A., Oshita, L., & Cook, B. G. (2017). Co-teaching for students with disabilities: A critical and updated analysis of the empirical literature. In J. M. Kauffman, D. P. Hallahan, & P. C. Pullen (Eds.), *Handbook of Special Education* (pp. 233–248). Routledge.

Cooper, H. M. (2007). *Battle over homework: Common ground for administrators, teachers, and parents* (3rd ed.). Corwin Press.

Covey, S. R. (2013). *The 7 habits of highly effective people.* Simon & Schuster.

Covey, S. R., & Covey, S. (2020). *The 7 habits of highly effective people: Revised and updated.* Simon & Schuster.

Covey, S. R., & Merril, R. R. (2018). *The SPEED of trust: The one thing that changes everything.* Free Press.

Coyne, P., Evans, M., & Karger, J. (2017). Use of a UDL literacy environment by middle school students with intellectual and developmental disabilities.

Intellectual and Developmental Disabilities, 55(1), 4–14.

Curwin, R. L., Mendler, A. N., & Mendler, B. D. (2018). Discipline with dignity. ASCD.

Dalton, E. (2017). Beyond Universal Design for Learning: Guiding principles to reduce barriers to digital and media literacy competence. Journal of Media Literacy Education, 9(2), 17–29.

Daly, E. J., III, Martens, B. K., Witt, J. C., & Dool, E. J. (1997). A model for conducting a functional analysis of academic performance problems. School Psychology Review, 26(4), 554–574.

de Greeff, J. W., Bosker, R. J., Oosterlaan, J., Visscher, C., & Hartman, E. (2017). Effects of physical activity on executive functions, attention and academic performance in preadolescent children: A meta-analysis. Journal of Science and Medicine in Sport, 21(5), 501–507.

de Jong, J. P., Curşeu, P. L., & Leenders, R. T. A. (2014). When do bad apples not spoil the barrel? Negative relationships in teams, team performance, and buffering mechanisms. Journal of Applied Psychology, 99(3), 514.

Dean, M. (2015). Superb social skills instruction. In W. W. Murawski & K. L. Scott (Eds.), What really works in secondary education (pp. 306–321). Corwin.

Den Heijer, A. E., Groen, Y., Tucha, L., Fuermaier, A. B. M., Koerts, J., Lange, K. W., Thome, J., & Tucha, O. (2017). Sweat it out? The effects of physical exercise on cognition and behavior in children and adults with ADHD: A systematic literature review. Journal of Neural Transmission, 124(1), 3–26.

Derman-Sparks, L. (1989). Anti-bias curriculum: Tools for empowering young children. National Association for the Education of Young Children.

Dickinson, D. K., & Porche, M. V. (2011). Relation between language experiences in preschool classrooms and children's kindergarten and fourth-grade language and reaching abilities. Child Development, 82(3), 870–886.

Dieker, L. A. (2007). Demystifying secondary inclusion: Powerful school-wide and classroom strategies. Dude Publishing.

Dieker, L., Finnegan, L., Grillo, K., & Garland, D. (2013). Special education in the science classroom: A co-teaching scenario. Science Scope, 37(4), 18–22.

Domitrovich, C. E., Durlak, J. A., Staley, K. C., & Weissberg, R. P. (2017). Social-emotional competence: An essential factor for promoting positive adjustment and reducing risk in school children. Child Development, 88(2), 408–416.

Donaldson, J. M., & Austin, J. L. (2017). Environmental and social factors in preventing, assessing, and treating problem behavior in young children. Policy Insights from the Behavioral and Brain Sciences, 4(1), 9–16.

Dostal, H., Gabriel, R., & Weir, J. (2017). Supporting the literacy development of students who are Deaf/Hard of Hearing in inclusive classrooms. The Reading Teacher, 73(8), 327–334.

Dunbar, F. (2016). 7 easy ways to improve school-wide communication. Edutopia. https://www.edutopia.org/article/7-ea sy-ways-to-improve-school-wide-comm unication-folwell-dunbar

Durlak, J. A. (2015). What everyone should know about implementation. In J. A. Durlak, C. E. Domitrovich, R. P. Weissberg, T. P. Gulotta, & T. P. (Eds.), Handbook of social and emotional learning (pp. 395–405). The Guilford Press.

Durlak, J. A., Weissberg, R. P., Dymnicki, A. B., Taylor, R. D. & Shellinger, K. B. (2011). The impact of enhancing students' social and emotional learning: A meta-analysis of school-based universal interventions. Child Development, 82(1), 405–432.

Elias, M. J., Zins, J. E., Weissberg, R. P., Frey, K. S., Greenberg, M. T., Haynes, N. M., Kessler, R., Schwab-Stone, M. E., & Shriver, T. P. (1997). Promoting social and emotional learning: Guidelines for educators. ASCD.

Embury, D. C., & Clarke, L. S. (2023) *Flipping the classroom as an inclusive practice* (Vol. 15, p. 3). TCARE Newsletter, California State University Northridge Center for Teaching and Learning.

Epstein, J. L., & Van Voorhis, F. L. (2001). More than minutes: Teachers' roles in designing homework. *Educational Psychologist, 36*(3), 181–193.

Ericsson, I. (2003). *Motorik, koncentrationsförmåga och skolprestationer: En interventionsstudie i skolår 1–3. (Motor skills, attention and academic achievements: An intervention study in school year 1–3).* Malmö University Library.

Evertson, C. M., & Weinstein, C. S. (Eds.). (2006). *Handbook of classroom management: Research, practice, and contemporary issues.* Lawrence Erlbaum Associates.

Flores, C. (2019) *Using visual schedules in your classroom* (Vol. 8, p. 5). TCARE Newsletter, California State University Northridge Center for Teaching and Learning.

Fallah, S., & Murawski, W. W. (2018). Special education and CLD families: Challenges and strategies for establishing strong partnerships. In K. E. L. Norris & S. Collier-Stewart (Eds.), *Social justice and parent partnerships in multicultural education contexts* (pp. 65–84). IGI Global.

Feitosa, J., Grossman, R., Kramer, W. S., & Salas, E. (2020). Measuring team trust: A critical and meta-analytical review. *Journal of Organizational Behavior, 41*(5), 479–501.

Fernandez-Rio, J., Sanz, N., Fernandez-Cando, J., & Santos, L. (2017). Impact of a sustained cooperative learning intervention on student motivation. *Physical Education and Sport Pedagogy, 22*(1), 89–105.

Flood, W. A., Wilder, D. A., Flood, A. L., & Masuda, A. (2002). Peer-mediated reinforcement plus prompting as treatment for off-task behavior in children with attention deficit hyperactivity disorder. *Journal of Applied Behavior Analysis, 35*(2), 199–204.

Flower, A., McKenna, J. W., Bunuan, R. L., Muething, C. S., & Vega, R., Jr. (2014). Effects of the Good Behavior Game on challenging behaviors in school settings. *Review of Educational Research, 84*(4), 546–571.

Franco, E. S., & Panhoca, I. (2008). Vestibular function in children under-performing at school. *Brazilian Journal of Otorhinolaryngology, 74*(6), 815–825.

Friend, M., & Cook, L. (1992). *Interactions: Collaboration skills for school professionals.* Longman Publishers.

Friend, M., & Cook, L. (2021). *Interactions: Collaboration skills for school professionals* (9th ed.). Pearson.

Friend, M., Cook, L., Hurley-Chamberlain, D., & Shamberger, C. (2010). Co-teaching: An illustration of the complexity of collaboration in special education. *Journal of Educational and Psychological Consultation, 20*(1), 9–27.

Fuchs, L., & Fuchs, D. (1986). Effects of systematic formative evaluation: A meta-analysis. *Exceptional Children, 53*(3), 199–208.

Gajda, R., & Koliba, C. (2007). Evaluating the imperative of intraorganizational collaboration: A school improvement perspective. *American Journal of Evaluation, 28*(1), 26–44.

Garten, J., Kennedy, B., Sagae, K., & Dehghani, M. (2019). Measuring the importance of context when modeling language comprehension. *Behavior Research Methods, 51*, 480–492.

Gear, A. (2018). *Reading power: Teaching students how to think while they read* (2nd ed.). Pembroke.

Gear, A. (2020). *Powerful writing structures: Brain pocket strategies for supporting a year-long writing program.* Pembroke.

Geertsen, S. S., Thomas, R., Joséen, M. N., Dahn, I. M., Andersen, J. N., Krause-Jensen, M., Korup, V., Nielsen, C. M., Wienecke, J., Ritz, C., Krustrup, P., & Lundbye-Jensen, J. (2016). Motor skills and exercise capacity are associated with objective measures of cognitive functions and academic performance in preadolescent children. *PLoS One, 11*(8), e0161960–e016196.

George, C. L. (2010). Effects of response cards on performance and participation in social studies for middle school students with emotional and behavioral disorders. *Behavioral Disorders, 35*(3), 200–213.

Gerlach, K. (2015). *Let's team up! A checklist for teachers, paraeducators, and principals.* Dude Publishing.

Ghaderi, A., Johansson, M., & Enebrink, P. (2017). *Pilotstudie av PAX i skolan: En kulturanpassad version av PAX Good Behavior Game. (Cultural adaptation and pilot study of PAX Good Behavior Game in Sweden).* http://paxiskolan.se/forskning/

Gillies, R. M. (2016). Cooperative learning: Review of research and practice. *Australian Journal of Teacher Education, 41*(3), 39–54.

Gimbert, B. G., Miller, D., Herman, E., Breedlove, M., & Molina, C. E. (2023). Social emotional learning in schools: The importance of educator competence. *Journal of Research on Leadership Education, 18*(1), 3–39.

Ginsburg-Block, M. D., Rohrbeck, C. A., & Fantuzzo, J. W. (2006). A meta-analytic review of social, self-concept, and behavioral outcomes of peer-assisted learning. *Journal of Education & Psychology, 98*(4), 732–749.

Glazier, J. A., Boyd, A., Hughes, K. B., Able, H., & Mallous, R. (2017). The elusive search for teacher collaboration. *The New Educator, 13*(1), 3–21.

Goleman, D. (1995). *Emotional intelligence: Why it can matter more than IQ.* Bantam Books.

Gonzalez-DeHass, A. R., Willems, P. P., & Holbein, M. F. D. (2005). Examining the relationship between parental involvement and student motivation. *Educational Psychology Review, 17*(2), 99–123.

Gordon, D. T., Gravel, J. W., & Shifter, L. A. (Eds.). (2009) *A policy reader in Universal Design for Learning.* Harvard Education Press.

Grabherr, L., Macauda, G., & Lenggenhager, B. (2015). The moving history of vestibular stimulation as a therapeutic intervention. *Multisensory Research, 28*(5–6), 653–687.

Graham-Clay, S. (2005). Communicating with parents: Strategies for teachers. *School Community Journal, 15*(1), 117–130.

Grant, S., Hamilton, L. S., Wrabel, S. L., Gomez, C. J., Auger, A., Tamargo, J., Unlu, F., Chavez-Herrerias, E., Baker, G., Barrett, M., Harris, M., & Ramos, A. (2017). *Social and emotional learning interventions under the Every Student Succeeds Act: Evidence review.* RAND Corporation. http://www.rand.org/t/RR2133

Greene, R. (2017). *Vilse i skolan—hur vi kan hjälpa barn med beteendeproblem att hitta rätt. (Lost at school—why our Kids with behavioral challenges are falling through the cracks and how we can help them).* Studentlitteratur.

Gribetz, S. K. (2018). The festival of every day: Philo and Seneca on quotidian time. *Harvard Theological Review, 113*(3), 357–381.

Guerra, N. G., & Smith, E. P. (Eds.). (2006). *Preventing youth violence in a multicultural society.* American Psychological Society.

Gulløv, C. (2017) *Social pedagogues in Denmark* (Vol. 5, p. 6). TCARE Newsletter, California State University Northridge Center for Teaching and Learning.

Haidt, J. (2006). *The happiness hypothesis: Finding modern truth in ancient wisdom.* Basic Books.

Handley, J. F. (2018). Fix your broken routines: Three rules to live by. *ASCD Express, 13*(21). https://www.ascd.org/el/articles/fix-your-broken-routines-three-rules-to-live-by

Hansen, A. (2016). *Hjärnstark: Hur motion och träning stärker din hjärna. (Brain* strong: How exercise and training strengthen your brain). Fitnessförlaget.

Hāøggblom, P. (2016). Universal Design for Learning—A Swedish programme for widening participation. *AHEAD Journal, 4*. https://www.ahead.ie/journal/Universal-Design-for-Learning-a-Swedish-programme-for-widening-participation

Hart, B., & Risley, T. R. (1995). *Meaningful differences in the everyday experience of young American children*. Paul H. Brookes Publishing.

Hastings, R. P., & Bham, M. S. (2003). The relationship between student behaviour patterns and teacher burnout. *School Psychology International, 24*(1), 115–127.

Hattie, J., & Clarke, S. (2019). *Feedback— så återkopplar du i klassrummet (Visual learning— Feedback)*. Natur & Kultur.

Hattie, J., & Timperley, H. (2007). The power of feedback. *Review of Educational Research, 77*(1), 81–112.

Hawkins, R. O., Haydon, T., Denune, H., Larkin, W., & Fite, N. (2015). Improving the transition behavior of high school students with emotional behavioral disorders using a randomized interdependent group contingency. *School Psychology Review, 44*(2), 208–223.

Henrich, J. (2020). *The WEIRDest people in the world: How the West became psychologically peculiar and particularly prosperous*. Farrar, Straus and Giroux.

Hoffman, J. D., Brackett, M. A., Bailey, S. B., & Willner, C. J. (2020). Teaching emotion regulation in schools: Translating research into practise with the RULER approach to social and emotional learning. *Emotion, 20*(1), 105–109.

Hoover-Dempsey, K. V., Walker, J. M., Sandler, H. M., Whetsel, D., Green, C. L., Wilkins, A. S., & Closson, K. (2005). Why do parents become involved? Research findings and implications. *The Elementary School Journal, 106*(2), 105–130.

Hott, B. L., & Limberg, D. (2015). Perfectly positive behavior. In W. W. Murawski & K. L. Scott (Eds.), *What really works with secondary education* (pp. 120–136). Corwin.

Hott, B. L., Randolph, K. M., & Martin, A. (2017). UDL and positive behavior interventions and supports: Making classroom management positive. In W. W. Murawski & K. L. Scott (Eds.), *What really works with exceptional learners* (pp. 111–122). Corwin.

Hughes, C. E. (2015). Great gifted education. In W. W. Murawski & K. L. Scott (Eds.), *What really works in secondary education* (pp. 234–254). Corwin.

Hyland, K. (2011). Learning to write: Issues in theory, research and pedagogy. In R. M. Manchón (Ed.), *Learning-to-write and writing to learn in an additional language* (pp. 17–35). John Benjamins.

Ivcevic, Z., & Brackett, M. A. (2014). Predicting school success: Comparing conscientiousness, grit, and emotion regulation ability. *Journal of Research in Personality, 52*, 29–36.

Jacobs, G. M., & Ivone, F. M. (2020). Infusing cooperative learning in distance education. *The Electronic Journal for English as a Second Language, 24*(1), 1–15.

Jacobs, G. M., & Renandya, W. A. (2019). *Student centered cooperative learning: Linking concepts in education to promote student learning*. Springer Nature.

Jenkins, M., & Murawski, W. W. (2023). *Connecting high-leverage practices to student success: Collaboration in inclusive classrooms*. Corwin.

Johansson, M., Biglan, A., & Embry, D. (2020). The PAX good behavior game: One model for evolving a more nurturing society. *Clinical Child and Family Psychology Review, 23*(4), 462–482.

Johnson, D. W., & Johnson, F. (2009). *Joining together: Group theory and group skills* (10th ed.). Allyn & Bacon.

Johnson, D. W., & Johnson, R. T. (n.d.). *An overview of cooperative learning*. Cooperative Learning. http://www.co-operation.org/what-is-cooperative-learning

Johnson, D., Maruyama, G., Johnson, R., Nelson, D., & Skon, L. (1981). Effects of cooperative, competitive, and individualistic goal structures on achievement: A meta-analysis. *Psychological Bulletin, 89*(1), 47–62.

Joslyn, R. P., Austin, J. L., Donaldson, J. M., & Vollmer, T. R. (2020). A practitioner's guide to the Good Behavior Game. *Behaviour Analysis: Research and Practice, 20*(4), 219–235.

Kanter, J. W., Manos, R. C., Bowe, W. M., Baruch, D. E., Busch, A. M., & Rusch, L. C. (2010). What is behavioral activation?: A review of the empirical literature. *Clinical Psychology Review, 30*(6), 608–620.

Kapp, S. K., Steward, R., Crane, L., Elliott, D., Elphick, C., Pellicano, E., & Russell, G. (2019). "People should be allowed to do what they like": Autistic adults' views and experiences of stimming. *Autism, 23*(7), 1782–1792.

Karlsson, P. (2018). *Positivt beteendestöd i omsorg och skola—en introduktion (Positive behavior support in social care and school—An introduction)*. Natur & Kultur.

Karten, T., & Murawski, W. W. (2020). *Co-teaching do's, don'ts, and do betters*. Association for Supervision and Curriculum.

Kazdin, A. (Ed.). (2012) *The token economy: A review and evaluation*. Springer Science & Business Media.

Keefe, E. B., & Moore, V. (2004). The challenge of co-teaching in inclusive classrooms at the high school level: What the teachers told us. *American Secondary Education, 32*(3), 77–88.

Kellmann, M., & Heidari, J. (2020). Changes in the perception of stress and recovery in German secondary school teachers. *Teacher Development, 24*(2), 242–257.

King-Sears, M. E., Brawand, A. E., Jenkins, M. C., & Preston-Smith, S. (2014). Co-teaching perspectives from secondary science co-teachers and their students with disabilities. *Journal of Science Teacher Education, 25*(6), 651–680.

Kiphard, E. J. (2009). *Motopädagogik (Psychomotor education)*. Verlag modernes lernen. Modern Learning Publishing House.

Koch, I., Poljac, E., Müller, H., & Kiesel, A. (2018). Cognitive structure, flexibility, and plasticity in human multi-tasking: An integrative review of dual-task and task-switching research. *Psychological Bulletin, 144*(6), 557–583.

Koutsandréou, F., Wegner, M., Niemann, C., & Budde, H. (2016). Effects of motor versus cardiovascular exercise training on children's working memory. *Medicine & Science in Sports & Exercise, 48*(6), 1144–1152.

Kyndt, E., Raes, E., Lismont, B., Timmers, F., Cascallar, E., & Dochy, F. (2013). A meta-analysis of the effects of face-to-face cooperative learning. Do recent studies falsify or verify earlier findings? *Educational Research Review, 10*, 133–149.

Lane, S. J., Mailloux, Z., Schoen, S., Bundy, A., May-Benson, T. A., Parham, L. D., Smith Roley, S., & Schaaf, R. C. (2019). Neural foundations of Ayres Sensory Integration. *Brain Sciences, 9*(7), 153.

Lauvås, P., & Jönsson, A. (2019). *Ren formativ bedömning (Purely formative assessment)*. Studentlitteratur.

LeGray, M. W., Dufrene, B. A., Sterling-Turner, H., Olmi, D. J., & Bellone, K. (2010). A comparison of function-based differential reinforcement interventions for children engaging in disruptive classroom behavior. *Journal of Behavioral Education, 19*(3), 185–204.

Lewis, T. J., Hatton, H. L., Jorgenson, C., & Maynard, D. (2017). What beginning special educators need to know about conducting functional behavioral assessments. *Teaching Exceptional Children, 49*(4), 231–238.

Liem, G. A., Ginns, P., Martin, A. J., Stone, B., & Herrett, M. (2012). Personal best goals and academic and social functioning: A longitudinal perspective. *Learning and Instruction, 22*(3), 222–230.

Linane, M. J. (2015). How to improve your school staff's communication: Tips and tricks from the classroom. *EdSurge News*. https://www.edsurge.com/news /2015-09-02-how-to-improve-your-sch ool-staff-s-communication-tips-and-tri cks-from-the-classroom

Lochner, W. W., Murawski, W. W., & True-Daley, J. (2019). The effect of co-teaching on student cognitive engagement. *Theory and Practice in Rural Education, 9*(2), 6–19.

Lochner, W. W., & Withrow, B. (2019) *Looking for school improvement? Get a diagnostic!* (Vol. 8, p. 2). TCARE Newsletter, California State University Northridge Center for Teaching and Learning.

Lott, E., Pukl, D., & Miller, T. (2018). How to avoid the direct instruction time trap. *ASCD Express, 13*(21). https://www.ascd.org/el/articles/how-to-avoid-the-direct-instruction-time-trap

Lyon, C. P., Hogan, E. K., & Kearns, D. M. (2021). Individualizing literacy instruction in co-taught classrooms through a station teaching model. *Intervention in School and Clinic, 56*(4), 224–232.

Ma, J., Kerulis, A. M., Wang, Y., & Sachdev, A. R. (2020). Are workflow interruptions a hindrance stressor? The moderating effect of time-management skills. *International Journal of Stress Management, 27*(3), 252–261.

Mager, R. F., & Pipe, P. (1997). *Analyzing performance problems.* The Center for Effective Performance.

Mahar, M. T. (2011). Impact of short bouts of physical activity on attention-to-task in elementary school children. *Preventive Medicine, 52*(1), 60–64.

Maheady, L., Mallette, B., & Harper, G. F. (2006). Four classwide peer tutoring models: Similarities, differences, and implications for research and practice. *Reading & Writing Quarterly, 22*(1), 65–89.

Maier, S. F., & Seligman, M. E. (1976). Learned helplessness: Theory and evidence. *Journal of Experimental Psychology: General, 105*(1), 3–46.

Mandel, S. (2003). *Cooperative work groups: Preparing students for the real world.* Corwin.

Mandel, S. (2015). Cool cooperative learning. In W. W. Murawski & K. L. Scott (Eds.), *What really works in secondary education* (pp. 154–169). Corwin.

Martin, A. J. (2007). Examining a multidimensional model of student motivation and engagement using a construct validation approach. *British Journal of Educational Psychology, 77*(2), 413–440.

Martin, A. J., & Elliot, A. J. (2016). The role of personal best (PB) goal setting in students' academic achievement gains. *Learning and Individual Differences, 45,* 222–227.

Martin, N., Wray, M., James, A., Draffan, E. A., Krupa, J., & Turner, P. (2019). *Implementing inclusive teaching and learning in UK higher education: Utilizing Universal Design for Learning (UDL) as a route to excellence.* Society for Research into Higher Education.

Mavilidi, M. F., Ruiter, M., Schmidt, M., Okely, A. O., Loyens, S., Chandler, P., & Paas, F. (2018). A narrative review of school-based physical activity for enhancing cognition and learning: The importance of relevancy and integration. *Frontiers in Psychology, 2018*(9), 2079.

McConnell, B. M., & Murawski, W. W. (2017). The importance of partnerships: School-to- home collaboration. In W. W. Murawski & K. L. Scott (Eds.), *What really works with exceptional learners* (pp. 338–355). Corwin.

McCray, E., Kamman, M., Brownell, M. T., & Robinson, S. (2017). *High-leverage practices and evidence-based practices: A promising pair.* CEEDAR.

Mccutchen, M. (2019). *10 strategies for improving home and school collaboration.* Classcraft. https://www.classcraft.com/resources/blog/strategies-for-improving-home-and-school-communication/

McIntosh, K., Brigid Flannery, K., Sugai, G., Braun, D. H., & Cochrane, K. L. (2008). Relationships between academics and problem behavior in the transition from middle school to high school. *Journal of Positive Behavior Interventions, 10*(4), 243–255.

McLeod, S. A. (2019). Constructivism as a theory for teaching and learning. *Simply Psychology*. https://www.simplypsychology.org/constructivism.html

Medina, J. (2014). *Brain rules*. Pear Press.

Meyer, A., & Rose, D. H. (2005). The future is in the margins: The role of technology and disability in educational reform. In D. H. Rose, A. Meyer, & C. Hitchcock (Eds.), *The universally designed classroom: Accessible curriculum and digital technologies* (pp. 13–35). Harvard Education Press.

Meyer, B., Schermuly, C. C., & Kauffeld, S. (2016). That's not my place: The interacting effects of faultlines, subgroup size, and social competence on social loafing behaviour in work groups. *European Journal of Work & Organizational Psychology, 25*(1), 31–49.

Midgley, C., Anderman, E., & Hicks, L. (1995). Differences between elementary and middle school teachers and students: A goal theory approach. *The Journal of Early Adolescence, 15*(1), 90–113.

Mitchell, B. S., Hirn, R. G., & Lewis, T. J. (2017). Enhancing effective classroom management in schools: Structures for changing teacher behavior. *Teacher Education and Special Education, 40*(2), 140–153.

Morgan, P. L., Frisco, M. L., Farkas, G., & Hibel, J. (2010). A propensity score matching analysis of the effects of special education services. *The Journal of Special Education, 43*(4), 236–254.

Morisano, D., Hirsh, J. B., Peterson, J. B., Pihl, R. O., & Shore, B. M. (2010). Setting, elaborating, and reflecting on personal goals improves academic performance. *Journal of Applied Psychology, 95*(2), 255–264.

Murawski, W. W. (2006). Student outcomes in co-taught secondary English classes: How can we improve? *Reading & Writing Quarterly, 22*(3), 227–247.

Murawski, W. W. (2009). *Collaborative teaching in secondary schools: Making the co-teaching marriage work!* Corwin Press.

Murawski, W. W. (2010). *Collaborative teaching in elementary schools: Making the co-teaching marriage work!* Corwin Press.

Murawski, W. W. (2012). 10 tips for using co-planning time more efficiently. *Teaching Exceptional Children, 44*(4), 8–15.

Murawski, W. W., & Dieker, L. A. (2013). *Leading the Co-teaching Dance*. Council for Exceptional Children.

Murawski, W. W., & Gaines, A. (2021). What really works with exceptional learners in distance learning situations (supplement). In W. W. Murawski & K. L. Scott (Eds.), *What really works with exceptional learners*. Corwin.

Murawski, W. W., & Goodwin, V. (2014). Effective inclusive schools and the co-teaching conundrum. In J. McLeskey, N. L. Waldron, F. Spooner, & B. Algozzine (Eds.), *Handbook of effective inclusive schools: Research and practice* (pp. 292–305). Routledge.

Murawski, W. W., & Hughes, C. E. (2021). Special educators in inclusive settings: Take STEPS for self-advocacy! *Teaching Exceptional Children, 53*(3), 184–193.

Murawski, W. W., & Lochner, W. W. (2011). Observing co-teaching: What to ask for, look for, and listen for. *Intervention in School and Clinic, 46*(3), 174–183.

Murawski, W. W., & Lochner, W. W. (2018). *Beyond basic co-teaching: A no-fail, data-driven continuous improvement model*. Association for Supervision and Curriculum.

Murawski, W. W., & Novak, K. (2019). UDL and change: Taking baby steps to success. In W. W. Murawski & K. L. Scott (Eds.), *What really works with Universal Design for Learning* (pp. 283–298). Corwin Press.

Murawski, W. W., & Ricci, L. A. (2019). UDL and co-teaching: Establishing the perfect union. In W. W. Murawski & K. L. Scott (Eds.), *What really works with Universal Design for Learning* (pp. 141–155). Corwin Press.

Murawski, W. W., & Scott, K. L. (Eds.). (2019). *What really works with Universal Design for Learning*. Corwin Press.

Murawski, W. W., & Spencer, S. A. (2011). *Collaborate, communicate, and differentiate!: How to increase student learning in today's diverse schools.* Corwin.

Närhi, V., Kiiski, T., & Savolainen, H. (2017). Reducing disruptive behaviours and improving classroom behavioural climate with class-wide positive behaviour support in middle schools. *British Educational Research Journal, 43*(6), 1186–1205.

Nel, N., Mohangi, K., Krog, S., & Stephens, O. (2016). An overview of grade R literacy teaching and learning in inclusive classrooms in South Africa. *Per Linguam, 32*(2), 47–65.

Nie, Y., Tan, G. H., Liau, A., Lau, S., & Chua, B. L. (2013). The roles of teacher efficacy in instructional innovation: Its predictive relations to constructivist and didactic instruction. *Educational Research for Policy and Practice, 12*(1), 67–77.

Nilsson, M., Blomqvist, K., & Andersson, I. (2016). Salutogenic resources in relation to teachers' work-life balance. *Work, 56*(4), 591–602.

Novak, K., & Rodriguez, K. (2018). *UDL progress rubric.* CAST. http://castpublishing.org/novak-rodriguez-udl-progression-rubric/

Nuthall, G. (2004). Relating classroom teaching to student learning: A critical analysis of why research has failed to bridge the theory-practice gap. *Harvard Educational Review, 74*(3), 273–306.

Oberle, E., Domitrovich, C. E., Meyers, D. C., & Weissberg, R. (2019). *Establishing systemic social and emotional learning approaches in schools: A framework for schoolwide implementation.* Routledge.

Office for Standards of Education. (2014). *Below the radar: Low-level disruptions in the country's classrooms.* http://www.gov.uk/government/publications/below-the-radar-low-level-disruption-in-the-countrys-classrooms

Organization for Economic Cooperation and Development. (2019) *TALIS 2018 results: Teachers and School Leaders as Lifelong Learners* (Vol. 1). OECD Publishing.

Palmis, S., Danna, J., Velay, J.-L., & Longcamp, M. (2017). Motor control of handwriting in the developing brain: A review. *Cognitive Neuropsychology, 34*(3–4), 187–204.

Paran, A., & Wallace, C. (2016). Teaching literacy. In G. Hall (Ed.), *The Routledge handbook of English language teaching* (pp. 441–455). Routledge.

Phillips, C. L., Iannaccone, J. A., Rooker, G. W., & Hagopian, L. P. (2017). Noncontingent reinforcement for the treatment of severe problem behavior: An analysis of 27 consecutive applications. *Journal of Applied Behavior Analysis, 50*(2), 357–376.

Pinker, S. (2013). *Learnability and cognition: The acquisition of argument structure* (2nd ed.). MIT Press.

Porche, M., Grossman, J., Biro, N., MacKay, N., & Rivers, S. (2014). *Collaboration to achieve whole school SEL across a large, urban district* [ED562719]. Society for Research on Educational Effectiveness.

Porter, A., & Bernhardt, P. E. (2018). *Digital citizenship: Promoting wellness for thriving in a connected world.* Vertex Learning.

Premo, J., Cavagnetto, A., & Davis, W. B. (2018). Promoting collaborative classrooms: The impacts of interdependent cooperative learning on undergraduate interactions and achievement. *CBE Life Science Education, 17*(32), 1–16.

Protheroe, N. (2009). Good homework policy = good teaching. *Principal, 89*(1), 42–45.

Puranik, H., Koopman, J., & Vough, H. C. (2020). Pardon the interruption: An integrative review and future research agenda for research on work interruptions. *Journal of Management, 46*(6), 806–842.

Puzio, K., Coby, G. T., & Algeo-Nichols, D. (2020). Differentiated literacy instruction: Boondoggle or best practice? *Review of Educational Research, 90*(4), 459–498.

Randolph, J. J. (2007). Meta-analysis of the research on response cards: Effects on test achievement, quiz achievement, participation, and off-task behavior.

Journal of Positive Behavior Interventions, 9(2), 113–128.

Rao, K., Currie-Rubin, R., & Logli, C. (2016). *UDL and inclusive practices in IB schools worldwide.* CAST Professional Learning.

Rappaport, S., Grossman, J., Garcia, I., Zhu, P., Avila, O., Granito, K., Chen, D., Kennedy, A., & Quinn, J. (2017). *Group work is not cooperative learning: A working paper from the Investing in Innovation (i3) evaluation.* MDRC.

Read, J. A., Einstein, G., Hahn, E., Hooker, S. P., Gross, V. P., & Kravitz, J. (2010). Examining the impact of integrating physical activity on fluid intelligence and academic performance in an elementary school: A preliminary investigation. *Journal of Physical Activity and Health, 7*(3), 343–351.

Redding, S. (2000). *Parents and learning.* UNESCO Publications. http://www.i-be.unesco.org/publications/EducationalPracticesSeriesPdf/prac02e.pdf

Regan, K., Evmenova, A. S., Good, K., Legget, A., Ahn, S. Y., Gafurov, B., & Mastropieri, M. (2018). Persuasive writing with mobile-based graphic organizers in inclusive classrooms across the curriculum. *Journal of Special Education Technology, 33*(1), 3–14.

Repertoire Productions. (2013). *The myth of average: Todd Rose at Tedx Sonoma County.* https://www.youtube.com/watch?v=4eBmyttcfU4

Richards, J. (2012). Teacher stress and coping strategies: A national snapshot. *The Educational Forum, 76*(3), 299–316.

Rimm-Kaufman, S. E., & Hulleman, C. S. (2015). SEL in elementary school settings; identifying mechanisms that matter. In J. A. Durlak, C. E. Domitrovich, R. P. Weissberg, & T. P. Gulotta (Eds.), *Handbook of social and emotional learning* (pp. 151–166). The Guilford Press.

Rodriguez, J. (2019). UDL and policy: Considering legal implications. In W. W. Murawski & K. L. Scott (Eds.), *What really works with Universal Design for Learning* (pp. 269–282). Corwin Press.

Rodriguez, J. A., & Murawski, W. W. (2022). *Special education law and policy: From foundation to application.* Plural Publishing.

Romaniuk, C., Miltenberger, R., Conyers, C., Jenner, N., Jurgens, M., & Ringenberg, C. (2002). The influence of activity choice on problem behaviors maintained by escape versus attention. *Journal of Applied Behavior Analysis, 35*(4), 349–362.

Ronfeldt, M., Farmer, S. O., McQueen, K., & Grissom, J. A. (2015). Teacher collaboration in instructional teams and student achievement. *American Educational Research Journal, 52*(3), 475–514.

Rose, D. H., Meyer, H., & Gordon, D. (2014). Reflections: Universal Design for Learning and the common core. *The Special Edge, 27*(2), 3–5.

Roseth, C. J., Johnson, D. W., & Johnson, R. T. (2008). Promoting early adolescents' achievement and peer relationships: The effects of cooperative, competitive, and individualistic goal structures. *Psychological Bulletin, 134*(2), 223–246.

Rothstein-Fisch, C., & Trumbull, E. (2008). *Managing diverse classrooms: How to build on students' cultural strengths.* ASCD.

Ruppar, A., Fisher, K. W., Olson, A. J., & Orlando, A. M. (2018). Exposure to literacy for students eligible for the alternate assessment. *Education and Training in Autism and Developmental Disabilities, 53*(2), 192–208.

Sabol, T. J., & Pianta, R. C. (2012). Recent trends in research on teacher–child relationships. *Attachment & Human Development, 14*(3), 213–231.

Salovey, P., & Mayer, J. D. (1990). Emotional intelligence. *Imagination, Cognition and Personality, 9*(3), 185–211.

Schaaf, R. C., Dumont, R. L., Arbesman, M., & May-Benson, T. A. (2018). Efficacy of occupational therapy using Ayres Sensory Integration: A systematic review. *American Journal of Occupational Therapy, 72*(1), 1–10.

Schad, E. (2019). No time to talk! Teachers' perceptions of organizational communication: Context and climate. *Educational Management Administration & Leadership, 47*(3), 421–442.

Scherrer, V., & Preckel, F. (2019). Development of motivational variables and self-esteem during the school career: A meta-analysis of longitudinal studies. *Review of Educational Research, 89*(2), 211–258.

Schoen, S. A., Lane, S. J., Mailloux, Z., May-Benson, T., Parham, L. D., Smith Roley, S., & Schaaf, R. C. (2019). A systematic review of ayres sensory integration intervention for children with autism. *Autism Research, 12*(1), 6–19.

Scriven, M. (1966). The methodology of evaluation. *Social Science Education Consortium, 110*, 1–140.

Seok, S., DaCosta, B., & Hodges, R. (2018). A systematic review of empirically based Universal Design for Learning: Implementation and effectiveness of universal design in education for students with and without disabilities at the post-secondary level. *Open Journal of Social Sciences, 6*(5), 171–189.

Sheninger, E. C., & Murray, T. C. (2017). *Learning transformed: Eight keys to designing tomorrow's schools, today.* ASCD.

Shogren, K. A., Faggella-Luby, M. N., Bae, S. J., & Wehmeyer, M. L. (2004). The effect of choice-making as an intervention for problem behavior: A meta-analysis. *Journal of Positive Behavior Interventions, 6*(4), 228–237.

Silva, A. P., Prado, S. O. S., Scardovelli, T. A., Boschi, S. R. M. S., Campos, L. C., & Frère, A. F. (2015). Measurement of the effect of physical exercise on the concentration of individuals with ADHD. *PLoS One, 10*(3), E0122119.

Simonsen, B., Fairbanks, S., Briesch, A., Myers, D., & Sugai, G. (2008). Evidence-based practices in classroom management: Considerations for research to practice. *Education & Treatment of Children, 31*(3), 351–380.

Skaalvik, E. M., & Skaalvik, S. (2017). Dimensions of teacher burnout: Relations with potential stressors at school. *Social Psychology of Education, 20*(4), 775–790.

Skinner, B. F. (1968). *The technology of teaching.* Appleton-Century-Crofts.

Slavin, R. E., & Madden, N. A. (2021). Student team learning and success for all: A personal history and overview. In *Pioneering perspectives in cooperative learning* (pp. 128–145). Routledge.

Smagorinsky, P. (2018). Literacy in teacher education: "It's the context, stupid." *Journal of Literacy Research, 50*(3), 281–303.

Smith, S. M., & Vela, E. (2001). Environmental context-dependent memory: A review and meta-analysis. *Psychonomic Bulletin & Review, 8*(2), 203–220.

Smith, N. L., & Waegerle, D. C. (2016). Chapter 32: Secondary education and content literacy in inclusive classrooms. In T. Petty, A. Good, & S. M. Putman (Eds.), *Handbook of research on professional development for quality teaching and learning* (pp. 678–705). IGI Global.

Snow, C. E., & Matthews, T. J. (2016). Reading and language in the early grades. *The Future of Children, 26*(2), 57–74.

Soares, D. A., Harrison, J. R., Vannest, K. J., & McClelland, S. S. (2016). Effect size for token economy use in contemporary classroom settings: A meta-analysis of single-case research. *School Psychology Review, 45*(4), 379–399.

Spaulding, L. S., Mostert, M. P., & Beam, A. P. (2010). Is Brain Gym® an effective educational intervention? *Exceptionality, 18*(1), 18–30.

Spencer, S. A. (2015). *Making the common core writing standards accessible through Universal Design for Learning.* Corwin Press.

Stone, D., & Heen, S. (2014). *Thanks for the feedback: The science and art of receiving feedback well.* Penguin Books.

Sugai, G., & Horner, R. H. (2020). Sustaining and scaling positive behavioral interventions and supports: Implementation drivers, outcomes, and considerations. *Exceptional Children*, *86*(2), 120–136.

Sugden, D., & Wade, M. (2013). *Typical and atypical motor development*. Mac Keith Press.

Taylor, F. W. (2003). *Scientific management*. Routledge.

Taylor, R. D., Oberle, E., Durlak, J. A., & Weissberg, R. P. (2017). Promoting positive youth development through school-based social and emotional learning interventions: A meta-analysis of follow-up effects. *Child Development*, *88*(4), 1156–1171.

Tilp, M., Scharf, C., Payer, G., Presker, M., & Fink, A. (2020). Physical exercise during the morning school break improves basic cognitive functions. *Mind, Brain, and Education*, *14*(1), 24–31.

Tingstrom, D. H., Sterling-Turner, H. E., & Wilczynski, S. M. (2006). The good behavior game: 1969–2002. *Behavior Modification*, *30*(2), 225–253.

Toews, S. G., & Kurth, J. A. (2019). Literacy instruction in general education settings: A call to action. *Research and Practice for Persons with Severe Disabilities*, *44*(3), 135–142.

True-Daley, J. (2021). Example response card made for 2Teach activities. *2Teach Consulting*. http://www.2TeachLLC.com

Trussell, R. P., Chen, H. J., Lewis, T. J., & Luna, N. E. (2018). Reducing escape-maintained behavior through the application of classroom-wide practices and individually designed interventions. *Education & Treatment of Children*, *41*(4), 507–531.

United Nations, Department of Economic and Social Affairs, Population Division. (2019). *International Migrant Stock 2019*. United Nations database, POP/DB/MIG/Stock/Rev. https://www.un.org/en/development/desa/population/migration/publications/migrationreport/docs/ MigrationStock2019_TenKeyFindings.pdf

Urdan, T., & Schoenfelder, E. (2006). Classroom effects on student motivation: Goal structures, social relationships, and competence beliefs. *Journal of School Psychology*, *44*(5), 331–349.

Van Ryzin, M. J., & Roseth, C. J. (2018a). Enlisting peer cooperation in the service of alcohol use prevention in middle school. *Child Development*, *89*(6), e459–e467.

Van Ryzin, M. J., & Roseth, C. J. (2018b). Cooperative learning in middle school: A means to improve peer relations and reduce victimization, bullying, and related outcomes. *Journal of Education & Psychology*, *110*(8), 1192–1201.

Van Ryzin, M. J., Roseth, C. J., & Biglan, A. (2020). Mediators of effects of cooperative learning on prosocial behavior in middle school. *International Journal of Applied Positive Psychology*, *5*(1), 37–52.

Vatterott, C. (2010). Five hallmarks of good homework. *Educational Leadership*, *68*(1), 10–15.

Walker, J. D., & Barry, C. (2022). *Behavior management: Systems, classrooms, and individuals*. Plural Publishing.

Walker, J. D., & Hott, B. L. (2017). Positive behavior intervention and supports in the inclusive classroom. In W. W. Murawski & K. L. Scott (Eds.), *What really works with exceptional learners* (pp. 133–151). Corwin.

Watson, A., Timperio, A., Brown, H., Best, K., & Hesketh, K. D. (2017). Effect of classroom-based physical activity interventions on academic and physical activity outcomes: A systematic review and meta-analysis. *International Journal of Behavioral Nutrition and Physical Activity*, *114*, 1–14.

Webb, N. M. (2008). Teacher practices and small-group dynamics in cooperative learning classrooms. In R. Gillies, A. Ashman, & J. Terwel (Eds.), *The teacher's role in implementing cooperative learning in the classroom* (pp. 201–221). Springer.

West, S. L., & O'Neal, K. K. (2004). Project DARE outcome effectiveness revisited.

American Journal of Public Health, 94(6), 1027–1029.

White, A. L., Hoppey, D., & Allsopp, D. H. (2024). IDEA discipline mandates and outcomes. In J. A. Rodriguez & W. W. Murawski (Eds.), *Special education law and policy: From foundation to application* (pp. 361–388). Plural Publishing.

White, M., & Mason, C. Y. (2006). Components of a successful mentoring program for beginning special education teachers: Perspectives from new teachers and mentors. *Teacher Education and Special Education, 29*(3), 191–201.

Wiggins, G., & McTighe, J. (2005). *Understanding by design* (2nd ed.). ASCD.

Wiliam, D. (2017). *Embedded formative assessment: Strategies for classroom formative assessment that drives student engagement and learning.* Solution Tree Press.

Wiliam, D. (2018). *Creating the schools our children need.* Learning Sciences International.

Wiliam, D., & Leahy, S. (2015). *Embedding formative assessment.* Learning Sciences International.

Wilson, D. A. (2004). *Strategies for classroom management K–6: Making magic happen.* Scarecrow Education.

Yarbrough, J. L., Skinner, C. H., Lee, Y. J., & Lemmons, C. (2004). Decreasing transition times in a second grade classroom: Scientific support for the timely transitions game. *Journal of Applied School Psychology, 20*(2), 85–107.

Yazzie-Mintz, E. (2010). *Charting the path from engagement to achievement: A report on the 2009 high school survey of student engagement.* Center for Evaluation and Education Policy. https://files.eric.ed.gov/fulltext/ED495758.pdf

Zigmond, N., Magiera, K., Simmons, R., & Volonino, V. (2013). Strategies for improving student outcomes in co-taught general education classrooms. In B. G. Cook & M. Tankersley (Eds.), *Research-based strategies for improving outcomes in academics* (pp. 116–124). Pearson.

INDEX

A Sage Company

CORWIN HAS ONE MISSION: to enhance education through intentional professional learning.

We build long-term relationships with our authors, educators, clients, and associations who partner with us to develop and continuously improve the best evidence-based practices that establish and support lifelong learning.

More From
Wendy W. Murawski...

What Really Works
With Exceptional
Learners

What Really Works
With Universal Design
for Learning

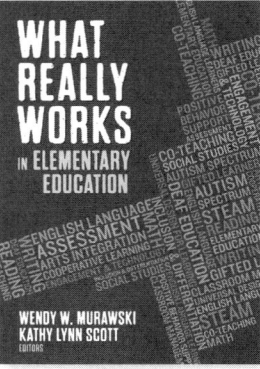

What Really Works
in Elementary
Education

What Really Works
in Secondary
Education

Connecting High-
Leverage Practices
to Student Success

Collaborate,
Communicate, and
Differentiate!

Collaborative
Teaching in
Secondary Schools

Collaborative
Teaching in
Elementary Schools

Order your copy at **corwin.com**